Educations in Ethnic Violence

In *Educations in Ethnic Violence*, Matthew Lange explores the effects education has on ethnic violence. Lange contradicts the widely held belief that education promotes peace and tolerance. Rather, Lange finds that education commonly contributes to aggression, especially in environments with ethnic divisions, limited resources, and ineffective political institutions. He describes four ways in which organized learning spurs ethnic conflicts. Socialization in school shapes students' identities and the norms governing intercommunal relations. Education can also increase students' frustration and aggression when their expectations are not met. Sometimes, the competitive atmosphere gives students an incentive to participate in violence. Finally, education provides students with superior abilities to mobilize violent ethnic movements. Lange employs a cross-national statistical analysis with case studies of Sri Lanka, Cyprus, the Palestinian territories, India, sub-Saharan Africa, Canada, and Germany.

Matthew Lange is Associate Professor of sociology at McGill University. He is the author of *Lineages of Despotism and Development* (2009) and coeditor of *States and Development* (2005) and *Oxford Handbook on the Transformation of States* (forthcoming).

Educations in Ethnic Violence

Identity, Educational Bubbles, and Resource Mobilization

MATTHEW LANGE
McGill University

CAMBRIDGE UNIVERSITY PRESS
Cambridge, New York, Melbourne, Madrid, Cape Town,
Singapore, São Paulo, Delhi, Tokyo, Mexico City

Cambridge University Press
32 Avenue of the Americas, New York, NY 10013-2473, USA

www.cambridge.org
Information on this title: www.cambridge.org/9781107602373

© Matthew Lange 2012

This publication is in copyright. Subject to statutory exception
and to the provisions of relevant collective licensing agreements,
no reproduction of any part may take place without the written
permission of Cambridge University Press.

First published 2012

Printed in the United States of America

A catalog record for this publication is available from the British Library.

Library of Congress Cataloging in Publication data

Lange, Matthew.
Educations in ethnic violence : identity, educational bubbles, and
resource mobilization / Matthew Lange.
p. cm.
Includes bibliographical references and index.
ISBN 978-1-107-01629-3 (hardback) – ISBN 978-1-107-60237-3 (paperback)   1. Ethnic conflict.   2. Ethnic relations.   3. Education – Sociological aspects.   4. Segregation in education.   5. Discrimination in education.   6. Students – Attitudes.   I. Title.
HM1121.L36   2012
305.8009172'4 – dc23   2011031553

ISBN 978-1-107-01629-3 Hardback
ISBN 978-1-107-60237-3 Paperback

Cambridge University Press has no responsibility for the persistence or accuracy of URLs for external or third-party Internet Web sites referred to in this publication and does not guarantee that any content on such Web sites is, or will remain, accurate or appropriate.

Contents

Figures		*page* vii
Tables		ix
Acknowledgments		xi
1	Introduction: Education and Ethnic Violence	1
2	Education and Ethnic Violence: A Theoretical Framework	12
3	Testing the Impact of Education on Ethnic Violence: A Cross-Sectional Time-Series Analysis	35
4	Education and Ethnic Violence in Sri Lanka	59
5	Education and Ethnic Violence in Cyprus	84
6	Education and Ethnic Violence in the Palestinian Territories, India, and Sub-Saharan Africa	113
7	Education and Ethno-Nationalist Conflict in Canada and Germany	154
8	Education and Ethnic Violence: Conclusions and Implications	189
Bibliography		207
Index		235

Figures

2.1	Model of education's impact on ethnic violence	*page* 16
2.2	Scope conditions affecting the impact of education on ethnic violence	30
4.1	Unemployment rate by age and education, 1969–1970	72
6.1	Percent of total unemployed by educational level among select African countries	143
7.1	Class and Nazi Party membership, 1923	172
7.2	Class of new Nazi Party members, 1933	172

Tables

2.1	Four educational mechanisms affecting ethnic violence	page 27
3.1	Summary statistics	44
3.2	Random-effects models of the determinants of ethnic violence, entire set	45
3.3	Random-effects models of the determinants of ethnic violence, set of high-income countries	47
3.4	Random-effects models of the determinants of ethnic violence, set of middle- and low-income countries	48
3.5	Random-effects models of the determinants of ethnic violence with fractionalization-education interaction, entire set	50
3.6	Random-effects models of the determinants of ethnic violence with fractionalization-education interaction, high-income countries	51
3.7	Random-effects models of the determinants of ethnic violence with fractionalization-education interaction, low-income and medium-income countries	52
3.8	Random-effects models of the determinants of ethnic violence, set of countries with high political effectiveness	53
3.9	Random-effects models of the determinants of ethnic violence, set of countries with low and medium political effectiveness	54
3.10	Random-effects models of the determinants of education	56
6.1	Random-effects models of determinants of ethnic violence, sub-Saharan Africa	140
6.2	Ethnic violence by colonial power, 1980–1999	140
6.3	Educational and economic development in sub-Saharan Africa, 2007	142

Acknowledgments

This project began as a study of the impact of colonialism on ethnic violence. During the course of my research, I began to accumulate diverse evidence suggesting that colonial education contributed to ethnic violence in different ways in different places. Because colonialism is popularly viewed as something that negatively affects diverse types of social relations, such findings were hardly unexpected. As I looked into the issue further, however, I found evidence that this educational effect is not limited to the colonial situation, a finding that is a bit more surprising.

In the end, I chose to drop my focus on colonialism and explore how education affects ethnic violence, and *Educations in Ethnic Violence* is the outcome of this switch. Two main factors pushed me to make the change. First, there is already a large literature on how colonialism affected ethnic relations, and my analysis was not uncovering anything exciting and new. Second, I believe that the social world is extremely complex and that this complexity makes Manichean categories of good and evil irrelevant. Yet, the literature on development commonly depicts education as universally beneficial and desirable. According to the World Bank (2011), for example:

Investment in education benefits the individual, society, and the world as a whole. Broad-based education of good quality is among the most powerful instruments known to reduce poverty and inequality. With proven benefits for personal health, it also strengthens nations' economic health by laying the foundation for sustained economic growth. For individuals and nations, it is key to creating, applying, and spreading knowledge – and thus to the development of dynamic, globally competitive economies. And it is fundamental for the construction of democratic societies.

Given my background as a sociologist and the much more critical view of education in the sociology of education, such claims appeared to me exaggerated and one-sided. I therefore wanted to investigate whether there was another darker side to the educational coin.

During the long process of researching and writing *Educations in Ethnic Violence*, several individuals and organizations assisted me in diverse ways. Monetarily, the Social Science and Humanities Research Council of Canada generously funded the project. My research was also assisted by the International Centre for Ethnic Studies at both Colombo and Kandy in Sri Lanka, the Centre for Development Studies in Kerala, the Public Records Office and British Library in the UK, the OKD Institute of Social Change and Development in Assam, the Archives of the Society of Missionaries of Africa in Rome, and the PRIO Cyprus Centre. Several individuals in these organizations offered considerable support, guidance, and friendship, most notably K.M. de Silva, Indranee Dutta, Sunil Mani, Thambirajah Ponnudurai, and Bhupen Sarmah. Outside of these organizations, Rena Choparou, Gopa Gopa Kumar, Yiannis Papadakis, Alexis Rappas, Michael Tharakan, Jandhyala Tilak, and Michalinos Zembylas, generously assisted with my fieldwork and offered wonderful advice; they also treated me to coffee, invited me to their homes to dine with their families, and performed several other extremely kind and generous acts. Closer to home, I am grateful for the assistance I received from friends, colleagues, and students. Among these, John A. Hall, Maurice Pinard, Eran Shor, and Matthias vom Hau offered invaluable comments at different stages of the research project, and T.V. Paul helped me establish contacts in Kerala. Most notably, I must recognize the valuable contributions made by several excellent research assistants at McGill University, including Samantha Berger, Andrew Dawson, Jason Settels, and Kalyani Thurairajah. Two former advisors who keep on advising – Patrick Heller and Dietrich Rueschemeyer – also offered valuable and generous assistance. Finally, I thank my wife for her patience and support throughout the research project, my son for his love and inspiration, and my parents for their love and guidance throughout my life. While all of these organizations and people have helped me enormously and improved the book in a variety of ways, the final product is hardly perfect. I am solely responsible for its faults.

Dedicated to Ursel Eggen, Dorwin Hansen, Patrick Heller, James Mahoney, and Dietrich Rueschemeyer, five teachers and mentors who have offered encouragement and guidance over the years.

1

Introduction

Education and Ethnic Violence

After the initial shock following the 9/11 attacks, many Americans stopped to consider why a group of young men would choose to take their own lives and kill thousands of innocent people. Whereas some looked in the mirror and focused on American foreign policy and economic dominance as a cause of widespread resentment, most considered the bombers themselves. Among the latter category, many quickly concluded that the bombers were evil and deranged lunatics, quite possibly the devil's underlings who were attempting to destroy God's chosen few. The more sociologically inclined considered how the social environment of the bombers influenced their actions. One explanation was that the bombers were impoverished and acted out of desperation. Another more common explanation was that they were uneducated and acted out of ignorance.

The educational hypothesis seems quite logical, as it coincides with the popular belief that education helps prevent extremism and violence by promoting critical-thinking skills, empathy, and tolerance. Indeed, the educational hypothesis is commonly used to explain diverse types of violence, such as why someone participates in gang violence or beats one's spouse. Along these lines, Nobel Laureate Elie Wiesel proclaimed that "[e]ducation is the way to eliminate terrorism" (Berrebi 2007: 3). Yet, Wiesel is a very educated and erudite man and a former member of Irgun,[1] which Hannah Arendt, Albert Einstein, and other Jewish intellectuals described as "a terrorist, right-wing, chauvinist organization" (Abramowitz et al. 1948). Indeed, in its struggle against Arab Palestinians

---

[1] Wiesel worked for an Irgun newspaper between 1947 and 1949, while he was a student at Sorbonne.

and the British colonial administration, the Zionist organization helped revolutionize modern "terrorist"[2] techniques, including the bombing of Arab markets and the King David Hotel in 1946, the latter of which killed ninety-one innocent men, women, and children (Walter and Sandler 2006: 250).

Coinciding with the Wiesel anecdote, there is growing evidence that members of organizations using terrorist techniques are, in fact, quite educated. If one looks at the educational backgrounds of the 9/11 bombers, they were not the ignoramuses that many assume. As one commentator notes, the 9/11 bombers "were adults with education and skill...[who had] spent years studying and training in the United States" (Wilgoren 2001). Mohammed Atta, the leader of the 9/11 bombers, provides a notable example. He was the son of a prominent Egyptian lawyer and brother of two university professors. He excelled in school, pursued postgraduate studies in Urban Planning in Germany, and appeared to be following in his family's professional footsteps (Pape 2005: 220). Individuals involved in the Glasgow Airport bombing were even more educated, albeit much less successful: seven of the eight perpetrators were either doctors or medical residents. Notably, these examples are not exceptions to the rule, as broader empirical analyses all find that militants using terrorist techniques are generally better educated than their peers (Berrebi 2007; Krueger and Maleckova 2003; Pape 2005; Russell and Miller 1978). Contrary to common assumptions, available evidence therefore suggests that education is not an elixir of peace but might actually increase one's risk of participating in terrorist violence.

In the pages that follow, I explore the impact of education on violence through a broad empirical analysis that combines qualitative and quantitative methods. Instead of focusing on terrorist violence, however, I consider how education affects a type of violence that only occasionally takes the form of terrorist attacks: ethnic violence. The analysis provides consistent evidence that education is more likely to contribute to ethnic violence than to restrain it and highlights four mechanisms through which education can promote ethnic violence.

---

[2] "Terrorism" is a politically and normatively loaded term, and I therefore attempt to avoid using it. Still, the term designates certain types of violent acts (mainly indiscriminate violence targeting civilians, attempting to inflict numerous casualties, and perpetrated in pursuit of a broader political goal), and presently there is no alternative term for this type of violence. I therefore continue to use the adjective "terrorist" to refer to acts of violence against civilians, which attempt to inflict mass casualties and are perpetrated in pursuit of a broader political goal.

The first three mechanisms help motivate individuals to act violently against members of other ethnic communities. Through the socialization mechanism, education imparts norms and identities that affect intercommunal relations. Whereas most people assume that education socializes students to respect difference and value human rights, I provide evidence that schools commonly do the opposite: by segregating education, teaching biased curricula, and discriminating against students based on their ethnicity, education frequently strengthens ethnic divisions and antagonisms and thereby increases the risk of violence. Second, I find that education commonly contributes to two psychological traits that have the potential to motivate violence: high aspirations and aggressiveness. As a source of merit, education is an important and legitimate means of status and mobility and actively cultivates aspirations for wealth, power, and respect. The status imparted by education, in turn, gives individuals both the confidence to address grievances and the belief that they have the legitimate right to do so, and both promote aggressive behavior when expectations are unmet. Recognizing this mechanism's similarity with previous works, I refer to it as the frustration-aggression mechanism (Dollard 1939; Gurr 1970). Third, education can promote ethnic violence by creating incentives to use violence as a means of resolving competition, something I refer to as the competition mechanism. When individuals find themselves – and their communities – in competitive relations over scarce resources, violence might be a means of eliminating rivals and thereby maximizing resources, and the educated frequently find themselves in very competitive relations. Moreover, individuals and communities commonly compete over education.

The fourth mechanism differs from the previous three in that it does not *motivate* individuals to participate in ethnic violence. Instead, it affects the ability of individuals to *mobilize* ethnic violence. Through the mobilization mechanism, education increases the resources that individuals possess, and these resources allow actors to organize broad-based and violent ethnic movements.

Each mechanism contributes to ethnic violence, but none is the sole – or even the most influential – determinant of ethnic violence, as multiple factors contribute to ethnic violence in each case. Moreover, multiple educational mechanisms are present and influential in each case, and the presence of one mechanism commonly reinforces another. Indeed, I do not find a single case where only one mechanism is active, and the presence of one mechanism commonly contributes to another. The competition mechanism, for example, is frequently weak on its own because the costs and benefits of participating in collective violence are unknown, but the frustration-aggression mechanism supplements it by bringing emotional antipathy into the equation. Similarly, the socialization mechanism supplements both the frustration-aggression and competition mechanisms by strengthening communal identities. Without strong communal identities, individuals neither focus their frustration and aggression on other ethnic communities nor perceive other ethnic communities as competitors. Finally, because the mobilization mechanism does not motivate people to participate in ethnic violence, it often depends on some combination of the socialization, frustration-aggression, and competition mechanisms to promote ethnic violence. At the same time, when educated individuals are motivated by one or more of the motivational mechanisms, their mobilizational resources allow them to organize violent movements that engage the educated and uneducated alike, showing that the ultimate impact of the motivational mechanisms depends heavily on the mobilization mechanism.

Although finding that education is more likely to promote ethnic violence than to limit it, I find that education only increases the risk of ethnic violence in certain environments and that the ultimate impact of education depends on three contextual factors. First, education is most likely to promote ethnic violence in resource-scarce environments. Most notably, an abundance of resources diminishes the risk of ethnic violence in two ways: it limits the frustration-aggression mechanism by increasing the likelihood that the educated will attain their expectations for status and mobility; and it impedes the competition mechanism by limiting the intensity of zero-sum competition over resources.

Second, I find that education is less likely to promote ethnic violence in environments with effective political institutions – that is, political institutions that are capable of engaging the population and implementing complex policy and that actively respect and protect basic rights. Most importantly, effective political institutions help limit the grievances of educated individuals and therefore restrain the frustration-aggression mechanism. For one thing, they offer formal and effective avenues of addressing grievances, thereby pushing individuals and communities to address their grievances through peaceful political channels instead of through the use of violence. In addition, ineffective political institutions are much more likely to formally discriminate and use violence against segments of their own populations, both of which cause very strong grievances and thereby strengthen the frustration-aggression mechanism. Similarly, ineffective political institutions are less capable of containing outbreaks of ethnic violence. In addition to the frustration-aggression mechanism, political institutions affect the strength of the competition mechanism. In particular, they intensify competition for political resources when they are ethnicized, clientelistic, and unstable.

Finally, the impact of education on ethnic violence depends on ethnic divisions and animosity. Without them, education does not likely contribute to ethnic violence in any way. For example, although socialization in schools could possibly construct ethnic divisions and hostilities, schools are most likely to socialize students in ways that promote ethnic violence when the elites controlling schools – to some minimal degree – share ideas of community and ethnic hostility. Their efforts, in turn, are greatly facilitated when teachers and students already perceive ethnic divisions and hold ethnic stereotypes. The frustration-aggression mechanism also depends on ethnic divisions and intercommunal animosity. Most notably, the frustration and aggression of aggrieved and educated individuals can be directed against any number of actors, but ethnic rivals are logical targets in social environments with preexisting ethnic divisions and antipathy. Along these exact same lines, ethnic cleavages promote the competition mechanism by causing people to consider other ethnic communities as competitive rivals. Finally, the mobilizational resources of education can be applied to diverse purposes but are most likely to coordinate violent ethnic movements when strong and antagonistic ethnic divisions are already present.

Thus, education interacts with the scarcity of resources, ineffective political institutions, and ethnic divisions and is most likely to promote ethnic violence in these contexts. This finding offers evidence that education is rarely an independent cause of ethnic violence but is usually a background condition that exerts its effect when combined with other factors. While suggesting that education is rarely a proximate or ultimate cause of ethnic violence, my conclusion in no way denies that education contributes to ethnic violence in influential ways. In particular, this book provides evidence that education commonly intensifies and disseminates ethnic antipathy; legitimizes violence against members of other ethnic communities; increases competition, frustration, and aggression; and provides mobilizational resources to coordinate violent ethnic movements. In so doing, many schools offer educations that heighten the risk of ethnic violence.

METHODOLOGY AND RESEARCH DESIGN

Social scientists increasingly recognize that considerable leverage can be gained from both qualitative and quantitative methods (Brady and Collier 2004; Huber and Stephens 2001; Stephens and Rueschemeyer 1997). They also note that each methodological tradition has limitations and that each helps compensate for the limitations of the other. Because of this potential for methodological complementarity, there is growing agreement that considerable insight can be gained by combining qualitative and quantitative methods. I share this position and use both statistical and comparative-historical methods to explore the impact of education on ethnic violence.

This book's first analytic section uses statistics to test the relationship between education and ethnic violence. Specifically, I provide a cross-sectional time-series analysis using random-effects models for 121 countries. This statistical technique gains insight from two types of comparison: it compares *different* countries to see if there is a relationship between level of education and level of ethnic violence, and it compares the *same country over time* to see if changes in education are related to subsequent changes in ethnic violence. The main advantages of statistical analysis are its ability to offer generalizable insight that applies to numerous cases and its ability to estimate causal effects. The method, however, is disadvantaged in other ways. Most notably, statistical analysis has difficulty analyzing processes and mechanisms, and one therefore cannot be sure whether statistical relationships are causal or spurious.

The book's second and much larger analytic section uses comparative-historical methods. This methodology's main disadvantage is its limited ability to provide generalizable insight. Thus, in combining comparative-historical methods with statistics, the main advantage of the latter helps make up for the main disadvantage of the former. Alternatively, the main strengths of comparative-historical methods are highlighting mechanisms and analyzing complex processes characterized by multiple interdependent causes. These strengths, in turn, supplement statistical findings by offering insight into whether statistical relationships are causal or spurious.

This book's comparative-historical analysis provides three types of insight into whether and how education affects ethnic violence: pattern matching, process tracing, and narrative comparison. It uses pattern matching, a qualitative technique that tests theories by seeing whether expected hypotheses are supported by in-depth case analysis

(Campbell 1975; Mahoney 2000: 410–412). I employ pattern matching in two ways. First, this book's statistical findings provide evidence that education promotes ethnic violence, and, if this is the case, one would expect that educated individuals play important roles instigating, coordinating, or participating in ethnic violence. I therefore use case studies to explore the roles educated individuals play in episodes of ethnic violence. If the comparative-historical case studies show that several educated individuals are actively involved in ethnic violence and contribute to it in influential ways, they provide evidence that the relationship is not spurious and that education contributes to ethnic violence in some way. If the comparative-historical case studies find that educated individuals play no or only marginal roles in episodes of ethnic violence, they offer evidence that the relationship between education and ethnic violence is spurious. My second use of pattern matching is based on the hypothesis that the risk of ethnic violence should increase markedly after periods of educational expansion if education contributes to ethnic violence. I therefore analyze the sequences of educational expansion and ethnic violence to see if they occur in the expected order. Notably, the statistical analysis already explores whether there is a relationship between educational expansion and ethnic violence, so this use of pattern matching is in some way superfluous. Yet, pattern matching allows one to analyze this relationship in greater detail by looking at the sequence of events and the social environment in which educational expansion occurred, and this qualitative evidence goes beyond simply establishing a statistical relationship. Even more, this use of pattern matching helps set up and strengthen the second qualitative method employed by this analysis – process tracing – by establishing a sequence whereby educational expansion is followed by ethnic violence.

Process tracing is a qualitative technique that attempts to discover mechanisms linking either independent and dependent variables or proximate factors in a causal sequence (George and Bennett 2005: 205–232; Mahoney 2000: 412–415; Roberts 1996: 105–133). To use process tracing, researchers must, first and foremost, establish a relationship or apparent causal sequence. Then, while paying special attention to the potential effects of one factor on another, they need to gather qualitative evidence about the process leading to the outcome in an effort to explore mechanisms linking the factors. I use process tracing to explore potential mechanisms linking education and ethnic violence. For this, I review evidence of the causes of specific episodes of ethnic violence, paying particular attention to whether education contributed to ethnic violence by motivating people to participate in ethnic violence, providing the mobilizational resources to organize collective violence, or both. If I discover mechanisms that coincide with and appear to explain the positive statistical relationship between education and ethnic violence, process tracing provides evidence that the relationship is not spurious and that education commonly contributes to ethnic violence in some way. If, on the other hand, the analysis fails to highlight a mechanism linking education to ethnic violence, the qualitative analysis supports claims that education does not contribute to ethnic violence.

Although methodological work on process tracing largely ignores the comparative-historical methods developed and used by Max Weber, my use of process tracing follows the Weberian tradition in two ways. First, mechanisms that motivate individuals to participate in ethnic violence must be viewed as ideal types that are abstracted from and only partially conform to reality. As Weber notes, it is impossible to know for sure why people act the way they do, and almost all individual actions are simultaneously shaped by multiple factors. In an effort to overcome these problems and create a sociology based on social action, he devises ideal types – analytic tools that are abstractions of reality and that help the researcher identify and compare recurring features in the social world to gauge their causal impact. For this analysis, I use three motivational mechanisms – the socialization, frustration-aggression, and competition mechanisms – as ideal types of social action and explore the extent to which they help explain ethnic violence in particular cases. In so doing, I recognize that no single mechanism or combination of mechanisms offers a complete explanation for ethnic violence and that, in reality, mechanisms causing social action will not completely conform to the ideal types. Still, in analyzing the extent to which the action orientations of individuals conform to the ideal types, one can gain insight into whether the mechanisms contribute to ethnic violence.

Second, I share Weber's focus on social carriers, or actors that have consequential effects on social relations by shaping and coordinating the action orientations of multiple actors (Kalberg 1994: 58–62). Weber focuses his ideal-typical analysis on social carriers because he realizes the impossibility of gaining insight into the action orientations of multiple individuals. He therefore focuses largely on institutions that shape the action orientations of many people over extended periods of time. In this same way, I focus on educational institutions and consider how they affect individual action. Specifically, I explore whether they help motivate people to participate in violence through the socialization, frustration-aggression, and competition mechanisms. Of equal importance, I also investigate whether educational institutions contribute to ethnic violence through the mobilization mechanism by providing the mobilizational resources that make possible collective action.

Narrative comparison is the third and final comparative-historical technique that I use to explore the impact of education on ethnic violence. As its name suggests, it compares the processes and mechanisms of different cases through narrative assessment. The main purpose of narrative comparison is to help highlight factors that contributed to the outcome by comparing processes, mechanisms, and social phenomena. In this book, I use narrative comparison to highlight the impact of education on ethnic violence and to explore scope conditions.

I use pattern matching, process tracing, and narrative comparison in a comparative-historical analysis of multiple cases: Sri Lanka, Cyprus, the Palestinian territories, India, sub-Saharan Africa, Canada, and Germany. Case selection was guided primarily by the fit of cases with the statistical findings and oversamples cases that experienced ethnic violence. Some might criticize this strategy for selecting on the dependent variable (see Geddes 1990; King, Keohane, and Verba 1994); however, their criticism about selection bias is only relevant when researchers attempt to apply quantitative methods to small-N analysis (Collier, Mahoney, and Seawright 2004). In this book, I do not attempt to establish a relationship based on small-N comparison; I use statistics for this. Conversely, I use comparative-historical methods to offer case-specific insight into the impact of education on ethnic violence. And, I selected several cases for the comparative-historical analysis that experienced ethnic violence because only they are able to highlight the educational mechanisms in action.

The first two cases – Sri Lanka and Cyprus – conform to the general findings of the statistical analysis: both were relatively educated and non-wealthy and possessed only moderately effective political institutions when their histories of intense ethnic violence began. If education does promote ethnic violence, these cases are therefore likely to shed light on mechanisms. As such, these *exploratory case studies* highlight potential mechanisms linking education and ethnic violence and thereby test causal hypotheses implied by the statistical findings.

The next three case studies are of the Palestinian territories, India, and sub-Saharan Africa. They are more abbreviated than the first two, and I include them to test whether the findings of the Sri Lankan and Cypriot case studies can be extended to additional cases. I select the Palestinian territories for two reasons. First, the case is also a very likely candidate of ethnic violence, as it has very high levels of education but is very impoverished and possesses very ineffective political institutions. Second, it has reliable data on individuals who participated directly in violence and therefore allows me to explore the education of individuals who directly participate in violence with greater rigor than the previous case studies.

I include the next two cases to test the generalizability of the previous findings more rigorously, as neither strongly conforms to the statistical findings. India does not appear at risk of education-induced ethnic violence because its level of education and rate of educational expansion are quite modest. I selected the case, however, because its relatively low aggregate educational record hides a large pool of educated individuals, as the Indian educational system has historically been elitist and concentrates resources at the upper levels of education (Ansell 2010; Nair 1981; Rudra 2008; Weiner 1991). Thus, the number of people receiving a basic education is limited, but an unusually high percentage of those who receive a basic education advance to the secondary and postsecondary levels. Further, the Indian economy has been unable to absorb many educated individuals, causing educated unemployment to be a severe problem and potentially promoting ethnic violence through the frustration-aggression and competition mechanisms. As such, India could be a statistical exception that helps highlight the influence of particular mechanisms.

Sub-Saharan Africa is the second case that does not strongly conform to the statistical findings, as the region has relatively high levels of ethnic violence but among the lowest levels of education in the world. Still, there is considerable variation in both education and ethnic violence among African countries, and I explore whether education offers any insight into variation in ethnic violence in sub-Saharan Africa. This case study employs both statistical comparison of sub-Saharan African countries and abbreviated case studies of two cases that experienced severe ethnic violence – Nigeria and Rwanda – and two cases that did not – Burkina Faso and Benin.

Finally, I selected two cases that have had relatively peaceful ethnic relations over the past half-century: Canada and Germany. I chose to include both cases because the statistical analysis finds that education is positively related to ethnic violence only among non-wealthy countries and countries with ineffective political institutions, and the case studies of Canada and Germany therefore provide insight into the apparent exceptionalism of countries with these characteristics. For the Canadian case, I focus on the Quebec separatist movement, explore whether educational expansion contributed to the movement, and investigate reasons why this movement was overwhelmingly nonviolent. The German case also considers why contemporary Germany has low levels of ethnic violence, but it differs from the Quebec case study because it compares ethno-nationalist movements in Germany during different periods: the Nazi movement prior to World War II and the neo-Nazi movement during the 1980s and 1990s. As such, the analysis of Germany includes two different cases – one with high levels of ethnic violence and one with low levels of ethnic violence. The analysis explores the educational attainment of Nazi and neo-Nazi activists and investigates why the educated were more likely to participate in the Nazi movement but less likely to participate in the neo-Nazi movement.

Based on this methodological design and case selection, the book's subsequent analysis is organized into seven chapters. In Chapter 2, I define ethnic violence and education and offer a theoretical framework. The framework describes potential mechanisms through which education affects ethnic violence, contextual factors that affect the mechanisms, and the interrelationships among the mechanisms. Chapter 3 uses statistical methods to explore the relationship between education and ethnic violence and potential contextual factors that interact with education to affect ethnic violence. Chapters 4 and 5 provide detailed case studies of Sri Lanka and Cyprus, respectively. Chapter 6 attempts to extend the findings from Chapters 4 and 5 by applying them to the Palestinian Territories, India, and sub-Saharan Africa. Chapter 7 provides case studies of Canada and Germany to explore why education is not related to ethnic violence in wealthy countries with effective political institutions. Finally, Chapter 8 summarizes the findings, considers whether they apply to other types of violence, and describes their policy implications.

2

Education and Ethnic Violence

A Theoretical Framework

All major theories of ethnic violence provide insight that is simultaneously limited and valuable. Each theory is limited because ethnic violence is so complex: it depends on the particular context and sequence of events; any number of factors can spark it; and the perpetrators of ethnic violence are all motivated by different combinations of grievances, aspirations, interests, obligations, and pressures. Because of this very complexity, however, multiple theoretical perspectives are able to simultaneously offer insight into ethnic violence, making them all valuable.

Noting the value and limitations of theories of ethnic violence, the goal of this chapter is not to construct a general theory of ethnic violence. Instead, I construct a more focused framework that considers how education affects ethnic violence. For this, I note mechanisms from a variety of theories, consider how the mechanisms affect one another, and explore scope conditions on which the mechanisms depend. This mid-range theoretical approach follows recent claims by diverse social scientists that theory is most useful when it explores mechanisms and scope conditions instead of covering laws (George and Bennett 2005; Hedstrom and Swedberg 1998; Rueschemeyer 2009; Tilly 2001). Before turning to the theoretical framework, however, it is instructive to first consider the two complex concepts that are its focus: ethnic violence and education.

ETHNIC VIOLENCE AND EDUCATION: DEFINITIONS

Any minimal definition of ethnic violence must consider what violence is and how ethnicity relates to it. Most broadly, violence involves action that intentionally harms others. Defined as such, violence can take three main forms: harassment, which harms one's psychological well-being; the destruction of property, which harms one's possessions; and physical violence, which harms one's body. In this book, I analyze violence in general but pay particular attention to its more extreme forms. As a consequence, I focus on the destruction of property and bodily injury, paying closest attention to violence resulting in deaths.

An ethnicity is a group of people who define themselves or are defined by others as sharing a common culture and heritage. Formal definitions of ethnic violence, in turn, usually have three components: it involves violence between civilians, these civilians live in the same country, and the violence is motivated – at least in part – by ethnic difference. Because one does not always know what motivates violence, ethnic violence can be a matter of interpretation. Indeed, it is sometimes unclear whether ethnicity motivates violence to some extent or whether economic, political, or personal grievances provide the sole motivational drive. Empirical analyses of ethnic violence must therefore pay close attention to the motivations of violence to analyze cases of violence that are motivated by ethnic difference. Such attention is especially important for violence involving only a few people, but the classification of violence as ethnic is usually much easier for collective violence, because ethnic organizations and leaders openly mobilize people to participate in violence by stressing communal grievances and interests.

As highlighted by these last remarks, ethnic violence can occur on a small scale through isolated individual attacks, on a medium scale through riots and pogroms, or on a large scale through well-organized ethnic-based movements and communal wars. In this book, I am most concerned with collective violence motivated by ethnicity and employ "ethnic violence" solely to refer to collective forms of violence, a restriction that generally coincides with the preexisting literature. As a form of collective violence, ethnic violence therefore involves multiple people and multiple incidents that lack independence from one another, allowing the collection of incidents to be categorized as a single collective event. Such interdependence might be caused by early incidents either sparking counterattacks or inspiring copycat violence. In addition, ethnic organizations frequently coordinate, mobilize, and maintain ethnic violence and thereby make possible ethnic violence on a large scale over a prolonged period of time.

Because ethnicity is an important basis of national identity, ethnic violence can sometimes be categorized simultaneously as nationalist violence (Brubaker and Laitin 1998; Calhoun 1993). For example, some civilians use violence against other civilians to gain independence for their ethnic nations, some states encourage their civilians to act violently against minorities who fail to conform to state-propagated ideas of nation, and both are simultaneously ethnic and nationalist violence. Yet, ethnic violence and nationalist violence are not synonymous for two reasons. First, only nationalist violence necessarily involves ideas of political community. Violence between Korean and African Americans in Los Angeles after the Rodney King trial, for example, was ethnic but lacked a nationalist component. Second, states frequently participate directly in nationalist violence, and nationalist violence commonly involves state-on-civilian violence. By definition, however, ethnic violence involves civilian-on-civilian violence. In this book, I focus on ethnic violence in general and only consider nationalist violence when it is simultaneously ethnic violence.

Despite being a word understood and employed by nearly everyone, education is almost impossible to define because it is an institution, a resource, a process, and an activity. In this book, I recognize that education is multifaceted but focus on three of its many characteristics: education as learning process, education as institution, and education as resource. Together, these three make education an influential social carrier that can shape diverse types of social relations, including ethnic violence.

In its broadest sense, education is a series of experiences that have a formative effect on the mind or physical abilities of an individual; that is, it is a learning process. As a learning process, education is very influential and shapes the cognitive abilities and frameworks of individuals. Through education, people learn techniques and "facts" and become acquainted with diverse materials. Moreover, and of greater relevance to this book, education socializes people to hold particular norms, outlooks, expectations, and identities.

As a learning process, education occurs constantly throughout one's life and in diverse settings. I do not employ such a broad conceptualization of education in this book but focus on formal education, that is, learning that occurs in institutions with the express purpose of passing knowledge, outlooks, and skills from teachers to students. Although recognizing that people learn a great deal in nonformal environments, I limit my conceptualization, because a broad definition would make an empirical study of the effects of education much more difficult and because popular conceptualizations of education only focus on formal education. And when one simply focuses on formal education, another important element of what education is also emerges: education as institution.

As an institution, education includes student and teacher roles and has the express purpose of passing knowledge, norms, skills, and other ideas from teacher to student. In educational institutions, teaching occurs through a system of rules governing the appropriateness of curricula; legitimate forms of teaching; student-teacher relations; the recognition of student achievement (grades, degrees, etc.); and proper behavior of students, teachers, and staff. These institutional rules enforce appropriate behavior and standardize the impact of education on a large and diverse student body. Although managed by educational administrators, educational institutions are almost always under the authority of officials from higher bodies with interests beyond imparting knowledge and skills. These are most commonly governments, religious organizations, communities, and charities. As a consequence, educational institutions are usually embedded in and influenced by larger institutional systems that frequently affect the curriculum and the mode of instruction.

Formal education in an institutional setting can teach a variety of material. In this book, I overlook education that simply teaches one subject, such as a language or a religion. Instead, I use the term "education" strictly to refer to colleges or educational institutions that teach multiple subjects. I restrict the concept because formal education has increasingly taken a multidisciplinary form over the last two centuries, and few single-subject schools remain. Along these lines, I use the term "educated" to designate individuals who have completed many years of formal education in multidisciplinary schools relative to their peers.

Besides being a learning process and an institution teaching a multitude of subjects, education is also an important resource. The skills, knowledge, and merit one gains from education can be strategically employed to pursue goals, a fact that usually explains why there is so much demand for education. Similarly, educational institutions include organizations and equipment that can be used by individuals in pursuit of their interests. The resources available in educational institutions do not usually motivate students to get an education but are frequently exploited by students to pursue their interests once they begin their educations.

THEORETICAL FRAMEWORK: EDUCATION AND ETHNIC VIOLENCE

Conceptualized as such, education can be a very influential social carrier that shapes diverse patterns of social relations. Indeed, education is a powerful socializing agent shaping the norms, interests, and outlooks of many individuals; is a major determinant of status and respect; and is an important resource that facilitates collective action. In this book, I employ

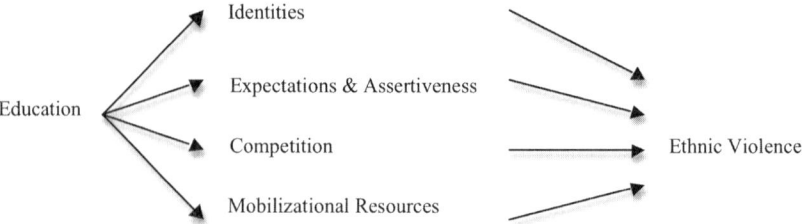

FIGURE 2.1. Model of education's impact on ethnic violence.

a theoretical framework that considers how education shapes ethnic violence in four ways. As depicted in Figure 2.1, I propose that education affects identities, expectations and assertiveness, competition, and mobilizational resources, and that each of these shapes ethnic violence through a distinct mechanism. I refer to these mechanisms as the socialization, frustration-aggression, competition, and mobilization mechanisms.

The Socialization Mechanism

Some scholars of ethnic violence take a constructivist approach.[1] They claim that ethnicity is constructed and that ethnic violence is promoted by discourses, symbols, and rituals that heighten communal identities and ideas of intercommunal antipathy. Mamdani (2001), for example, explores how colonial officials and missionaries helped construct the Hutu-Tutsi cleavage in Rwanda. He also analyzes how discourses, rituals, and the ethnicization of power created intercommunal fear and hostility, something that simultaneously belittled, dehumanized, and provoked the "other." Whereas Mamdani focuses on ethnogenesis, many constructivists take a more moderate approach that simply considers how factors strengthen preexisting ethnic divisions and hostilities. Brass's (1997) work on communal violence in India offers an example of the latter. He highlights the importance of coding violence as communal or noncommunal and finds that categorization affects both the strength of communal identity and the likelihood of communal violence.

Ultimately, the constructivist approach focuses on socialization as an underlying cause of ethnic violence: it claims that socialization contributes to ethnic violence by strengthening ethnic identities and intensifying intercommunal animosity. Recognizing that education is a very powerful

---

[1] See Brass 1997; Fearon and Laitin 2000; Gaborieau 1985; Roosens 1989; Tambiah 1996.

socializing institution, constructivists commonly conclude that education can have important effects on ethnic violence through its impact on identities. Depending on the form and content of education, such socialization can either increase or reduce the risk of ethnic violence.[2]

Socialization that occurs in educational institutions can promote peaceful ethnic relations in different ways. Most notably, it can help construct common communal identities among populations that formerly perceived themselves as part of different communities. This can occur when education promotes a common language among a multilingual population (Miguel 2004; Weber 1976). Indeed, a shared language not only allows people to communicate with one another, but it is also a very important basis of communal identity. Education can also promote a shared collective identity by emphasizing a common heritage. History and civics courses frequently impart ideas of a shared history and the glories of nation. Rituals – such as flag ceremonies, the national anthem, and convocations – are a third notable way through which education can help construct a common collective identity.

These examples all suggest that education can promote unity by assimilating the population into a homogeneous mass. Yet, the construction of a common communal identity does not necessitate the elimination of difference, as a multicultural approach can also help unify a diverse population but does not provoke the same backlash as a homogenizing policy. In fact, a multicultural approach is likely the only option available for most countries in the world today, as preexisting and irretractable subnational identities prevent the construction of homogeneous nation states (Stepan, Linz, and Yadav 2011).

Along with promoting a shared identity, education can also limit ethnic violence by socializing students to hold common norms that promote more peaceful social relations. Durkheim (1934; 1973), for example, believed education plays an important role building consensus in modern society. According to this view, education facilitates consensus building by teaching general norms that govern daily interactions and thereby providing the grease that helps limit conflict. These norms deal with such mundane things as walking on a particular side of the hall or sidewalk. They also include broader norms, such as respecting diversity and the rights of others. Along these lines, the UNESCO Declaration of the

---

[2] See Bryan and Vavrus 2005; Bush and Saltarelli 2000; Coulby and Jones 2001; Davies 2004; Gallagher 2004; Graham-Brown 1994; Harber 1996; Ichilov 2004; Johnson and Stewart 2007.

Principles of Tolerance claims that "[e]ducation is the most effective means of preventing intolerance" and proposes that the "first step in tolerance education is to teach people what their shared rights and freedoms are, so that they may be respected, and to promote the will to protect those of others" (UNESCO 1995).

A third way through which education can promote peaceful ethnic relations is by increasing empathy. Certain forms of education enhance the ability of individuals to think critically and connect ideas, and these cognitive skills allow individuals to empathize with and extend norms to people from different backgrounds. As a consequence, people are more likely to respect differences instead of acting in prejudiced ways.

Socialization at schools can contribute to peaceful intercommunal relations in these ways, but it does not always do so. Indeed, instead of critical thinking, education frequently focuses on rote memorization and mindlessly following authority. Moreover, education might socialize students to accept norms of a particular culture and reject those of others. Finally, and most notably, education can strengthen ideas of ethnic difference and disfavor in several ways.

One way education might heighten ethnic divisions and intercommunal animosity is through the ethnic-based segregation of schools. Educational segregation is quite common when ethnic identities are based on language, religion, or both because segregation allows the instruction of students in their native tongue and religion. Although desirable in some ways, ethnic segregation usually increases social distance between communities, thereby limiting intercommunal friendships and marriages, contributing to misunderstandings about individuals from different communities, and helping create or enforce ethnic divisions. At the extreme, segregated education can fail to provide a common language and thereby prevent individuals from different communities from being able to communicate with one another.

School curriculum can also socialize students to strengthen exclusive ethnic identities. Indeed, political and religious bodies frequently run schools and explicitly attempt to construct ethno-national identities.[3] Although having the potential to create communal unity among some, such a policy is based on an us-them dichotomy and necessarily removes people from the community and stresses their difference. Beyond textbooks, teachers and administrators choose what text to read, emphasize particular aspects of the text, and lead discussions. Instructors therefore

---

[3] See Gellner 1983; Ichilov 2004: 65; Weber 1976.

help bring life to the curriculum and have the potential to play an important role strengthening ideas of ethnic difference. In this way, both the material and mode of instruction can socialize students to perceive ethnic differences and categorize people accordingly, thereby creating necessary conditions for ethnic violence.

Even more than increasing divisions, the curriculum can exacerbate intercommunal antagonisms by villainizing others and socializing students to place members of other ethnic communities "beyond the perimeter within which moral values and rules of justice and equity apply" (Bryan and Vavrus 2005: 186). For instance, schools can teach that a country is the true homeland of only one ethnic community, or that certain ethnic communities are inherently inferior in some way (evil, less intelligent, cowardly, etc.). Less formally, teachers can ridicule and discriminate against students from different ethnic communities, thereby encouraging and legitimizing ethnic discrimination and disfavor.

Education therefore has the potential to promote either ethnic peace or violence through socialization. Still, one must be careful not to overstate the impact of educational socialization on intercommunal relations. Previous research on the impact of education on political socialization is mixed.[4] Sociologists find that students do not simply accept whatever they are taught in school but choose between the views and norms that they are exposed to on a daily basis. Their acceptance of the educational message therefore depends greatly on whether their greater social environment reinforces the educational message. Importantly, if ideas, norms, and attitudes are present outside of school, education does not construct them: it simply has the potential to strengthen and legitimize them. Strong constructivist claims about education causing ethnogenesis thus appear overstated.

The Frustration-Aggression Mechanism

Whereas constructivist theory focuses on how ethnic identities and intercommunal antipathy are created, other theories assume the presence of ethnic cleavages and focus on how grievances cause ethnic violence. Materialist theories, for example, claim that economic inequalities and limited opportunities cause aggrieved individuals to act violently.[5] Similarly,

---

[4] See Langton and Jennings 1968; Merelman 1971; Rodgers 1973; Torney-Purta 2000; Torney-Purta and Schwille 1986.
[5] See Blalock 1967; Bonacich 1973; Gurr 1970; Hechter 1975; Hewitt 1977; Melson and Wolpe 1970; Midlarsky 1988; Muller and Seligson 1987; van den Berghe 1981.

political theories of ethnic violence focus on how power differentials and political discrimination create grievances that motivate violence.[6] Although not explicit, grievance-based theories commonly draw on the frustration-aggression mechanism.[7]

As originally formulated by Dollard (1939) and subsequently used by others in different reformulations, the frustration-aggression mechanism motivates aggressive and potentially violent action through emotion. Such emotive action is sparked when individuals are unable to meet their expectations, especially when their expectations were almost attained. As such, people with high and seemingly attainable expectations are severely aggrieved when hardships prevent them from meeting their aspirations. These aggrieved individuals, in turn, are at a heightened risk of acting violently.

Any number of grievances can spark the frustration-aggression mechanism, and analyses of frustration-induced violence usually focus on grievances. Besides the actual grievances, some factors increase the expectations of individuals and heighten the risk that an individual will react aggressively to frustration. Of particular relevance to this analysis, education commonly increases both expectations and assertiveness and thereby places the educated at a heightened risk of frustration-induced violence.

Education is an important credential and source of status and is one of the most influential determinants of social mobility. One notable side effect of these educational effects is that educated individuals commonly have high expectations for mobility and respect. Indeed, individuals actively pursue educations to become upwardly mobile, and they expect to be mobile once they have completed their schooling. Bourdieu (1984) goes even further, suggesting that educational institutions actually create these aspirations. He describes how education stresses the value of white-collar employment, stigmatizes blue-collar work, and emphasizes that education is the means of avoiding the latter and finding the former.

---

[6] See Gurr 1993, 2000; Hechter 2000; Horowitz 1985, 2001; Sambanis 2001; Wimmer Cederman, and Min 2009.

[7] Although popular in the 1970s, the frustration-aggression mechanism is presently largely overlooked by studies of ethnic violence within political science and sociology. While some claim that the mechanism has been disproved, critical reviews of the mechanism find that it appears to provide considerable insight into ethnic violence (just not as much as originally claimed) and that the theory has not been adequately tested (Brush 1996; Sayles 2007). The mechanism has remained quite prominent in psychology, however, and recent analyses provide evidence that the mechanism has an influential impact on violence.

At the same time, Bourdieu suggests that the aspirations of the educated are commonly unmet and that this mismatch between expectations and reality promotes enormous anger and frustration. Along these same lines, scholars of rebellions, revolutions, anticolonial movements, domestic violence, and ethnic violence all find that the inability of the educated to attain their aspirations promotes grievances that, in turn, contribute to violence.[8]

Another side effect of the status and mobility-generating effects of education is assertiveness. The status and prestige imparted via education strengthens one's self-esteem. High self-esteem, in turn, gives individuals the confidence to confront others and assertively pursue their interests. Similarly, self-esteem causes people to view their grievances as important, legitimate, and in need of redress. As a consequence, they are more likely to act assertively to address their problems. Supporting these claims, numerous psychological analyses find that individuals with high self-esteem are much more likely to react aggressively to grievances than individuals with lower self-esteem.[9]

Education can therefore increase the risk of frustration-induced violence because it heightens expectations – thereby leading to more intense frustration when expectations are unmet – and increases assertiveness – thereby promoting aggressive reactions to frustration. The focus of such frustration-induced aggression can be determined randomly and might be a matter of convenience. Such aggression can also be vengeful and focus on individuals who are directly implicated in the grievance. Finally, preexisting stereotypes can promote scapegoating by directing frustration and aggression against entire categories of people. Of these three, frustration-induced scapegoating contributes most greatly to collective violence for two reasons. First, and most obviously, it creates many potential targets. Second, scapegoating usually occurs when grievances are perceived as collective (that is, affecting an entire community), and collective grievances can motivate a large number of individuals to address them.[10]

---

[8] See Abernethy 2000: 337–341; Anstey 1970; Boyden and Ryder 1996; Callaway 1963; Goldstone 1991; Hornung, McCullough, and Sugimoto 1981; Huntington 1968; Lange 2003; Majumdar 2005; McCully 1940; Riga 2008; Seitz 2004; Tambiah 1996: 17.

[9] See Barry et al. 2007; Baumeister, Smart, and Boden 1996; Burton, Mitchell, and Lee 2005; Bushman and Baumeister 1998; Goldberg, et al. 2007; Kernis, Grannemann, and Barclay 1989; Locke 2009; Sandstrom and Jordan 2006; Svindseth et al. 2008; Thomaes et al. 2008.

[10] See Belanger and Pinard 1991: 450; Blau and Schwartz 1984: 174; Horowitz 1985; Wimmer 2002: 101–104.

Ethnic violence provides a preeminent example of how the frustration-aggression mechanism can promote scapegoating. Ethnicity is a very salient basis of identity, and people commonly view the world through ethnic lenses: individuals actively look for ethnic markers, believe they are treated differently because of their ethnicity, compare the status and wealth of their ethnic community with others, and so forth. As a consequence, ideas of discrimination become popularized, ethnic inequalities become a political issue, and ethnic prejudices are widespread – these are ideal conditions for scapegoating. Thus, "where people tend to think of themselves foremost as members of a particular caste, religious, ethnic, or language group, feelings of anger and frustration emanating from economic and social problems (that would usually be directed at the government) are often aimed at another group" (Bryjak 1986: 49). By contributing to the frustration-aggression mechanism, education therefore has the potential to contribute to ethnic scapegoating and violence.

The Competition Mechanism

Ultimately, the frustration-aggression mechanism contributes to ethnic violence through emotive action. Several scholars of ethnic violence, however, take a rational-choice perspective and focus on the impact of rational action. That is, individuals calculate the costs and benefits of participating in ethnic violence and choose to participate when the expected benefits outweigh the expected costs. The literature suggests it is frequently rational to participate in ethnic violence in environments with high levels of competition, as the vanquishing or elimination of ethnic rivals helps maximize individual and communal resources. Throughout this book, I refer to the rational-choice-based mechanism of ethnic violence as the competition mechanism.

Although anyone might have incentives to participate in ethnic violence, the literature commonly points to the educated as particularly prone to violence because they find themselves in more competitive situations and have more to gain from eliminating rivals. According to instrumentalist theory, elites – who are usually very educated – sometimes choose to instigate and lead ethnic violence when faced with stiff competition for power. This perspective notes that elites can benefit from ethnic violence because it allows them to gain support from their ethnic communities. Several works on the former Yugoslavia, for example, note how Slobodan Milosevic stressed ethnic difference and mobilized his Serbian constituency to participate in violence against non-Serbs to increase his power in the uncertain and competitive political environment following the collapse of the Soviet Union (Bozic-Roberson 2004; Oberschall 2000; Petersen 2002).

Competition theory makes a similar argument but focuses on economic competition instead of politics.[11] According to this view, ethnic competition is greatest in "modernizing" societies because of the growing number of educated individuals who desire a limited number of high-status white-collar jobs. This competition, in turn, creates incentives to weaken or eliminate rivals and thereby promotes violence and movements that seek to advantage one's ethnic community. Notably, the incentives that can motivate individuals to participate in violent ethnic movements are commonly selective – that is, they benefit the individual directly by eliminating rivals. They are also frequently communal, as individuals are worried about the well-being of their community and its representation in elite occupations. Logically, the competition mechanism is strongest when both individual and communal incentives are present and reinforce one another.

A number of scholars from diverse theoretical backgrounds claim that the educated face considerable competition for jobs and power and that this competition frequently pushes them to organize and participate in violent ethnic movements. Bates (1974), for example, claims that the educated are more embroiled in ethnic competition for jobs and resources and "organize collective support to advance their position in the competition for the benefits of modernity" (468). Similarly, Horowitz (1985) describes how education breaks down ethnic-based divisions of labor and promotes ethnic competition for jobs, thereby causing ethnic antagonism and violence to be greatest among the educated (113, 134). Goldstone (1997) makes similar claims linking education to revolutionary violence. He writes:

In a healthy society that is rich in resources and is building its institutions and its economy, there is usually room to accommodate a growing elite. But what happens if a country does not have a growing economy, but has invested in universities that are trying to develop an elite for the future, and that future does not come?... The result is a heightened competition between elites to see who is going to control what wealth there is, and what government there is. (107)

According to this view, education increases competition by giving the educated the credentials to compete for limited power and resources, as those

---

[11] See Hannan 1979; Olzak 1992; Olzak and Nagel 1986; Melson and Wolpe 1970.

without the appropriate credentials are removed from the competition. Thus, it is not education per se that causes ethnic violence through the competition mechanism; it is social environments with scarce resources that place the educated in more competitive positions. Still, education can contribute to ethnic violence more directly through its impact on confidence and assertiveness, both of which heighten the intensity and aggressive character of competition. Education can also have a more direct impact on ethnic violence when competition is over education itself. Indeed, education is an extremely valuable resource and is frequently the object of competition. For example, access to education is often restricted, and individuals therefore compete for enrollment. Similar to competition over jobs, competition over educational access is commonly promoted by both individual interests – individuals desiring greater education for themselves – and communal interests – individuals desiring greater education for their communities. People also compete for education because it can be employed to protect and disseminate culture and allows actors to disregard, disrespect, and disparage the cultures of others. Recognizing this, Geertz (1973) claims that primordial battles over the control of schools are both common and heated. Language provides an important example. Because language is an important marker of community and affects the ability of individuals to succeed in school and find employment, all ethnic communities have an interest in making their language the lingua franca of education (Horowitz 1985).

The Mobilization Mechanism

Most theories of ethnic violence focus on factors that motivate violence. In this way, the socialization, frustration-aggression, and competition mechanisms all appear to contribute to ethnic violence by providing motivation. Resource mobilization theory is quite unique in this regard, as it focuses on mobilizational capacity. It starts with the position that the mobilization of collective action is a difficult task and considers how individuals can successfully organize social movements. According to this perspective, education greatly expands the mobilizational capacity of individuals and thereby promotes movement success (Edwards and McCarthy 2004; Gamson 1987; McCarthy and Zald 1987). Although largely overlooked by scholars of ethnic violence, resource mobilization theory is very relevant because ethnic-based social movements frequently contribute to episodes of ethnic violence and because ethnic violence is a form of collective action. Throughout this book, I refer to education's impact on mobilizational capacity as the mobilization mechanism.

Since the Middle Ages, schools have been hotbeds of social movements and collective violence (Boren 2001). Indeed, in dozens of countries throughout the world, schools have been bases for social revolutions, coups, nationalist struggles, and political movements (Altbach 1989). In France, mass student protests brought the country to a standstill in 1968 and nearly toppled the de Gaulle government, and American students were a core component of the civil rights movement. In Russia and Cuba, student activists played major roles in revolutionary movements and thereby directly contributed to the rise of each country's communist regime. Indeed, in his analysis of leftist guerrilla movements in Latin America, Wickham-Crowley (1992) finds that students founded and formed the core memberships of most movements and that the movements – not coincidentally – commonly followed periods of educational expansion.

In exploring the causes of active student participation in social movements, several scholars find that education provides diverse resources that can be exploited to organize collective movements. For example, participation in movements requires time, and students generally have a lot of it because of their relatively flexible academic schedules and limited responsibilities. As a consequence, they are able to participate in social movements without having to worry about losing a job, angering a spouse, or neglecting children. Second, broad-based collective action requires considerable cognitive skills that are enhanced by formal education. According to Morris and Staggenborg (2004), these skills include "framing grievances and formulating ideologies, debating, interfacing with the media, writing, orating, devising strategies and tactics, creatively synthesizing information gleaned from local, national and international venues, dialoguing with internal and external elites, improvising and innovating, developing rationales for coalition building and channeling emotions" (175). Third, the educational environment provides exceptional communication resources that are vital for collective action. Most basically, schools bring hundreds – if not thousands or even tens of thousands – of people into close proximity with one another and therefore facilitate communication and coordinated action. Furthermore, the actual educational facilities offer communication resources in the form of student newspapers, poster-boards, telephones, computers, printers, and copiers. Finally, schools have a number of diverse organizations and associations. Examples include sports teams, political groups, cultural associations, student governance organizations, fraternities, and academic associations. While providing another important means of communication, these student groups also provide a formal organizational structure that facilitates collective decision making and the coordination of members.

Notably, mobilizational resources do not predispose the educated to ethnic violence; they simply provide resources that facilitate collective action of any type, including ethnic violence (Allardt 1981). Thus, in ethnically stratified and competitive societies, people can employ educational resources to mobilize either violent or peaceful ethnic movements. Even the latter, however, have the potential to promote ethnic violence because they commonly spark violent backlashes. Student involvement in the civil rights movement provides an example, as students frequently exploited mobilizational resources in their nonviolent pursuit of racial equality (Morris 1981). Their nonviolent tactics, however, sparked violent opposition from many whites who favored the status quo.

Education, Empowerment, and Ethnic Violence

Whereas most scholars of ethnic violence view the phenomenon as completely undesirable, others recognize that it can be a means of subordinate-community advancement. This more critical conflict perspective views ethnic violence as the result of adjustments in communal power that either threaten dominant communities and thereby spark violence against minorities, strengthen subordinate communities and thereby spark movements forcefully pursuing greater equality, or – most commonly – some combination of the two. Education, in turn, is an important means of subordinate-group empowerment, and this is another way through which education can contribute to ethnic violence.

Although a distinct theoretical view with a particular normative orientation, this empowerment perspective does not offer any new mechanism linking education to ethnic violence. Instead, the frustration-aggression and mobilization mechanisms underlie the impact of empowerment on ethnic violence. As noted previously, education is a means of merit and self-esteem, both of which promote frustration and aggression when expectations are unmet. At the same time, merit and self-esteem are important elements of empowerment, and frustration-induced action demonstrates this empowerment and has the potential to contribute to further empowerment. Different works, for example, find that cognitive liberation is vital for social movements – especially for movements mobilizing subordinate groups – and occurs when people gain the self-confidence to organize assertive movements. Along these lines, McAdam (1982) analyzes the American civil rights movement and provides evidence that the growing self-confidence of African Americans directly affected the movement's emergence and success. He notes, in turn, that the expansion of education among African Americans promoted greater self-confidence and thereby contributed to a social movement that peacefully yet aggressively demanded racial equality.

The social movement literature also notes that mobilizational resources are a very important means of empowerment. Indeed, by providing knowledge, skills, communication technologies, and organizations, education actively empowers. Along these lines, the expansion of education among African Americans contributed to the civil rights movement by endowing them the mobilizational resources to organize a broad-based movement that did not employ violence but that ultimately provoked it (Morris 1981).

EDUCATIONAL MECHANISMS: INTERACTIONS AND SCOPE CONDITIONS

As shown in Table 2.1, education therefore appears to affect ethnic violence in four different ways. First, education shapes identities and intercommunal antipathy and can either promote or deter ethnic violence through the socialization mechanism. Second, education promotes both aspirations and assertiveness, and both can contribute to ethnic violence through the frustration-aggression mechanism. Next, education can intensify competition and thereby promote ethnic violence through the

TABLE 2.1. *Four Educational Mechanisms Affecting Ethnic Violence*

Mechanism	Educational Effect	Effect on Ethnic Violence
Socialization	Shapes identity and intercommunal animosity	Positive or Negative
Frustration-Aggression	Shapes expectations and assertiveness	Positive
Competition	Shapes incentives to eliminate competitors	Positive
Mobilization	Shapes capabilities to mobilize movements	Positive or Negative

competition mechanism. Finally, education expands the mobilizational resources of actors, and these resources make possible collective action that can either promote or deter ethnic violence.

Given the presence of four educational mechanisms and the fact that two mechanisms are capable of either promoting or deterring ethnic violence, the relationship between education and ethnic violence appears rather complex. To make more sense of this complexity, it is helpful to consider how the mechanisms affect one another and the conditions that shape how the mechanisms affect ethnic violence.

Mechanistic Complementarity

With four educational mechanisms, it is possible that education affects ethnic violence in multiple ways. In addition, if multiple mechanisms are active simultaneously, the presence of one mechanism might affect the impact of another. It is possible that some mechanisms compete with and counteract the effect of one another. If schools socialize students to be more tolerant of other ethnic communities at the same time that the frustration-aggression and competition mechanisms are present, for example, the mechanisms likely reduce or cancel the effects of one another: the socialization mechanism might prevent the competition and frustration-aggression mechanisms from focusing on ethnic others, and the competition and frustration-aggression mechanisms might prevent tolerance education from successfully shaping the norms and cognitive frameworks of students.

When multiple mechanisms simultaneously promote ethnic violence, the mechanisms logically complement and reinforce one another. The most obvious example of mechanistic complementarity pairs the frustration-aggression and competition mechanisms. Indeed, limited opportunities promote both frustration over impeded mobility and competition over scarce resources, and each intensifies the other. For example, competition alone rarely drives individuals to participate in collective violence (Belanger and Pinard 1991). Two reasons for this are imperfect information and risk: the benefits of violence are unpredictable, and the costs are potentially enormous (i.e., one's life or a long prison sentence). Yet, the emotional influence of the frustration-aggression mechanism can help overcome uncertain cost-benefit calculations and cause one to have a lower risk threshold. Similarly, the competition mechanism can strengthen the frustration-aggression mechanism. For example, communal competition can promote discriminatory acts that advantage one community over another, and discrimination creates powerful grievances that promote violence through the frustration-aggression mechanism.

Besides the frustration-aggression and competition mechanisms, other educational mechanisms also appear to complement and reinforce one another. Both the frustration-aggression and competition mechanisms can strengthen the socialization mechanism. Indeed, the educational curriculum is most likely to be divisive and to increase intercommunal antipathy when communities are angry over hardships, compete for scarce resources, and blame ethnic rivals for their grievances. Such complementarity also runs in the opposite direction, as the socialization mechanism strengthens the frustration-aggression and competition mechanisms when it heightens ethnic difference and presents other communities in a negative light. In so doing, socialization helps strengthen ethnic-based cognitive categories and intercommunal disfavor, both of which are necessary for ethnic rivalries and scapegoating.

Lastly, the mobilization mechanism is also greatly affected by the other mechanisms. It differs from the previous three because it helps *mobilize* violence instead of *motivating* it. As a consequence, the mobilization mechanism does not strengthen the motivational impulse of the socialization, frustration-aggression, and competition mechanisms but provides a means of broad-based violence when such motivation is already present. The mobilization mechanism is therefore most likely to contribute to ethnic violence in the presence of one or more educational mechanisms that motivate people to participate in ethnic violence. When the educational system socializes students to be tolerant toward other communities and when the frustration-aggression and competition mechanisms are weak, however, the mobilizational resources offered by education are more likely to mobilize peaceful ethnic relations instead of violence.

Conversely, the impact of the three motivational mechanisms also depends greatly on the mobilization mechanism. Whereas the socialization, frustration-aggression, and competition mechanisms promote ethnic violence when large numbers of individuals are simultaneously motivated by them, collective violence almost always depends on mobilizational resources, as the latter are needed to frame and popularize grievances and coordinate collective action. Educational resources are commonly used for such purposes, and the ultimate influence of the three motivational mechanisms therefore greatly depends on the mobilization mechanism. Indeed, without their mobilizational resources, educated individuals would be less capable of organizing ethnic movements regardless

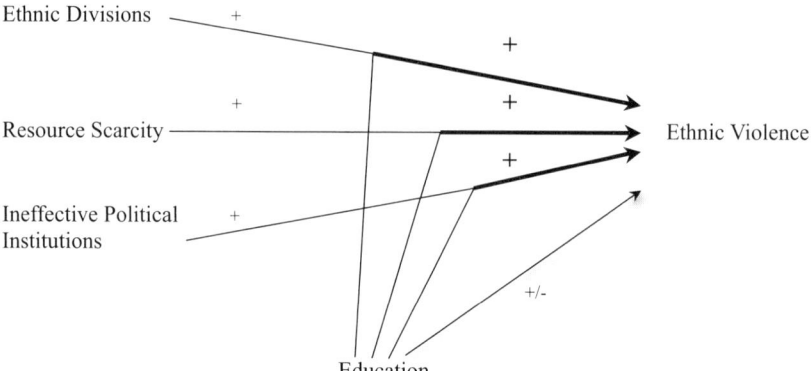

FIGURE 2.2. Scope conditions affecting the impact of education on ethnic violence.

of their motivation, suggesting that the impact of the three motivational mechanisms is much more limited in the absence of the mobilization mechanism.

Scope Conditions and Interactions

Mechanisms are frequently context-dependent (Falleti and Lynch 2009). That is, some social environments activate and intensify mechanisms, and some mechanisms exert their effect by magnifying the impact of other contextual factors. It is therefore instructive to consider whether any contexts affect the four educational mechanisms. Ultimately, the four educational mechanisms appear to depend on and magnify the impact of other factors. Thus, if education contributes to ethnic violence, it is not likely a direct cause. Instead, as depicted in Figure 2.2, the four educational mechanisms interact with and increase the impact of three more proximate causes of ethnic violence: ethnic divisions and antagonisms, resource scarcity, and ineffective political institutions.

All four educational mechanisms logically depend on preexisting ethnic divisions and antagonisms. That is, if a population lacks ethnic cleavages, the four educational mechanisms would not likely promote ethnic violence for the simple reason that each requires at least two ethnic communities. Moreover, much of the impact of the educational mechanisms lies in their abilities to increase the salience of ethnic divisions.

The frustration-aggression mechanism, for example, can be focused on any number of actors, but ethnic rivals are common targets in social environments with preexisting divisions. Most importantly, collective grievances against other ethnic communities are vital for scapegoating, but they cannot be easily constructed from scratch and therefore depend on preexisting ethnic divisions and disfavor. Ethnic scapegoating, in turn, further increases the salience of ethnic divisions, heightens intercommunal antipathy, creates an emotive drive for aggression, and thereby promotes ethnic violence. Similarly, the competition mechanism depends on ethnic divisions because the mechanism requires that many people perceive an ethnic community as a competitor. Once present, however, the competition mechanism promotes ethnic violence by further strengthening ethnic cleavages, creating incentives to eliminate ethnic competitors, and increasing intercommunal disfavor. Finally, intercommunal divisions are necessary for the mobilization of educational resources against another ethnic community, and ethnic-based mobilization subsequently increases the chance of violence in ethnically divided environments.

Different from the other three mechanisms, the socialization mechanism might not depend on preexisting divisions, as the strong constructivist position suggests that powerful elites with effective means of mass communication can transform communal identities and intercommunal relations (see Mamdani 2001). Although possible, sociologists find that attempts to socialize students in schools frequently fail but are most successful when the educational message reflects the larger social environment. As such, socialization is most likely to promote ethnic violence in environments with preexisting divisions and to contribute to peaceful ethnic relations in environments with only limited intercommunal divisions. Although the socialization mechanism depends on ethnic divisions in this way, similar to the other mechanisms, it is not an intervening variable that simply transmits the impact of preexisting ethnic divisions. Instead, it has the potential to increase the effect of ethnic divisions by further strengthening ethnic divisions, intensifying antipathy, and legitimizing violence.

Along with ethnic cleavage, some of the mechanisms also appear to both depend on and increase the effect of resource scarcity. Most notably, the competition mechanism promotes violence when there is a shortage of resources, forcing individuals and communities to compete for them. In resource-rich environments, such competition still occurs but is rarer and less intense, because most people are able to attain their material needs and basic material wants. Education, in turn, appears to exacerbate competition in resource-scarce environments by constituting a highly desirable resource that is an influential means to material wealth. When there is an oversupply of educated workers, education also increases competition for high-status jobs, thereby magnifying the impact of resource scarcity on ethnic violence.

The availability of resources also appears to affect the presence and strength of the frustration-aggression mechanism. Because education greatly increases expectations for economic mobility and respect, educated individuals who are not upwardly mobile experience great frustration, placing them at a heightened risk of frustration-induced violence. The ability to be upwardly mobile and attain a job aligned with one's educational credentials, in turn, depends on the strength of the economy and the presence of a large number of white-collar jobs. Thus, where economies are poor and white-collar jobs are rare, the frustration-aggression mechanism should be powerful, especially among the educated unemployed and underemployed. And when many people have high levels of frustration and aggression, resource scarcity is more likely to provoke ethnic violence, suggesting that the frustration-aggression mechanism magnifies the impact of resource scarcity on ethnic violence.

Notably, the competition and frustration-aggression mechanisms are most dependent on resource scarcity when it is combined with another condition: a large supply of educated individuals. Indeed, in poor economies with few educated individuals, the educated will have greater opportunities finding a job than in a poor economy with many educated individuals, thereby reducing both competition and frustration among the educated. The competition and frustration-aggression mechanisms therefore appear particularly dependent on educational bubbles, where a poor economy and an oversupply of educated individuals promotes high levels of educated unemployment and underemployment.

The socialization mechanism might also depend on the availability of resources, albeit to a much lesser degree. In particular, the absence of resources does not appear to cause the socialization mechanism to promote ethnic violence, but the availability of resources seems to increase the likelihood that the socialization mechanism contributes to peaceful ethnic relations in one way: tolerance education requires considerable resources to develop an appropriate curriculum and train teachers, and it therefore appears to be a luxury that schools in nonwealthy environments are less capable of offering.

In addition to ethic cleavages and the availability of resources, the political context also appears to shape the educational mechanisms. Tilly (2003), for example, finds that strong states and robust democracies are powerful deterrents of collective violence. They do so, in part, by limiting both grievances and zero-sum competition, suggesting that the frustration-aggression and competition mechanisms depend on political institutions.

Political institutions affect grievances in many ways. Effective states, for example, are often capable of stopping violence before it gets out of control, and violence is an important source of grievances. Moreover, ineffective states that are not governed by robust democracies frequently use violence against their own citizens, and state violence causes very powerful grievances. A robust democracy also allows individuals to address their grievances through formal and peaceful political channels. Similarly, a robust democracy protects basic rights and helps prevent political discrimination, and the latter is a major source of grievances. For all of these reasons, the frustration-aggression mechanism should be most common and powerful in places lacking both robust democracies and highly effective states.

Whereas political institutions affect grievances and thereby the frustration-aggression mechanism, it also appears that education intensifies the impact of political grievances. Most notably, because education increases the aspirations and assertiveness of people, political grievances are most likely to provoke the frustration-aggression mechanism among the educated. Moreover, because educated individuals possess greater mobilizational resources, they are more capable of organizing violent movements over political grievances.

The competition mechanism might also depend on political institutions. Most importantly, competition for political power is very intense when the government is clientelistic and only offers goods and services to a select group of clients. Ethnic-based clientelism therefore strengthens the competition mechanism and promotes ethnic violence. Political instability also strengthens the competition mechanism by creating incentives to compete for political power. Most importantly, it places the government at risk and creates openings for the realignment of political power. And while clientelistic and unstable political institutions promote competition, it is commonly educated individuals who have the most to gain from transformations in political power that benefit their ethnic community: they take control of the government, gain greater access to public-sector jobs, and are better placed to become clients of state patronage. Clientelism and political instability are therefore most likely to intensify competition – and thereby create the strongest incentives to eliminate ethnic rivals – among more educated segments of the population.

SUMMARY

Education has the potential to affect ethnic violence in many ways. The socialization and mobilization mechanisms can either positively or negatively affect ethnic violence. The impact of the socialization mechanism depends on the content of education, whereas the motives of those who control educational resources shape the mobilization mechanism. Alternatively, the frustration-aggression and competition mechanisms promote ethnic violence but do not logically contribute to peaceful intercommunal relations.

All four mechanisms appear to affect one another, and several mechanisms might therefore shape ethnic violence simultaneously. When the mechanisms affect ethnic violence in opposite ways, they likely reduce the effect of each mechanism. Alternatively, when the mechanisms affect ethnic violence in the same way, they reinforce one another.

Different contextual factors appear to affect the strength of the educational mechanisms. Most notably, all four mechanisms depend on and magnify the impact of ethnic cleavages. In addition, the frustration-aggression and competition mechanisms are most powerful in resource-scarce environments and environments with ineffective political institutions. Because the mechanisms complement one another, the socialization and mobilization mechanisms are also more likely to promote ethnic violence in environments with limited economic opportunities and ineffective political institutions. In this way, education is most likely to promote ethnic violence in environments that are ethnically divided, are nonwealthy, and possess ineffective political institutions – three characteristics that are quite common throughout much of the world, especially outside of Europe and North America. Throughout the remainder of this book, I test these propositions, beginning with a cross-national statistical analysis.

3

Testing the Impact of Education on Ethnic Violence

A Cross-Sectional Time-Series Analysis

Statistical methods explore generalizable causal arguments and are based on the assumption that A should be related to B if there is a causal relationship between A and B. Thus, if heavy rain triggers mudslides, mudslides should be more common during or shortly after heavy rain, and this can be tested statistically. One should not expect a perfect one-to-one relationship, however, as mudslides also depend on hilly terrain, deforestation, earth quakes, volcanic eruptions, and other factors. Along these lines, if education is a common determinant of peaceful ethnic relations, one would expect that educational attainment is usually lower among populations that experience ethnic violence and higher in regions with peaceful intercommunal relations. Alternatively, if education promotes ethnic violence, places with higher levels of education should – on average – experience higher levels of ethnic violence. Although there are many analyses that use statistics to provide insight into the causes of ethnic violence, very few actually explore whether education is related to it (see Lange and Balian 2008; Lange and Dawson 2010). The present chapter does just this. Based on the theoretical framework presented in Chapter 2, it also explores whether the impact of education on ethnic violence depends on ethnic diversity, the availability of resources, and the effectiveness of political institutions.

DATA AND METHODS

To explore the relationship between education and ethnic violence, I perform a cross-sectional time-series analysis. This methodology combines and simultaneously exploits two different types of statistical comparison to investigate the correlates of ethnic violence. First, it *compares different countries* to explore whether particular country-level characteristics are related to ethnic violence. Thus, if countries that experienced ethnic violence, on average, had populations with higher levels of education than countries that did not, it provides evidence that education contributes to ethnic violence. Second, the time-series element takes into consideration whether educational changes *within a particular country over time* are related to changes in ethnic violence within that same country over time. Thus, if ethnic violence is more common after periods of rapid educational expansion, this also provides evidence that education promotes ethnic violence.

Notably, the use of aggregate, national-level measures of education and ethnic violence are hardly ideal for the purposes of this analysis. Indeed, data on the educational levels of individuals, whether and how individuals participate in ethnic violence, educational and economic differentials between ethnic communities, the content of education, unemployment and underemployment by education level and ethnicity, and the level of unmet expectations by education level would all provide better insight into the relationship between ethnic violence and education. Unfortunately, such data do not exist. As a consequence, I use aggregate data on education, ethnic violence, and other factors, a problematic second-best approach but one that still provides evidence into the impact of education on ethnic violence. In particular, the statistical analysis provides insight into whether or not a country's level of educational attainment and pace of educational expansion affect the risk of ethnic violence.

The cross-sectional time-series data for this analysis cover the period from 1960 to 1999, and the set includes countries with more than 500,000 people and available data. Data on the level of ethnic violence are only available for decades: they score the highest level of ethnic violence within a country during the 1960s, the 1970s, the 1980s, and the 1990s. For the remaining variables, I take the average score throughout the decade. Different from most time-series analyses, I therefore score variables decennially instead of annually.

Pooled ordinary least squares regression is often inappropriate for cross-sectional time-series analysis, because multiple observations from the same country at different periods of time are likely more similar than the observations between countries. The Breusch and Pagan (1979) Lagrange Multiplier statistic tests for the presence of these unmeasured country effects, or unobserved heterogeneity. My tests confirm the presence of unobserved heterogeneity in the models. Consequently, the use of pooled regression may result in *heterogeneity bias*, where unmeasured country effects result in inconsistent or meaningless estimates of pooled regression parameters (Hsiao 2003). Two common strategies that statistically control for unmeasured heterogeneity using panel data are the random-effects model and the fixed-effects model. The Hausman (1978) test of the two modeling strategies indicates that the random-effects model is the most efficient and consistent estimator for all models presented later in the chapter and is thus employed to analyze the data.[1]

Dependent Variable

I employ data from the Minorities At Risk Project (MAR) to measure ethnic violence (Bennett and Davenport 2003). In particular, I use the MAR variable measuring intercommunal conflict, which occurs when civilians from a communal – or ethnic – group are involved in open conflict with civilians from another communal group living within the same country (Bennett and Davenport 2003). The severity of intercommunal conflict is measured on a seven-point scale: 0 = no conflict evident, 1 = individual acts of harassment, 2 = political agitation, 3 = sporadic violent attacks, 4 = anti-group demonstrations, 5 = communal rioting, and 6 = communal warfare. Thus, when violence between Hutus and Tutsis escalated into communal warfare during the 1990s, Rwanda had a score of 6 for the decade. Alternatively, Canada had a score of 0 for the 1980s because there was no known communal conflict, but there were incidents of communal harassment between First Nation and European Canadians during the 1990s, giving the country a score of 1 during the decade. Because many countries have more than one communal group experiencing violence in any given decade, I score a country's level of ethnic violence by using

---

[1] To test the robustness of the results, I consider two alternative estimation strategies: OLS using panel-corrected standard errors (Beck and Katz 1995) and OLS using cluster-correlated robust estimates of variance (Williams 2000). Given that I am able to confirm but not correct for autocorrelation owing to the data structure, I use the more conservative cluster-correlated robust estimates of variance. All the models using cluster-correlated estimates produce substantively similar results as the random-effects models, but I only present the results of the latter.

Whereas tests suggest the appropriateness of random effects, the results using fixed effects might also be of interest. When running models using fixed effects, the coefficients of the educational variables parallel the results using random effects, as all coefficients of the education variables are positively related to ethnic violence and have roughly the same magnitude as the education variables in the models using random effects. The fixed-effects models differ, however, in that the relationships between ethnic violence and education are not statistically significant.

the maximum score of all communal groups within a country for a given decade.

It is potentially problematic to assume that this measure of ethnic violence is continuous because the intervals between each point of the scale are not of equal size. For example, the difference between no ethnic violence (0) and acts of harassment (1) is not the same as the difference between communal rioting (5) and communal warfare (6). To test for the significance of this problem, I also code the MAR variable dichotomously and use logistic regression, and the results achieved using various dichotomous thresholds are very similar to those achieved using the continuous scoring.[2] Moreover, I ran the models using ordered logit, which is the most appropriate technique for models using an ordinally scored dependent variable. The results of the ordered logit analysis are also nearly identical to those using random effects.[3] For ease of interpretation and space constraints, I simply present the results using the random-effects models using the seven-point measure as a continuous variable.

Another potential problem is that the MAR dataset only includes countries with politically active ethnic communities at risk of violence – a situation that excludes countries with limited potential for ethnic violence and therefore results in a biased set of cases. To limit this problem, I include countries that are excluded from the MAR dataset when they meet all of the conditions for being included in the set except one: they lack minority communities either facing discrimination or actively pursuing community interests through collective mobilization. For the cases that are excluded from the MAR dataset, I assume that countries without a risk of ethnic violence have no ethnic violence and score them as zero.

Focal Independent Variables

To test whether or not education affects the risk of ethnic violence, I use three different measures of education and test the relationship between each educational measure and ethnic violence in separate models.

---

[2] I created the dichotomous variable in three different ways: (1) a Minorities at Risk (MAR) score of 0 equals 0, and a MAR score of 1 through 6 equals 1; (2) a MAR score of 0 and 1 equals 0, and a MAR score of 2 through 6 equals 1; and (3) a MAR score of 0 through 2 equals 0, and a MAR score of 3 through 6 equals one. All three scorings produce similar results.

[3] There is only one significant change that results from using ordered logit: secondary completion rate is negatively related to ethnic violence using the set of high-income countries when using ordered logit but is unrelated when using random effects.

The first measure is the total enrollment in secondary education, regardless of age, expressed as a percentage of the population in the official secondary school age group (World Bank 2002). It will be henceforth referred to as the "Secondary Enrollment Rate." The next two indicators are taken from Barro and Lee (2000). "Secondary Completion Rate" examines the percentage of the population aged twenty-five years and older, which has successfully completed secondary school. The final indicator measures the average years of schooling of the population aged twenty-five years and older and is labeled "Average Years of Education." I chose these measures because all three provide insight into a country's relative level of education. When measuring rates of educational enrollment and completion, I focus on secondary instead of primary or postsecondary education because the latter two have much less variation, with several countries having universal or near-universal primary education and most of the world having very limited levels of postsecondary education. In addition, secondary and postsecondary education appears to have the greatest impact on all four of the educational mechanisms (in particular, the frustration-aggression, competition, and mobilization mechanisms).

Control Variables

To test the relationship between a country's level of education and its level of ethnic violence, I include twelve additional independent variables as controls.

> *Level of Political Discrimination*: Following past analyses finding that political discrimination against ethnic communities provokes ethnic-based violence, I use data from the MAR dataset to control for the highest level of political discrimination experienced by any ethnic community in a given country during a given decade (Bennett and Davenport 2003). The data range is from 0 to 4: 0 = no significant discrimination, 1 = slight discrimination, 2 = substantial discrimination, 3 = major discrimination, and 4 = extreme discrimination.
>
> *Ethnic Diversity*: I use a fractionalization measure derived from the confirmatory factor analysis of Fearon's (2003) ethnic fractionalization and cultural diversity scores. This variable attempts to control for ethnic diversity, which is arguably a necessary condition for communal violence. The ethnic fractionalization variable measures the chance that two randomly selected individuals from a country

speak different languages. The cultural diversity index, on the other hand, measures the cultural distance between peoples in a given country by scoring the extent of similarity between languages spoken in the country. The data range from − 1.84 to 1.47, with higher values showing greater diversity. Notably, many scholars of ethnic violence note that the measure is problematic, as politicized ethnic cleavages and intercommunal animosity are not directly measured by the variable. Instead, it only provides a very crude indicator of the level of ethnic diversity.

Per Capita Gross Domestic Product (log): I use the natural log of per capita gross domestic product to control for level of economic development. Different theories suggest that ethnic violence depends on the level of economic development, and several studies find that it is negatively and significantly related to it. The variable is taken from the Penn World Tables (Heston, Sommers, and Aten 2002).

Total Population (log): Past studies consistently find that population size is an important determinant of ethnic violence, and I therefore include the natural log of total population. The data are taken from the Penn World Tables (Heston, Sommers, and Aten 2002).

Level of Democracy: I control for the level of democratization by using the "Polity2" variable in the *Polity IV* dataset (Marshall and Jaggers 2003). I include the variable because regime type might shape the form and extent of ethnic conflict and mobilization.

History of Colonialism: The sixth variable controls for a country's history of overseas colonization, as past analyses find that former colonies exhibit higher rates of ethnic violence than noncolonies, and numerous qualitative analyses provide evidence that colonialism promoted ethnic violence in diverse ways.[4] The data are taken from Lange and Dawson (2009) and are dichotomous, measuring whether or not a country was a formal overseas colony for at least ten consecutive years at any time between 1648 and 1999.

Mountainous Land (log): Following Fearon and Laitin (2003), I control for the percent of mountainous territory within each country, a geographical factor that potentially facilitates the escalation of collective violence by limiting state infrastructural power.

Communism: The eighth variable is dichotomous and controls for whether or not a country had a communist regime during at least

---

[4] See Berman 1998; Lange and Dawson 2009; Mamdani 2001; Weiner 1978.

ten consecutive years between 1960 and 1999. I employ it because communist regimes generally have relatively high rates of education, a factor that might cause a spurious relationship between education and ethnic violence if left uncontrolled.

Youth Population: I include a variable measuring the percentage of the total population that is between fifteen and twenty-four years of age, an age group that might be more inclined to participate in extremist and violent acts. The data are from *UN Population Division Quinquennial Estimates and Projections* (United Nations 2007).

Period Effects: Finally, I employ three variables to control for period effects, as different studies find that the prevalence of ethnic violence has increased since the 1950s. For the analysis, the 1960s is the reference group, and I include three dichotomous variables measuring whether or not the set of data observations is from the 1970s, 1980s, or 1990s.

Interactions with Education

The theoretical framework in Chapter 2 describes how the impact of education potentially depends on three contextual factors: ethnic diversity and antipathy, the availability of resources, and political institutions. I therefore explore whether education interacts with these factors.

For ethnic diversity, I simply add an interaction term between education and ethnic fractionalization in the models. Theoretically, the fractionalization measure is not ideal for exploring interactions because it is a rather crude and imprecise measure. Moreover, the impact of education on ethnic violence seems to depend more on intercommunal antipathy than diversity. Because intercommunal antipathy depends on diversity, however, the variable should measure ethnic antipathy to some extent.

As described previously, the frustration-aggression and competition mechanisms appear to depend on the availability of resources and opportunities for mobility, as impeded mobility increases both frustration and competition for resources. I therefore investigate whether education and per capita GDP interact in nonlinear ways to promote ethnic violence. Because of high levels of multicollinearity, I am unable to include an interaction term for education and per capita GDP. I therefore pursue an alternative strategy of running models with different sets – one with mid-to-low-income countries, the other with high-income countries – and compare the results to see if the relationship between education and ethnic violence is similar for the two sets of cases.[5] If the frustration-aggression and competition mechanisms promote ethnic violence, one would expect education to be unrelated or negatively related to ethnic violence among wealthy countries but positively related to ethnic violence among non-wealthy countries. Despite separating the countries into two sets according to income, I still employ per capita GDP as a control because there remains great variation within each income category.[6]

Finally, the impact of education might depend on political institutions – specifically, their respect for basic rights, political responsiveness, stability, capacity to implement complex policy, and non-clientelistic relations. Because of the diverse political elements that appear relevant, it is difficult to include all in one variable of political effectiveness. Several of these political characteristics, however, are at least partially operationalized by different World Bank Governance Indicators, especially variables measuring government effectiveness, rule of law, and government responsiveness and accountability. I therefore combine and equally weight the indicators for an aggregate measure of political effectiveness. Unfortunately, the World Bank Governance Indicators are only available after 1996 and therefore cannot be employed as a control in models using panel data. As a consequence, I follow the strategy used to explore interactions between education and economic development: I divide the cases into two sets – high political effectiveness and medium-to-low levels of political effectiveness – based on the aggregate World Bank Governance

---

[5] To separate high-income from mid-to-low-income countries, I used the World Bank's (2008a) classification of high-income countries in 2007. However, I realize that some countries that are currently classified as high income may not have had high incomes throughout the entire time period under investigation. As such, I also categorized countries according to Western cultural heritage (i.e., Western Europe, Australia, Canada, New Zealand, and the United States), as these countries had high levels of income throughout the period of analysis. The results between the two classification schemes were nearly identical, so I simply present the income-based classification because of my interest in the interaction between national income and education.

Notably, the variations in the values of each measure of education within these two sets of countries are quite similar. Comparing the ranges between the income categories, I find that the Secondary Completion Rate ranges from 2 to 44.2 for the high-income category, as compared to 0.1 to 25.8 for the low-to-mid-income category; the Average Years of Education ranges from 2.2 to 12.1 for high-income countries and 0.1 to 10.4 for the other countries; lastly, the Secondary Enrollment Rate ranges from 33.8 to 136.1 as compared to 0.9 to 95.7 for high-income and mid-to-low-income countries, respectively.

[6] The range of the logged per capita GDP values is 7.56 to 10.25 for high income-countries and 5.99 to 9.30 for mid-to-low-income countries.

Indicator data from 1998.[7] Using these sets, I run the models to see whether the relationship between education and ethnic violence depends on the level of political effectiveness.[8] I use an aggregate score of 0.4 as the dividing line between countries with high and medium-to-low levels of political effectiveness. Notably, 0 is the average of all countries in the world, and the use of the 0.4 cutoff results in a high-effectiveness set that has one-third of the cases. I chose this relatively high point because political effectiveness likely limits grievances only at relatively high levels. Moreover, this division also facilitates comparison with the models disaggregated by income level, as the numbers of cases in the two sets are roughly equivalent to the sets disaggregated by per capita GDP.

Data Summary and Diagnostics

Summary statistics for each variable are presented in Table 3.1. Although I collected data for 160 countries, the models use between 100 and 121 cases because some cases have missing scores for at least one variable during all time periods and are therefore dropped from the set.[9] In addition, some of the remaining cases are missing at least one of the four data observation points, causing the models to be unbalanced. I conduct tests of nonlinearity and influence in the models. Concerning nonlinearity, per capita gross domestic product, total population, and the percent of mountainous territory within each country are best modeled by their natural log. I identified influential cases by examining the residuals of each

---

[7] The World Bank Governance indicators are constructed following a normal distribution with a mean of zero and unit standard deviation, so that the global average is 0, with 68 percent of the world's countries having scores between −1 and 1 and 95 percent of the world's countries having scores between −2 and 2. Positive scores represent better-than-average governance and negative scores represent worse-than-average governance.

[8] This strategy is potentially problematic because a country's level of political effectiveness undoubtedly varied between 1960 and 1999, but comparative-historical analyses find that political effectiveness is quite stable. Lange (2009), for example, explores the determinants of state capacity using statistical methods and finds that the correlation between political effectiveness in 1955 and 2000 is more than 0.7 among former British colonies.

[9] A comparison of levels of intercommunal conflict and education highlights that the countries excluded from the set are very similar to those included in it. For example, the average level of intercommunal violence was 1.29 for the countries included in the analysis and 1.04 for those countries excluded from it, and the average secondary completion rate was 14.79 for the included countries and 13.25 for those countries excluded from it (the differences are very similar using the other two education variables as well). Those countries excluded from the set therefore tend to have similar but slightly lower levels of both ethnic violence and education.

TABLE 3.1. *Summary Statistics*

Dependent Variables	N	Mean	Std. Dev.	Min	Max
Communal Conflict	505	1.21	2	0	6
Focal Independent Variables					
Secondary Completion Rate	428	8.57	8.49	0.1	44.2
Average Years of Education	424	4.65	2.94	0.1	12.1
Secondary Enrollment Rate	538	43.78	32.00	27.0	136.1
Control Variables					
Political Discrimination	547	2.17	1.66	0	4
Fractionalization	533	−0.29	0.93	−1.84	1.47
Overseas Colony Status	550	0.7	0.46	0	1
Population (log)	457	16.02	1.47	12.9	20.9
% Mountainous (log)	547	1.15	2.92	−4.61	4.55
Democracy	547	0.37	7.17	−10	10
GDP (log)	457	8.15	1.04	5.99	10.26
Communist Heritage	550	0.2	0.4	0	1
% Population aged 15–24 yrs.	533	0.18	0.02	0.12	0.23
1970s	550	0.25	0.43	0	1
1980s	550	0.25	0.43	0	1
1990s	550	0.29	0.45	0	1

observation of the random-effects models (using the combined residual, which includes both the random-error and overall error components). The exclusion of the observations with the largest residuals does not substantively alter the findings presented below. I also conduct tests of collinearity on the pooled regressions prior to running their corresponding random-effects models. Multicollinearity between the independent variables is at tolerable levels, as all variance inflation factors (VIF) are less than six. In the models that prove to be the most important for this analysis (the models in Tables 3.4, 3.7, and 3.9), VIF scores are less than 3.

RESULTS

Table 3.2 lists the results when using the entire set of cases and includes three models. The models differ according to the focal independent variable: the first model uses secondary completion rate as the focal independent variable, the second model uses average years of education as the focal independent variable, and the third model uses secondary enrollment rate as the focal independent variable. Of the three educational

TABLE 3.2. *Random-Effects Models of the Determinants of Ethnic Violence, Entire Set*

Regressors	Secondary Completion	Avg. Years of Education	Secondary Enroll. Rate
Education	0.007	0.190**	0.022***
	(0.013)	(0.080)	(0.007)
Political Discrimination	0.302***	0.316***	0.364***
	(0.081)	(0.080)	(0.072)
Fractionalization	0.247*	0.264*	0.234*
	(0.142)	(0.141)	(0.131)
Overseas Colony Status	0.330	0.281	0.887***
	(0.365)	(0.356)	(0.326)
Population (logged)	0.396***	0.387***	0.353***
	(0.092)	(0.091)	(0.081)
% Mountainous (logged)	−0.027	−0.029	−0.017
	(0.044)	(0.043)	(0.040)
Democracy	0.003	−0.008	0.003
	(0.018)	(0.018)	(0.017)
GDP (logged)	−0.234	−0.546**	−0.588***
	(0.202)	(0.223)	(0.199)
Communist Heritage	−0.558	−0.887*	−0.463
	(0.467)	(0.482)	(0.389)
% Population between 15–24	−9.842	−9.527	−11.708*
	(6.556)	(6.381)	(6.112)
1970s	0.116	0.152	−0.045
	(0.246)	(0.247)	(0.238)
1980s	−0.040	−0.078	−0.339
	(0.266)	(0.262)	(0.264)
1990s	1.464***	1.370***	0.966***
	(0.273)	(0.266)	(0.276)
Constant	−2.646	−0.672	0.086
	(2.614)	(2.657)	(2.443)
Observations	349	345	402
Number of Countries	101	100	121
R-squared (Overall)	0.343	0.359	0.351

Standard errors in parentheses
* p. < .10, ** p< .05, *** p < .01

variables, two (average years of education and secondary enrollment rate) are positively and significantly related ethnic violence whereas the third (secondary completion rate) is unrelated to it. The coefficients of the variables measuring average years of education and secondary enrollment rate suggest that an increase in education by one standard deviation is associated with an increase in the level of ethnic violence by between

0.6 and 0.7. With the average decennial level of ethnic violence being 1.2 for all countries during all decades, these increases are quite substantial. Overall, the findings are therefore mixed but offer evidence that education increases the risk of ethnic violence.

Besides the education variables, several control variables are significantly related to ethnic violence. As expected, political discrimination, ethnic fractionalization, a history of colonialism, population density, and the dummy for the 1990s are all positively related to ethnic violence, suggesting that they promote ethnic violence. Alternatively, per capita GDP is negatively related to it, showing that wealthy countries are at lower risk of ethnic violence.

Tables 3.3 and 3.4 use the same models as Table 3.2 but employ different sets of cases. Specifically, because of the potential interaction between education and per capita GDP but an inability to use an interaction term, I separate the countries into two sets – mid-to-low-income countries and high-income countries – to see if the results differ depending on national income. The results in Table 3.3 clearly show that education has a weak relationship with ethnic violence in high-income countries, as none of the education variables are significantly related to ethnic violence. Education therefore does not appear to affect ethnic violence in wealthy environments.

The results for the mid-to-low-income countries in Table 3.4 tell a much different story. The three educational variables are all positively and significantly related to ethnic violence. A comparison of the results using the set of non-wealthy countries in Table 3.4 with the results using the complete set in Table 3.2 shows several marked differences. When the set is restricted to non-wealthy countries, the significance levels of all three educational variables are statistically significant (the p-values for all three are below .001), and their coefficients increase considerably. In addition, the R-squared values of the model increase markedly. The coefficients of the educational variables in Table 3.4 show that an increase by one standard deviation is associated with an increase in ethnic violence by between 0.6 (secondary completion) and 0.9 (years of education and secondary enrollment). This effect is considerable, as the average level of ethnic violence is only 1.2. The findings therefore suggest that the impact of education on ethnic violence depends on the availability of resources, with education having a strong and positive impact on ethnic violence in non-wealthy countries but no net effect in wealthy countries.

The finding that national income level shapes the impact of education on ethnic violence offers strongest support to the frustration-aggression

TABLE 3.3. *Random-Effects Models of the Determinants of Ethnic Violence, Set of High-Income Countries*

Regressors	Secondary Completion	Avg. Years of Education	Secondary Enroll. Rate
Education	−0.031	−0.097	0.004
	(0.020)	(0.168)	(0.013)
Political Discrimination	0.298*	0.331**	0.392**
	(0.156)	(0.157)	(0.158)
Fractionalization	0.625	0.688	0.485
	(0.483)	(0.481)	(0.443)
Overseas Colony Status	0.171	−0.061	0.217
	(0.794)	(0.810)	(0.665)
Population (logged)	0.338	0.329	0.233
	(0.227)	(0.229)	(0.216)
% Mountainous (logged)	0.090	0.057	0.025
	(0.098)	(0.096)	(0.090)
Democracy	0.071**	0.076**	0.088**
	(0.035)	(0.036)	(0.036)
GDP (logged)	−0.001	−0.225	−0.375
	(0.743)	(0.803)	(0.708)
Communist Heritage	0.665	0.803	0.820
	(1.051)	(1.075)	(1.014)
% Population between 15–24	0.975	1.540	−2.659
	(10.943)	(11.204)	(10.826)
1970s	0.134	0.054	−0.057
	(0.427)	(0.430)	(0.483)
1980s	0.487	0.298	0.083
	(0.536)	(0.526)	(0.616)
1990s	1.617**	1.365**	0.939
	(0.630)	(0.615)	(0.769)
Constant	−4.762	−2.560	−0.261
	(7.420)	(7.717)	(7.069)
Observations	102	102	102
Number of Countries	29	29	30
R-squared (Overall)	0.344	0.338	0.344

Standard errors in parentheses
* p. < .10, ** p < .05, *** p < .01

and competition mechanisms. The frustration-aggression mechanism suggests that the educated are more likely to act violently in resource-scarce environments because they are less likely to meet their expectations for mobility. Similarly, the competition mechanism proposes that a scarcity of resources contributes to ethnic violence by heightening competition. Along these lines, countries with levels of education that are

TABLE 3.4. *Random-Effects Models of the Determinants of Ethnic Violence, Set of Middle- and Low-Income Countries*

Regressors	Secondary Completion	Avg. Years of Education	Secondary Enroll. Rate
Education	0.067***	0.301***	0.029***
	(0.022)	(0.095)	(0.008)
Political Discrimination	0.330***	0.309***	0.389***
	(0.085)	(0.087)	(0.078)
Fractionalization	0.207	0.242*	0.206
	(0.136)	(0.143)	(0.134)
Overseas Colony Status	0.983**	1.043**	1.482***
	(0.438)	(0.454)	(0.417)
Population (logged)	0.479***	0.518***	0.399***
	(0.091)	(0.095)	(0.086)
% Mountainous (logged)	−0.067	−0.059	−0.021
	(0.047)	(0.049)	(0.045)
Democracy	−0.032*	−0.038*	−0.027
	(0.019)	(0.020)	(0.018)
GDP (logged)	−0.725***	−0.764***	−0.779***
	(0.225)	(0.236)	(0.218)
Communist Heritage	−0.916*	−1.183**	−0.592
	(0.504)	(0.543)	(0.436)
% Population between 15–24	−12.289	−12.944	−15.313*
	(9.274)	(9.452)	(8.903)
1970s	0.206	0.264	0.054
	(0.310)	(0.317)	(0.285)
1980s	−0.188	−0.136	−0.358
	(0.337)	(0.343)	(0.317)
1990s	1.459***	1.531***	1.260***
	(0.363)	(0.369)	(0.333)
Constant	−0.859	−1.532	0.526
	(2.920)	(2.901)	(2.828)
Observations	247	243	300
Number of Countries	72	71	91
R-squared (Overall)	0.444	0.449	0.417

Standard errors in parentheses
* p. < .10, **p < .05, *** p < .01

high relative to their national income levels and that experience rapid increases in education are most prone to ethnic violence, a situation that is likely characterized by both a relatively large pool of unemployed and underemployed individuals with relatively high levels of education and heightened competition among educated individuals for high-status jobs. The results in Table 3.4 clearly show this pattern.

Similar to the models in Table 3.2, several control variables are strongly related to ethnic violence in Table 3.4. The population and the 1990 decennial control variables are both strongly and positively related to ethnic violence in most models; and fractionalization, colonial heritage, and the logged value of per capita GDP are significantly related in some models; and all relationships are in the expected directions. The only major differences between the control variables in Tables 3.2 and 3.4 are that the fractionalization variable loses its significance in two models and colonial heritage and per capita GDP gain significance in some models.

To test whether education and ethnic fractionalization interact to affect ethnic violence, I add an interaction term multiplying education and ethnic fractionalization in Tables 3.5 through 3.7. Table 3.5 uses the entire set of cases, Table 3.6 uses the set of high-income countries, and Table 3.7 uses the set of medium- and low-income countries. In Table 3.5, one of three interaction terms – using the average years of education variable – is significantly related to ethnic violence, offering only limited evidence that education and ethnic diversity interact. When analyzing the high-income countries in Table 3.6, none of the interaction terms are significant, suggesting that no interaction occurs among wealthy countries. Alternatively, all three interaction terms are positively and significantly related to ethnic violence when the set is limited to non-wealthy countries in Table 3.7, although the relationship is only significant at the 0.05-level in one of the models. Although supporting the theoretical framework in Chapter 2, these findings are relatively weak. Still, considering that the ethnic fractionalization variable is imprecise and a poor proxy for intercommunal antipathy, measurement error might very well account for the relative weakness of the findings.

Aside from the availability of resources and ethnic divisions, the theoretical framework in Chapter 2 claims that the impact of education on ethnic violence depends on the effectiveness of political institutions. Specifically, states that have the capacity to implement complex policy, are responsive to the population, are stable, and protect basic rights are more likely to limit grievances and competition among of the educated. Alternatively, states without these characteristics are more likely to discriminate against ethnic communities, to lack the capacity to stop ethnic violence, to use violence against its citizens, to promote ethnic competition, and to fail to provide effective political channels through which citizens can address grievances. As a consequence, the educated are more likely affected by the frustration-aggression and competition mechanisms in environments with ineffective political institutions. To explore whether

TABLE 3.5. *Random-Effects Models of the Determinants of Ethnic Violence with Fractionalization-Education Interaction, Entire Set*

Regressors	Secondary Completion	Avg. Years of Education	Secondary Enroll. Rate
Education	0.016	0.235***	0.024***
	(0.015)	(0.082)	(0.007)
Fractionalization	0.108	−0.118	0.067
	(0.181)	(0.234)	(0.192)
Educ*Fract	0.012	0.099**	0.004
	(0.009)	(0.048)	(0.004)
Political Discrimination	0.300***	0.303***	0.354***
	(0.081)	(0.079)	(0.072)
Overseas Colony Status	0.252	0.174	0.830**
	(0.371)	(0.358)	(0.326)
Population (logged)	0.400***	0.402***	0.359***
	(0.092)	(0.091)	(0.081)
% Mountainous (logged)	−0.034	−0.039	−0.020
	(0.045)	(0.043)	(0.040)
Democracy	0.004	−0.007	0.003
	(0.018)	(0.018)	(0.017)
GDP (logged)	−0.304	−0.609***	−0.623***
	(0.210)	(0.224)	(0.199)
Communist Heritage	−0.603	−0.866*	−0.502
	(0.469)	(0.480)	(0.386)
% Population between 15–24	−10.822	−12.274*	−13.706**
	(6.603)	(6.487)	(6.275)
1970s	0.136	0.197	−0.019
	(0.246)	(0.247)	(0.240)
1980s	−0.018	−0.026	−0.315
	(0.267)	(0.262)	(0.265)
1990s	1.471***	1.398***	0.984***
	(0.273)	(0.266)	(0.276)
Constant	−1.964	0.105	0.658
	(2.675)	(2.668)	(2.456)
Observations	349	345	402
Number of Countries	101	100	121
R − squared (Overall)	0.348	0.369	0.357

Standard errors in parentheses
* p. < .10, ** p < .05, *** p < .01

education interacts with effective political institutions, I combine and equally weight three World Bank Governance Indicators measuring voice and accountability, government effectiveness, and rule of law. Because the data are only available from 1996 to the present, I cannot use the variable

TABLE 3.6. *Random-Effects Models of the Determinants of Ethnic Violence with Fractionalization-Education Interaction, High-Income Countries*

Regressors	Secondary Completion	Avg. Years of Education	Secondary Enroll. Rate
Education	−0.050**	−0.200	0.002
	(0.025)	(0.205)	(0.014)
Fractionalization	1.302*	1.699	0.718
	(0.756)	(1.263)	(0.891)
Educ*Fract	−0.019	−0.121	−0.003
	(0.016)	(0.139)	(0.009)
Political Discrimination	0.235	0.280*	0.389**
	(0.164)	(0.167)	(0.160)
Overseas Colony Status	0.215	−0.075	0.224
	(0.823)	(0.818)	(0.651)
Population (logged)	0.436*	0.393	0.237
	(0.246)	(0.242)	(0.215)
% Mountainous (logged)	0.119	0.083	0.027
	(0.105)	(0.101)	(0.089)
Democracy	0.065*	0.075**	0.089**
	(0.035)	(0.036)	(0.036)
GDP (logged)	−0.238	−0.497	−0.496
	(0.774)	(0.869)	(0.778)
Communist Heritage	0.593	0.677	0.782
	(1.091)	(1.096)	(1.002)
% Population between 15–24	−0.218	−0.353	−4.011
	(10.929)	(11.441)	(11.204)
1970s	0.236	0.143	−0.014
	(0.434)	(0.443)	(0.495)
1980s	0.636	0.420	0.140
	(0.552)	(0.546)	(0.630)
1990s	1.784***	1.481**	0.972
	(0.648)	(0.632)	(0.773)
Constant	−3.206	0.173	1.136
	(7.668)	(8.446)	(7.743)
Observations	102	102	102
Number of Countries	29	29	30
R-squared (Overall)	0.335	0.347	0.349

Standard errors in parentheses
* $p < .10$, ** $p < .05$, *** $p < .01$

for an interaction term in the models. I therefore follow the strategy used in Tables 3.3 and 3.4 and divide the set by level of political effectiveness, thereby allowing me to explore whether the impact of education varies according to level of political effectiveness.

TABLE 3.7. *Random-Effects Models of the Determinants of Ethnic Violence with Fractionalization-Education Interaction, Low-Income and Medium-Income Countries*

Regressors	Secondary Completion	Avg. Years of Education	Secondary Enroll. Rate
Education	0.080***	0.362***	0.032***
	(0.024)	(0.097)	(0.008)
Fractionalization	−0.026	−0.261	−0.068
	(0.192)	(0.252)	(0.206)
Educ*Fract	0.029*	0.164**	0.009*
	(0.017)	(0.069)	(0.005)
Political Discrimination	0.321***	0.276***	0.368***
	(0.084)	(0.087)	(0.077)
Overseas Colony Status	0.945**	0.911**	1.434***
	(0.438)	(0.450)	(0.400)
Population (logged)	0.498***	0.534***	0.411***
	(0.092)	(0.094)	(0.083)
% Mountainous (logged)	−0.079*	−0.072	−0.025
	(0.048)	(0.049)	(0.043)
Democracy	−0.034*	−0.040**	−0.028
	(0.019)	(0.020)	(0.018)
GDP (logged)	−0.775***	−0.789***	−0.812***
	(0.227)	(0.232)	(0.211)
Communist Heritage	−0.927*	−1.117**	−0.600
	(0.503)	(0.535)	(0.420)
% Population between 15–24	−16.071*	−20.096**	−19.774**
	(9.498)	(9.816)	(9.138)
1970s	0.248	0.333	0.093
	(0.310)	(0.315)	(0.288)
1980s	−0.140	−0.060	−0.320
	(0.336)	(0.342)	(0.318)
1990s	1.483***	1.575***	1.297***
	(0.362)	(0.365)	(0.332)
Constant	−0.063	−0.161	1.469
	(2.950)	(2.915)	(2.786)
Observations	247	243	300
Number of Countries	72	71	91
R-squared (Overall)	0.450	0.461	0.425

Standard errors in parentheses
* $p < .10$, ** $p < .05$, *** $p < .01$

TABLE 3.8. *Random-Effects Models of the Determinants of Ethnic Violence, Set of Countries with High Political Effectiveness*

Regressors	Secondary Completion	Avg. Years of Education	Secondary Enroll. Rate
Education	−0.030	−0.027	0.019
	(0.019)	(0.155)	(0.012)
Fractionalization	0.617	0.662*	0.663*
	(0.378)	(0.378)	(0.377)
Political Discrimination	0.247*	0.295**	0.365**
	(0.149)	(0.150)	(0.152)
Overseas Colony Status	0.010	−0.274	−0.054
	(0.676)	(0.687)	(0.656)
Population (logged)	0.310	0.287	0.222
	(0.203)	(0.207)	(0.204)
% Mountainous (logged)	0.064	0.033	0.028
	(0.084)	(0.082)	(0.081)
Democracy	0.046	0.046	0.043
	(0.032)	(0.033)	(0.033)
GDP (logged)	0.280	−0.117	−0.499
	(0.619)	(0.694)	(0.591)
Communist Heritage	0.336	0.362	0.431
	(0.893)	(0.941)	(0.890)
% Population between 15–24	0.801	1.908	0.341
	(9.592)	(9.718)	(9.646)
1970s	0.096	0.029	−0.215
	(0.379)	(0.383)	(0.406)
1980s	0.476	0.307	−0.076
	(0.445)	(0.436)	(0.488)
1990s	1.497***	1.282***	0.644
	(0.502)	(0.488)	(0.618)
Constant	−6.627	−3.147	0.239
	(6.290)	(6.751)	(6.079)
Observations	122	122	121
Number of Countries	33	33	33
R-squared (Overall)	0.333	0.327	0.352

Standard errors in parentheses
* $p < .10$, ** $p < .05$, *** $p < .01$

Tables 3.8 gives the results for the set of countries with high political effectiveness, and Table 3.9 gives the results for the set of countries with medium and low political effectiveness. The results in Table 3.8 are very similar to those in Table 3.3, the only significant difference being that the relationship between democracy and ethnic violence loses its significance. Thus, education has no impact on violence among countries with high

TABLE 3.9. *Random-Effects Models of the Determinants of Ethnic Violence, Set of Countries with Low and Medium Political Effectiveness*

Regressors	Secondary Completion	Avg. Years of Education	Secondary Enroll. Rate
Education	0.058**	0.345***	0.026***
	(0.024)	(0.102)	(0.008)
Fractionalization	0.172	0.199	0.168
	(0.153)	(0.151)	(0.145)
Political Discrimination	0.324***	0.307***	0.381***
	(0.092)	(0.091)	(0.082)
Overseas Colony Status	1.023**	1.059**	1.603***
	(0.481)	(0.468)	(0.427)
Population (logged)	0.493***	0.548***	0.418***
	(0.099)	(0.098)	(0.090)
% Mountainous (logged)	−0.046	−0.048	−0.007
	(0.054)	(0.053)	(0.050)
Democracy	−0.025	−0.040*	−0.021
	(0.020)	(0.021)	(0.020)
GDP (logged)	−0.775***	−0.900***	−0.835***
	(0.239)	(0.235)	(0.223)
Communist Heritage	−0.864	−1.210**	−0.537
	(0.548)	(0.561)	(0.452)
% Population between 15–24	−10.271	−14.330	−14.994
	(10.507)	(10.443)	(9.882)
1970s	0.186	0.292	0.067
	(0.327)	(0.336)	(0.300)
1980s	−0.280	−0.232	−0.411
	(0.358)	(0.364)	(0.333)
1990s	1.438***	1.452***	1.252***
	(0.385)	(0.384)	(0.344)
Constant	−1.059	−0.833	0.545
	(3.158)	(3.057)	(2.992)
Observations	227	223	281
Number of Countries	68	67	88
R-squared (Overall)	0.434	0.451	0.407

Standard errors in parentheses
* $p < .10$, ** $p < .05$, *** $p < .01$

levels of political effectiveness. Alternatively, the results in Table 3.9 mirror those in Table 3.4 and show that education is strongly and positively related to ethnic violence in countries *without* highly effective political institutions. The tables therefore provide evidence that the impact of education depends on political effectiveness. This finding supports the frustration-aggression mechanism most strongly, as ineffective political institutions are a common cause of grievances among the educated. It also supports the competition mechanism, as ineffective political institutions increase political competition among the educated. Yet, the extreme similarities between Tables 3.3 and 3.8 and between Tables 3.4 and 3.9 suggest that per capita GDP and the aggregate measure of political effectiveness might measure the same thing. Indeed, the correlation between political effectiveness in 1998 and the log of average per capita GDP during the 1990s is 0.80. One therefore cannot be certain whether the impact of education depends on the availability of resources, the effectiveness of political institutions, or both.

Although the findings in Tables 3.2 through 3.9 suggest that education contributes to ethnic violence in particular environments, it is possible that the direction of causation actually goes from ethnic violence to education: ethnic violence might promote communal competition for education and thereby increase demand for it. To explore this possibility, I run a lagged statistical analysis testing whether past ethnic violence is related to subsequent levels of education, something one would expect if the direction of causation runs from ethnic violence to education. For this, I employ the same data and methods as the previous models (i.e., random-effects models using decennially scored data) but use education as the dependent variable and ethnic violence as the focal independent variable. Another major difference is that the analysis is lagged: the independent and dependent variables are measured in different decades, with the independent variables measured in time one and the dependent variables measured in time two. Because of the lag, the analysis only uses panel data from three decades – the 1970, 1980s, and 1990s. In addition to the focal independent variable, I employ per capita GDP (logged) and level of democracy as independent variables. I also control for temporal effects, using the 1970s as the reference category.

Table 3.10 shows the results using three different dependent variables: models 1 and 2 use secondary completion rate, models 3 and 4 use average years of education, and models 5 and 6 use secondary enrollment rate. In turn, the first model of each dependent variable includes the full set of cases, and the second model of each dependent variable includes the set of non-wealthy countries. The results show that the models account for much of the variation in education, with R-squared values ranging between 0.5 and 0.75. Per capita GDP and the decennial dummies for the 1980s and 1990s are all positively and significantly related to education in all models. Alternatively, communal conflict is unrelated to education in five of the six models. The exception is the model using secondary

TABLE 3.10. *Random-Effects Models of the Determinants of Education*

	Secondary Completion		Avg. Years of Education		Secondary Enrol. Rate	
Regressors	1	2	1	2	1	2
Communal Conflict	0.260	0.244	0.002	0.002	0.786*	0.496
	(0.221)	(0.197)	(0.029)	(0.028)	(0.427)	(0.406)
Democracy	0.065	0.107*	0.010	0.007	0.249*	0.009
	(0.070)	(0.062)	(0.009)	(0.009)	(0.146)	(0.146)
GDP (logged)	11.106***	7.262***	1.716***	1.177***	23.798***	16.961***
	(0.789)	(0.762)	(0.121)	(0.138)	(1.470)	(1.856)
1980	2.271***	2.042***	0.368***	0.545***	4.086***	6.404***
	(0.563)	(0.551)	(0.073)	(0.076)	(1.147)	(1.167)
1990	5.538***	5.501***	0.956***	1.283***	10.427***	11.765***
	(0.609)	(0.581)	(0.083)	(0.085)	(1.214)	(1.247)
Constant	−77.256***	−48.824***	−9.582***	−6.101***	−149.570***	−102.159***
	(6.297)	(5.806)	(0.971)	(1.050)	(11.691)	(14.052)
Observations	262	186	262	186	289	213
Number of Countries	97	71	97	71	106	80
R-squared (Overall)	0.649	0.532	0.720	0.494	0.752	0.5

Standard errors in parentheses
* $p < .10$, ** $p < .05$, *** $p < .01$

enrollment rate for the entire set of cases, and ethnic violence is positively related to education, albeit with limited significance (p. < .10). So, not only is past ethnic violence weakly related to subsequent education, but the one model with some significance includes the entire set cases. And if the relationships in the previous models were driven by the impact of ethnic violence on education, one would have expected much stronger relationships between education and ethnic violence, especially among non-wealthy countries. The analysis therefore fails to strongly support the hypothesis that ethnic violence promotes education and thereby offers evidence that any causal relationship highlighted in Tables 3.2 through 3.9 runs primarily from education to ethnic violence.

CONCLUSION

In this chapter, I investigate the relationship between the average educational attainment of a country's population and its level of ethnic violence and find that three different measures of education are positively and significantly related to ethnic violence when controlling for diverse variables. The statistical results therefore suggest that countries with more educated populations and rapid educational expansion are at a higher risk of ethnic violence than countries with less educated populations and slower educational expansion. I provide evidence, however, that the impact of education on ethnic violence is not the same for all countries but depends on three structural factors. First, the impact of education depends on the availability of resources, with education having no relationship with ethnic violence among wealthy countries but a very strong and positive effect among non-wealthy countries. Second, the analysis provides evidence that education – at least among non-wealthy countries – interacts with ethnic diversity. Finally, education is unrelated to ethnic violence among countries with high political effectiveness but positively and strongly related to ethnic violence among countries with medium-to-low levels of political effectiveness.

Aside from simply showing a relationship between ethnic violence and education, the statistical analysis also checks the direction of causation. In particular, I run a lagged analysis to see if past ethnic violence explains subsequent levels and changes in education. I find that ethnic violence is only weakly related to education in one of six models, and the analysis therefore fails to support claims that the relationship between education and ethnic violence runs from ethnic violence to education.

Despite robust findings that offer strong support to the theoretical framework presented in Chapter 2, any interpretation of the results must be questioned for at least two reasons. Most importantly, I use national-level data, but the theoretical mechanisms I describe occur at diverse levels of analysis. The results simply show that environments with more educated individuals and more rapid expansions in education are more likely to experience ethnic violence, and one cannot be certain that any of the mechanisms described in Chapter 2 underlie the relationship between education and ethnic violence. Second, it remains possible that the relationship is inaccurate because of missing variables or measurement error, as both problems commonly afflict cross-national statistical analysis. Because of these potential problems, further analysis is needed. To provide additional insight into whether any of the four educational mechanisms underlie the positive statistical relationship between level of education and level of ethnic violence, I now turn to comparative-historical methods and analyze the impact of education on ethnic violence in multiple cases, beginning with Sri Lanka.

4

Education and Ethnic Violence in Sri Lanka

According to Jayasuriya (2004), Sri Lanka – known as Ceylon until 1972 – was characterized by impressive social *welfare* in the 1940s, 1950s, and 1960s but has experienced intense social *warfare* since the 1970s. In this chapter, I explore whether the two are causally related. I begin by reviewing the country's history of ethnic violence and educational expansion. Next, I analyze whether educated individuals contributed to ethnic violence in influential ways. Finally, I investigate whether any of the educational mechanisms promoted ethnic violence.

ETHNICITY AND ETHNO-NATIONALIST VIOLENCE IN SRI LANKA

Sri Lanka is located on an island off the southern tip of India and is inhabited by 20 million people from diverse linguistic and religious backgrounds. The Sinhalese are the largest ethnic community and comprise nearly three-quarters of the island's total population. The Sinhalese speak Sinhala, an Indo-European language, and are nearly all Buddhist. Their progenitors emigrated from India approximately 3,000 years ago and gradually absorbed other peoples (including communities already living on the island and other more recent immigrants from the Indian mainland). Although sharing the same religion and language, the Sinhalese are divided between the Kandyan and Low-Country Sinhalese, an internal division with only limited social significance that resulted primarily from geography and historical differences in the extent of European colonial influence.

The Tamils are the second-largest ethnic community in Sri Lanka and comprise approximately 17 percent of the total population. They speak

Tamil, a Dravidian language, and are predominantly Hindu. Like the Sinhalese, the Tamils emigrated from the Indian subcontinent and are divided into two communities – Sri Lankan and Indian Tamils. The Sri Lankan Tamils comprise approximately 10 percent of the population and settled in Sri Lanka in different streams long before European colonialism. Many assimilated with the Sinhalese, but those settling in northern and eastern Sri Lanka retained a distinct Tamil culture and identity. The Indian Tamils, on the other hand, immigrated to Sri Lanka to work on the plantations in the central highlands during the British colonial period. Despite their common language and religion, both Tamil groups remain distinct from one another because they live in different regions of the island, because the Indian Tamils are generally from lower castes, and because the Sri Lankan Tamils frequently view the Indian Tamils as nonnatives. It is therefore appropriate to speak of each as separate ethnic communities. Throughout the remainder of this book, I use "Tamil" strictly to refer to Sri Lankan Tamils.

Muslims and Burghers comprise most of the remainder of the Sri Lankan population. The Muslims claim diverse origins – including Arab, Indian, and Malay – and make up 7 percent of the population. Historically, they have been active traders and merchants. The Burghers have mixed European and Sri Lankan heritage. They are usually Christian, speak English, and live in urban areas. The Burghers were conspicuous during the colonial period for their economic and political prominence. Since colonial independence in 1948, their privileged position disappeared, and many emigrated, leaving those who stayed a tiny minority.

Although Sri Lanka experienced several bouts of ethnic violence between Sinhalese and Tamils since 1956 and a deadly ethnic-based civil war between Sinhalese-dominated governments and Tamil separatist organizations between 1983 and 2009, conflict between both ethnic communities was very rare prior to colonial independence. Two relatively minor incidents of ethnic violence occurred during the colonial period, one of which pitted Sinhalese Buddhists against Christians in 1883, the other of which pitted Sinhalese against Muslims in 1915. Both were linked to a Sinhalese revival movement that attempted to increase the economic and political status of Sinhalese relative to more advantaged minority communities (Jayawardena 2004). Tension between the Sinhalese and Tamil communities began to grow in the 1920s because of constitutional changes preparing the colony for self-rule (de Silva 1984a: 115; de Silva 1986: 98). Prior to the first universal elections in 1931, the British designated representatives from the major ethnic communities, a situation that greatly advantaged the Tamils and the Burghers but left the Sinhalese heavily underrepresented. With the colonial declaration of democratic elections under universal suffrage, Tamil leaders actively protested and demanded that Tamils (along with other minority communities) be allotted half of all legislative positions, a demand that Sinhalese politicians strongly opposed and that caused more acrimonious relations between the political elites of both communities. This conflict never turned violent and diminished over time as Tamils came to accept the new political reality.

Conflict between the Sinhalese and Tamil communities reemerged in 1956 and 1958 but turned violent in both years. The violence pitted Sinhalese civilians against Tamil civilians and included individual attacks, mob violence, and arson. It was countrywide, killed hundreds, and dislocated tens of thousands. National language was the main issue that sparked intercommunal violence. In 1956, the Sinhalese-dominated government passed a law making Sinhala the national language, an act with considerable symbolism and that also limited the ability of non-Sinhalese to find white-collar employment. Sinhalese nationalistic demands to make Sinhala the sole national language, in turn, were fueled by the fact that English had been the dominant language within the Sri Lankan state and by a growing Sinhalese national fervor caused by the 2,500th anniversary of Buddha's death in 1956, a year predicted in Buddhist tradition to begin the spiritual awakening and the global proliferation of Buddhism (de Silva 1986: 162; Manogaran 1987: 47–48). Tamils strongly and openly opposed the policy, resistance that increased Sinhalese resentment against them and caused many Sinhalese to attack Tamils.

After a twenty-year lull, intercommunal violence returned in 1977 and, once again, involved Sinhalese civilians attacking Tamils. The most proximate cause was an attack on Sinhalese police forces by Tamil militants, but growing competition and animosity between Sinhalese and Tamils over education and employment and incompatible ethno-nationalist ideologies were important underlying causes. When the violence ended, at least 100 people were dead and 25,000 people were dislocated (de Silva 1986: 288; Pfaffenberger 1990: 243–244).

Sporadic episodes of violence continued after 1977 and primarily involved Sinhalese security forces combating Tamil militants. Then, intense communal violence erupted once again in 1983 after thirteen soldiers were ambushed and killed by Liberation Tigers of Tamil Eelam (LTTE, or the Tamil Tigers) forces, a group of young militants who used violent methods in pursuit of an independent Tamil homeland. In the resulting violence, as many as 4,000 Tamils were killed, nearly 300,000 became internal refugees, and 18,000 houses and 5,000 shops were destroyed (Winslow and Woost 2004: 2). The violence was intense and prolonged because the security forces did not stop Sinhalese attacks of Tamils and actually supported the violence in some locations (de Silva 1986: 339; Horowitz 2001: 352–353; Tambiah 1996: 99).

With the state's complicity in the violence, many Tamils became convinced that their grievances could not be addressed through formal politics, causing Tamil separatist organizations to strengthen and become more radical. In this way, the 1983 riots ultimately pushed the Tamil separatist movement to expand their activities and begin a violent civil war. After prolonged and deadly Tamil infighting, the LTTE emerged as the dominant Tamil separatist organization. The battle between the LTTE and the government vacillated over the years, with the government finally gaining ascendency in 2009. An estimated 100,000 Sri Lankans were killed during the war.

A HISTORY OF EDUCATION IN SRI LANKA

Although schools predated European conquest, the present system of education in Sri Lanka has strong colonial roots. After the British took over Sri Lanka in 1802, many of the preexisting missionary schools (established by the Dutch and Portuguese) were maintained, and the new colonial power allowed Christian missionaries from Great Britain and the United States to open additional schools. In particular, the American Ceylon Mission, the Church Missionary Society, and the Wesleyan Mission quickly established footholds on the island. In 1833, the government began to inspect schools to assure a certain standard, opened government schools, and gave financial assistance to others. By 1900, the government ran 484 schools in Sri Lanka and provided grants-in-aid to 1,328 others (de Silva 1997: 231).

The colonial educational system was hierarchical and heavily ethnicized, with English schools attracting Christian and Burgher students on top, missionary schools serving mainly Tamils in the middle, and the Sinhalese and Tamil vernacular schools at the bottom (Dharmadasa 1992: 195). English schools were concentrated in Colombo, the political and economic capital. They catered to the wealthy, especially Europeans, Burghers, and Christians. These schools were the colony's elite schools, and their graduates had access to elite positions in the colonial economy and civil service. In the 1880s, the government privatized all but one English school, a move that further restricted English education to the wealthy (Fernando 1979: 34–35).

The second tier of education was comprised of missionary schools that taught in English and either Sinhala or Tamil. Because they imparted English-language skills and had advanced curricula, these schools provided an opportunity for postsecondary education and white-collar employment. Relative to the English-only schools, however, they were much less prestigious and less geared toward advanced studies. Geographically, missionary schools were concentrated in Jaffna, a region in the north of the island and inhabited almost exclusively by Tamils. This unequal distribution was promoted by colonial policy: the British encouraged the missionaries to work in the north but forbid their presence elsewhere out of fear that their activities might provoke conflict in the Sinhalese-dominated south, which was more successful at thwarting Portuguese and Dutch colonial efforts and was only completely conquered by the British in 1815. Although rarely converting to Christianity, the Tamils were also more receptive to missionary education, which was the primary tool missionaries used to encourage conversion. This greater receptivity appears to have been caused by the fact that precolonial education among the Tamils was more secularized than Sinhalese education, the latter of which was focused exclusively on Buddhism. In addition, the Tamil revival movement encouraged education as a means of communal advancement.

The final tier of education included the overwhelming majority of the colony's schools and consisted of vernacular schools that taught in either Sinhala or Tamil. The government first opened vernacular schools in 1847 and helped construct a large system of vernacular education that stretched throughout the island. Unlike their English and mixed-vernacular counterparts, vernacular schools did not offer opportunities for advanced education and provided "a cheap, inferior education to the lowest socio-economic strata" (Jayaweera 1971: 162).

The educational system grew considerably in terms of both schools and students throughout the British colonial period. This expansion accelerated during the first half of the twentieth century and grew at a phenomenal pace after Sri Lanka's independence in 1948. One important cause of educational explosion was finance, as education – including higher education – was made free of charge in 1945. In addition, the government made Sinhala and Tamil the official languages of education after independence, allowing students from non-English schools greater opportunity to continue their schooling beyond primary levels. Demonstrating this expansion, the number of students enrolled in government and state-assisted schools was 360,000 in 1920, 800,000 in 1945, and 2.7 million in 1970 (Kearney 1979: 59). University education also expanded during the late colonial and early independence periods from a measly 904 in 1942 to 14,343 in 1968 (Jayaweera 1979: 140).

Thus, Sri Lanka has a history of both ethnic violence and impressive educational expansion, with the latter preceding the former. Educational expansion began in the early 1900s and accelerated even further in the 1940s, and the first episode of severe ethnic violence occurred in 1956. This sequence suggests that educational expansion might have contributed to ethnic violence, a possibility we now explore in greater detail. In particular, the next section investigates whether educated individuals contributed to violence in Sri Lanka and explores potential mechanisms linking education to violence.

EDUCATION, ETHNO-NATIONALISM, AND VIOLENCE

Only a tiny fraction of the Sri Lankan population participated in ethnic violence, and no data set exists on who participated in ethnic violence and why they did so. The available evidence suggests that ethno-nationalist violence in Sri Lanka involved civilians from diverse educational backgrounds. Among them, however, a number of highly educated individuals were implicated in the violence in two primary ways: they led ethno-nationalist revival movements and mobilized and actively participated in violent ethnic movements. Without the participation of educated individuals in these two ways, violence would likely have been much less severe.

At the heart of violence in Sri Lanka are two competing ideas of nation (one Sinhalese and one Tamil), and educated individuals played instrumental roles in promoting each. During the final three decades of the nineteenth century, the intelligentsia from the Sinhalese and Tamil communities began revival movements. The movements were spearheaded by highly educated literary figures who strove to increase the national consciousnesses of their respective ethnic communities. According to Farmer (1963), the revivalist associations of both Sinhalese and Tamil communities "formed part of a reaction from complete submission to Westernization and hence an important ingredient in the movement towards nationalism and national independence. From the communal point of view, they served to perpetuate differences between Sinhalese and Tamil, between Buddhist and Hindu" (52–53). Similarly, Tambiah (1996) claims that they "heightened, made self-conscious, and deepened the communal and ethnic consciousness, solidarity, and exclusiveness" of Sinhalese and Tamil communities (39).

Among the Tamils, the revivalist intelligentsia championed Tamil literature and art and popularized the Saiva doctrines of Hinduism, thereby helping create a "heightened cultural and linguistic consciousness" opposed to that of the Sinhalese (Tambiah 1986: 108). Arumuga Navalar (1822–1879) was the key figure among the Tamil-Hindu revival movement in Sri Lanka. Navalar viewed Tamil culture as severely threatened by colonialism and missionaries and actively preached the need for a Hindu revival. In pursuit of this goal, he ran a printing press, promoted the use of Tamil, and wrote poetry. His greatest concern, however, was with education, and he believed that "education was the indispensable instrument of religious recovery" (de Silva 2007: 147). The movement therefore played an important role expanding education among Tamils and providing an education that strengthened Tamil nationalism.

The Sinhalese revivalist movement began a generation after its Tamil counterpart. The movement also focused on the protection and strengthening of culture in the face of foreign interference. Anagarika Dharmapala (1864-1933) and Munidasa Cumaratunga (1887-1944) provide two of the movement's most influential leaders. Dharmapala focused his energy on the revival of Buddhism and played an important role constructing a Sinhalese-Buddhist identity that was opposed to Hindus and Muslims. He suggested that Sri Lanka had been unfairly taken from the Buddhists and declared the dire need for Sinhalese Buddhists to reinstate their great culture before its demise. Highlighting these elements, he declared:

This bright, beautiful island was made into a Paradise by the Aryan Sinhalese before its destruction was brought about by the barbaric vandals. Its people did not know irreligion.... Christianity and polytheism [i.e. Hinduism] are responsible for the vulgar practices of killing animals, stealing, prostitution, licentiousness, lying and drunkenness.... The ancient, historic, refined people, under the diabolism of vicious paganism, introduced by the British administrators, are now declining slowly away. (Guruge 1965: 482)

Cumaratunga lived a generation after Dharmapala and spent much of his life fighting to protect the Sinhala language instead of Buddhism. He claimed, "Language without dignity produces men and women without dignity. Men and women without dignity are as base as beasts and can be made to stoop to any meanness" (Dharmadasa 1972: 133–134). Cumaratunga's ideas and leadership were instrumental in the rise of the Hela movement, which sought to return Sinhalese culture to its past splendor by shunning Indian, colonial, and other alien influences. The movement's primary base of support was the Sinhalese intelligentsia, including monks and, especially, teachers, the latter of whom frequently joined out of a feeling of relative deprivation: they viewed themselves as impoverished and with low status relative to English teachers (Dharmadasa 1992: 275; Jayawardena 2004; Tambiah 1996: 40–42). The movement helped "instill confidence and self-respect into the minds of the Sinhalese literati who hitherto had suffered from a sense of inferiority" and was "a landmark in the rise of Sinhalese language nationalism" (Dharmadasa 1972: 141; Dharmadasa 1992: 281). Roberts (1977) notes that the Hela movement used many tools to promote their goals: "not merely the association, the conference, the magazine and pamphlet, the press, the *vadaya* (debates), the protest memorandum, the postal service, the protest meeting, and the symbolic event, but also the riot, the play, the gramophone record and the song" (xc). Movement participants also succeeded in embedding their message in Sinhalese schools, thereby influencing the next generation of Sinhalese literati.

Besides playing an instrumental role in the construction and invigoration of oppositional ethno-nationalist identities, educated individuals also took a prominent part in organizing and orchestrating acts of ethnic violence. Jayawardena (2004) finds that the Sinhalese nationalist elites were the leading figures in violence against Christians in 1883 and against Muslims in 1915. And, although they were able to mobilize the masses during the violence against Tamils in the 1950s and afterward, she notes that they also played a very prominent role in this violence. Indeed, public servants participated in violence in 1958, several Sinhalese doctors and lawyers attacked and drove out their Tamil counterparts during the ethnic violence of 1983, and several educated and unemployed individuals actively participated in the 1983 riots (Tambiah 1986: 52, 99; Vanniasingham 1988: 16). Most importantly, university students and young university graduates formed the core memberships of two notoriously violent organizations – the People's Liberation Front (JVP) and the Tamil Tigers (LTTE) – that actively promoted ethno-nationalist violence in Sri Lanka.

The JVP was a Maoist-inspired, ethno-nationalist organization that was organized to use extremely violent means to address inequalities present in Sri Lanka. Its members were almost exclusively ethnic Sinhalese, and the organization pursued a strongly pro-Sinhalese and anti-Tamil agenda. In its effort to gain political power, however, its waged violence primarily against ethnic Sinhalese, not Tamils. The obscure group gained international attention when it staged an unsuccessful coup against the Sri Lankan government in April 1971. JVP members attacked police stations and government buildings throughout much of the island but were repelled after long and violent battles with security forces. During this violence and subsequent government reprisals, approximately 6,000 people were killed and 14,000 arrested (Pfaffenberger 1990: 254). After the insurrection, the JVP survived by going underground. In the face of growing separatist pressures among the Tamil community in the early 1980s, the JVP strengthened its anti-Tamil leanings to become the most anti-Tamil of all political organizations, and JVP members helped insight the 1983 violence and thereby the ethnic-based civil war (Chandraprema 1991: 60, 101; de Silva 1995: 60; Peiris 1999: 177; Perera 1991: 14–15). In addition, the Indo-Sri Lankan Accord, which saw the Sri Lankan government make concessions to the LTTE in 1987, motivated the JVP to orchestrate a second insurrection lasting from 1987 to 1989, as it believed the government was disregarding Sinhalese interests in favor of the dreaded Tamils. During this insurrection, the JVP used terrorist tactics to intimidate the population and organized general strikes to oppose a government. Through JVP violence and government reprisals, approximately 50,000 people died. Notably, this was political violence with an ethnic component but not ethnic violence, as JVP members were ethnonationalist extremists who used violence to attack a Sinhalese-dominated government (and its supporters) that they saw as being overly elitist and too accommodating to the Tamils. Still, both the 1971 and 1987–89 insurrections contributed to ethno-nationalist violence indirectly by pushing governments to take more radical pro-Sinhalese and anti-Tamil positions.

Scholars of the JVP note that its membership had three main characteristics: they were overwhelmingly Sinhalese, youthful, and – of interest to this book – educated (Fernando 1979; Kearney 1975, 1978). Considering the latter, the JVP used universities as recruiting grounds and either coopted or organized different student associations to pursue their political objectives during both the 1971 and 1987–1989 movements, allowing the JVP "to effectively control the universities" (Bush 2003: 115; see also Alles 1990; Chandraprema 1991: 159–160; de Silva 1995: 54, 59–60). Supporting this view, individuals incarcerated for their affiliation with the JVP were considerably more educated than their non-JVP peers. Kearney (1975) finds that despite the fact that the educated are better able to avoid arrest because of their knowledge and social contacts, those arrested for possible participation in the JVP insurrection in 1971 were three times as likely to have passed their O-level exams (taken after the eleventh year of school and necessary for continuing studies) than their peers when controlling for age (749). During the 1987–1989 insurrection, JVP membership was equally, if not more, educated. Even when individuals with low-levels of education participated in JVP violence at the local level in the 1987–1989 insurrection, the educated members commonly played a vital role, as they collected weapons and distributed them to local thugs who could help in their violent activities (Chandraprema 1991: 169–170).

Among the Tamil community, several nationalist organizations copied the militant tactics of the JVP, the most notable example being the LTTE. Mirroring the JVP, the LTTE was also dominated by disheartened and relatively educated youths (Thangarajah 2002: 185). Early on, its core membership was university students and graduates, and the LTTE grew out of dozens of student-based organizations, including the Tamil Students' Federation, the TUF Youth Organisation (the youth organization of the dominant Tamil political party), the Unemployed Graduates Union (an organization of disgruntled university and secondary-school graduates), and EROS (a student organization of Tamil university students studying in London) (Hellmann-Rajanayagam 1994: 176; Pfaffenberger 1990: 254–255). In this way, educated Tamil youth founded and directed the organizations that used violence to pursue Tamil communal interests, comprised most of the members of these organizations during the initial phase of separatist violence, and thereby played a vital role in instigating the separatist movement.

EDUCATIONAL MECHANISMS

Given that violence followed educational expansion and that educated individuals played influential roles in ethno-nationalist movements and violence, the Sri Lankan case provides evidence that the relationship between ethnic violence and education runs from education to ethnic violence and might be causal. If education does promote ethnic violence, however, education must have contributed to their participation in some way.

The preceding analysis hints at the importance of the mobilization mechanism. Universities were hotbeds of activism, and the JVP and LTTE both recruited large segments of their memberships on university campuses.[1] Universities proved such an important base of recruitment

---

[1] See Alles 1990: 34; Balasingham 2004: 20–22; Bush 2003: 115; Chandraprema 1991: 160; de Silva 1995: 59–60; Peiris 1995.

because they concentrated thousands of youths in a small area. They were also important given the organizational resources available at universities. For example, Chandraprema (1991) notes that the Socialist Students Union (SSU) served as the central umbrella organization used by the JVP to organize students and nonstudents during the second insurrection (160).[2] The SSU proved so important because its presence reached beyond universities down to the district level, where its members included divisional leaders, a women's representative, a representative of an underground student organization (*Nimal Balasuriya Balakaya*), and university representatives (Chandraprema 1991: 160). This structure, in turn, allowed the JVP to coordinate its violent, student-led activities throughout large sections of the country (Chandraprema 1991: 160). Similarly, the LTTE relied heavily on universities for mobilizational resources. It and several other militant Tamil separatist organizations used student associations as a means of recruiting members and, in fact, trace their origins to these associations. The Tamil Students' Federation is arguably the most important example. It was formed in 1970 and, according to one high-ranking LTTE official, "moulded the emergence of the armed resistance movement of the Tamils" (Balasingham 2004: 20). The organization preached militancy, organized protests against the government, and arranged conferences to gain support and encourage Tamils to take up arms against the government (Balasingham 2004: 22). Within two years of its creation, members of the association began orchestrating acts of violence (Jayawardene and Jayawardene 1987: 5).

Besides mobilization, several experts also claim that the socialization mechanism contributed to ethnic violence in Sri Lanka by exacerbating preexisting ethnic divisions and antipathy. According to one former official in the Ministry of Education, the educational system was more divisive than unifying and utterly "failed to foster a national consciousness which enables us to live in harmony" (Udagama 1990: 9). Similarly, Jayaweera (1990) recognizes that the education promoted cultural exclusivism instead of multiculturalism and thereby "hastened social conflict" (69). Udagama (1990) goes so far as to claim that the many dualities and divisions within the Sri Lankan school system "laid the foundations... for a divisive society and a nation at war" (13).

Socialization at schools appears to have contributed to ethnic divisions in different ways. For one thing, schools in Sri Lanka usually segregated ethnic communities (Perera 1991: 63–71; Tampoe 2006: 225; Wijesinghe

---

[2] Alles (1990) also notes that it was vital to the organization of the first insurrection (34).

2004: 252). In itself, such segregation helped strengthen oppositional identities and prejudice by limiting intercommunal interactions. Moreover, the linguistically divided education system impeded Sinhalese and Tamil interactions even further by hindering intercommunal communication, as Sinhalese were not taught Tamil and Tamils were not taught Sinhala (Phadnis 1984: xxii; Wijesinghe 2004: 252). Finally, the educational curricula furthered this process by strengthening distinct communal identities. Sinhalese and Tamil schools taught different histories that emphasized different historic events, imparted particular communal biases, and "perpetually reinforced cultural prejudice and racial distrust" (Phandis 1984: xxii). Given the influence of Sinhalese and Tamil nationalist movements on the educational system, schools also socialized Sinhalese and Tamil students to hold different national identities. Prior to the 1960s, Tamil textbooks strongly reinforced a Tamil identity and paid closer attention to Tamil Nadu than Sri Lanka (Siriwardena et al. 1985: 35). After the government took control of Tamil vernacular education, however, the textbooks focused more on Sri Lankan national unity, although teachers commonly imparted negative attitudes toward Sinhalese during the lessons (Nissan 1996: 36). The textbooks in Sinhalese schools were strongly pro-Sinhalese and anti-Tamil (Hellmann-Rajanayagam 1986: 142; Perera 1991; Siriwardena et al. 1985: 5–33). "In Sinhala language schools," Nissan (1996) writes, "the texts used for teaching Buddhism, Sinhala language and social studies were found to contain the most damaging messages for ethnic relations, conveying negative images of Tamils as the historical enemies of the Sinhalese and celebrating ethnic heroes who are presented as having vanquished Tamils in ethnic wars" (36). Siriwardena et al. (1985) analyze Sinhalese textbooks and arrive at a similar conclusion: "[T]he Sinhala books not only fail to [project the sense of a common national identity] but contain an abundance of material which will strengthen communal attitudes and reinforce communal antagonisms" (59). In this way, schools actively taught Sinhalese that Tamils were outside the moral community, thereby legitimizing ethnic violence (Perera 1991).

The Frustration-Aggression and Competition Mechanisms

Although the socialization and mobilization mechanisms appear to have influenced ethnic violence and help explain the prominent role played by educated individuals, previous works on ethnic violence in Sri Lanka focus much more on the frustration-aggression and competition mechanisms. Both mechanisms were promoted by an educational bubble, which in turn was caused by the combination of a stagnant economy and rapid educational expansion. In fact, the frustration-aggression and competition mechanisms interacted and reinforced one another to such an extent that one might combine them into the competition-frustration-aggression mechanism: competition created incentives for eliminating rivals, frustration and aggression created the emotional motivation to do just that, and people therefore participated in violence for both instrumental and emotional reasons. While recognizing this interdependence, the analysis below separates them as much as possible in order to highlight their distinctiveness, as the frustration-aggression mechanism is based on emotion and the competition mechanism is based on rational calculation.

The Frustration-Aggression Mechanism. As a source of merit, education commonly increases the status expectations of pupils. During the period of British colonialism in Sri Lanka, English vernacular schools were used to create an indigenous elite class with access to political power and white-collar jobs. As a result, education was an extremely important means of social advancement, and Sri Lankans actively pursued it to get ahead (de Silva 1986: 93–95; Jayaweera 1979: 134; Pfaffenberger 1990: 253). Such was the emphasis placed on education as a source of advancement that some complained it had lost any focus on knowledge acquisition and self-growth (Emmerij 1972: 487).

Because many Sri Lankans pursued education as a means of advancement, a large number of educated individuals expected and believed that they had the legitimate right to climb the socioeconomic ladder. There was a general expectation that education would give access to white-collar jobs, which were relatively well paid, stable, and imparted considerable status in a country where the overwhelming majority was manual laborers. In fact, teachers commonly preached the merits of white-collar employment and the demerits of manual labor, thereby increasing student aversions toward the latter (Hettige 1991: 61).

During the British colonial period, white-collar expectations were usually met because of a shortage of educated individuals. As independence approached, the ascendency of Sri Lankans to the highest positions in the administrations caused the expectations of students to increase even further. Unfortunately for educated Sri Lankans, the combination of three factors severely restrained their mobility by the 1950s and, especially, the 1970s. First, the education explosion in Sri Lanka created a very large number of newly educated individuals in a relatively short period of time.

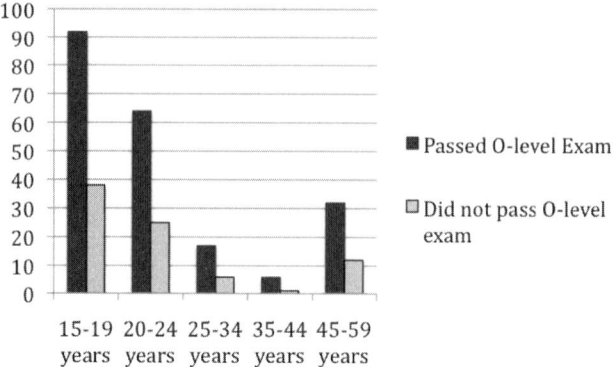

FIGURE 4.1. Unemployment Rate by Age and Education, 1969–1970. *Source:* Emmerij 1972: 487. *Note:* The O-level exams are taken after the eleventh year of education and must be passed in order to continue one's education.

Second, the overall size of the population grew rapidly. For instance, the total population aged twenty-five years of age and younger increased from 3.8 million in 1946 to 7.2 million in 1968 (de Silva 1986: 166–167). Finally, Sri Lanka experienced very limited economic growth during and after the education and population explosions. The country's per capita growth rate between 1950 and 1975 averaged less than 2 percent per year, expanding from $1,274 to only $1,901 (in constant 2005 U.S. dollars) over that period (Heston, Summers, and Aten 2009).

Due to the convergence of all three, the market for white-collar employment was swamped with qualified applicants, and the mass of educated youth experienced a decrease in relative wages. Between 1963 and 1982, the earnings ratio of employed individuals with up to O-level education (eleven years) and employed university graduates declined from 1:3.6 to 1:1.3 (Peiris 1999: 186). The educated with low-paying jobs were actually lucky, as many had a very difficult time finding any job whatsoever. Indeed, the unemployment rate soared among the educated, making the country an "outstanding example of the global phenomenon of educated unemployment" (de Silva 1986: 167).

Figure 4.1 shows the unemployment rates by education level and age group in 1969–1970. Specifically, it notes the unemployment rates of two educational categories: individuals who passed their O-level exams, and individuals who either did not take or did not pass their O-level exams. O-level exams are taken after the eleventh year of education, and students must pass it in order to continue their education. The figure clearly shows that unemployment was greater among the more educated for all age groups, with the more educated in each age group having an unemployment rate that was more than double that of the less educated. It also shows that educated youths were particularly hard hit, with unemployment rates of 92 percent for educated individuals aged between 15 and 19 and 64 percent for educated individuals aged 20-24. Whereas the figure shows that individuals who had passed their O-level exams after the eleventh year of schooling had much higher unemployment than those who had either not taken or failed the O-level exams, Kearney (1979) finds that the unemployment rate was even higher for individuals who had thirteen or more years of education: it was 23 percent for individuals aged between twenty-five and thirty-four years with thirteen or more years of education versus only 17 percent for individuals in the same age group who had successfully completed their eleventh year of education (74). Notably, the unemployment figure for individuals who successfully completed eleven years of education does not remove individuals who continued their studies and completed thirteen or more years of education. The difference in unemployment rates between individuals who stopped after eleven years of schooling and who completed at least thirteen years of schooling is therefore even greater than the statistics suggest.

Although experts of ethno-national violence in Sri Lanka point to a number of causes, it is commonly accepted that the employment problem among the educated youth was one of the most influential.[3] This line of argument suggests that the inability of the educated youth to find white-collar jobs caused anxiety, frustration, and anger, all of which increased their chances of acting violently. According to Kearney (1975):

> It is not difficult to imagine the consternation and despair of a youth who, after completing an education that had always in the past led to employment as a clerk or school-teacher, is advised to return to the mud of his father's paddy field. Even this prospect might not be open. The family plot may have been sold or given to his less-educated older brothers since his education was presumed to have removed him from dependence on agriculture. Population growth, in any case, had inexorably produced increasing pressure on the land, fragmentation of holdings, and landlessness. (737)

Similarly, Wijesinghe (1969, 1973), a psychologist at a Sri Lankan university, describes how the poor economic prospects of students caused

---

[3] See Alles 1990; Attanayake 2001; Bandarage 1998; de Silva 1986; Hettige 1991; Jayawardena 2004; Kearney 1975, 1978; Manogaran 1987; Moore 1981; Pfaffenberger 1990, 1994; Senaratne 1997; Shastri 1994; Tambiah 1986.

extreme angst and promoted a dramatic increase in student violence. He notes that this frustration-induced violence was directed against a variety of targets, including themselves.[4] The most common focuses of frustration and aggression, however, were the government and rival ethnic communities.

Many educated youth who were frustrated over their limited mobility blamed the government because they saw it as elitist and nepotistic. These sentiments and subsequent antistate violence are most evident in the JVP and the LTTE. As noted previously, the JVP was an extremely violent Maoist and ethno-nationalist organization that led rebellions against the government. Whereas all young and educated Sinhalese were prone to JVP membership, this was particularly the case for rural Sinhalese because they usually came from modest backgrounds and lacked the connections that proved so necessary to find white-collar jobs (Pfaffenberger 1990: 253). Indeed, Tiruchelvam (1984) describes how state employment in postcolonial Sri Lanka evolved into a spoils system in which who one knows means everything (189–191). In addition, the primary and secondary schools in rural areas generally lacked the facilities that allowed the students to study science, engineering, medicine, and other programs that offered the best job prospects (Kearney 1975: 733; Moore 1981: 97; Wijesinghe 1973: 315). As a consequence of these factors, the rural Sinhalese who managed to get high levels of education found that it was often for nothing and experienced extreme angst. Bandarage (1998), for example, interviewed several rural Sinhalese university graduates and found that their unmet aspirations caused enormous anguish:

Frustration, anger, and despair about social inequalities and blocked opportunities are greatest among the educated unemployed. Rural youth... along with their families, feel utterly betrayed after making great sacrifices to get a university education. They ask why they need a degree to pick tea, make masks, or cut stone. They wonder if they could have done better without the piece of paper. (17)

Several scholars, in turn, recognize that such frustration and aggression helps explain why JVP members were disproportionately educated and rural.[5]

Educated Tamils also despised the government but for a different reason: they held it accountable for discriminatory policy that restricted their

---

[4] Similarly, Kearney and Miller (1985) find that frustration among the educated over limited mobility promoted high rates of suicide in Sri Lanka.
[5] See Alles 1990: 337; Attanayake 2001: 77; Kearney 1975; Senaratne 1997: 30–31; Wijesinghe 1973.

mobility. As a consequence, they vented their frustration and aggression on the government in the form of a separatist movement.[6] Indeed, the "most militant agitators for separatism were the educated unemployed" (de Silva 1986: 261–262). Demonstrating the link between the unmet expectations of educated Tamils and separatist violence most clearly is the fact that the separatist movement grew out of Tamil student associations and, most notably, the Unemployed Graduates' Union, a Tamil organization comprised of unemployed high school and university graduates (Pfaffenberger 1990: 254–255).

The Sinhala Only Act is a notable discriminatory policy that caused educated Tamils to blame the government for their hardship and focus their frustration and aggression on it. The act made Sinhala the only official language of Sri Lanka, and all public servants were required to speak it, something that most educated Tamils could not do and that placed them at a fundamental disadvantage for coveted white-collar jobs in the public sector (Jayawardene and Jayawardene 1987: 162). In addition, it legitimized Sinhalese political dominance and discriminatory hiring practices. Thus, Tamils received only 1,000 of the 140,000 jobs offered by the government in 1978, and the percentage of Tamil civil servants declined considerably (Samarasinghe 1984: 178; Tiruchelvam 1984: 186). The percentage of Tamils employed by the state in general clerical service, for example, declined from 41 percent in 1949 to only 5 percent 30 years later, and the Tamil share of professional and managerial posts plummeted from 60 and 30 percent, respectively, in 1956 to only 10 and 5 percent in 1979 (Samarasinghe 1984: 178; Thangarajah 2002: 175). Pfaffenberger (1994), in turn, notes that limited employment opportunities intensified frustration and anger, because unemployed Tamil males "could not marry, at least not respectably; they could not obtain lands because they could not marry; and, indeed in Jaffna's puritanical culture, they could not even find sexual partners" (10).

Besides the government, educated Sinhalese and Tamils scapegoated one another for their grievances. Ethnic scapegoating was caused by the strength of ethnic identities, high levels of ethnic-based inequalities and discrimination, and extreme ethnic competition. Indeed, because of the salience of ethnicity and competition over scarce jobs, each community

---

[6] See Balasingham 2004: 19–20; Bhasin 2004; de Silva 1986; Kearney 1979: 79; Manogaran 1987: 119; Phadnis 1984; Pfaffenberger 1990, 1994; Sahedevan and DeVotta 2006: 56; Shastri 1994; Wijesinghe 2004: 266.

kept track of ethnic-based representation in elite jobs and education and felt aggrieved when their community was underrepresented or marginalized. In this way, individual grievances over unmet expectations pushed Sri Lankans to search for scapegoats, ethnic-based collective grievances caused people to blame rival ethnic communities for the general hardship faced by their community, and both individual and collective grievances promoted ethnically oriented frustration and aggression among the educated.

Notably, Tamil antigovernment violence simultaneously had an ethnic component since, in the eyes of Tamils, the government represented all Sinhalese Sri Lankans. Moreover, Tamils faced violence at the hands of Sinhalese civilians and did not refrain from attacking Sinhalese civilians. Notable LTTE attacks against Sinhalese civilians include the Kebithigollewa massacre, killing 62; the Gonagala massacre, killing 54; the Kallarawa massacre, killing 42; the Anuradhapura massacre, killing 146; and the Kent and Dollar Farm massacres, killing 52.

For the Sinhalese, on the other hand, the government was anything but Tamil, making Tamils a distinct target of aggression. Even before the education explosion caused an enormous oversupply of educated labor, ethnic inequality and limited mobility caused educated Sinhalese elites to instigate violence against advantaged communities, including violence against Christians in 1883 and against Muslims in 1915 (Jayawardena 2004). In a similar fashion, it contributed to the first round of Sinhalese-Tamil violence shortly after independence (Jayawardena 2004: 71–73). During all episodes of ethnic violence, educated Sinhalese were at a heightened risk of attacking ethnic rivals because of their greater sensitivity to ethnic inequalities, the latter of which directly affected their upward mobility. The shortage of white-collar jobs after independence, in turn, only intensified resentment and frustration over ethnic inequalities (de Silva 1986: 85). According to Tambiah (1986), frustration over unemployment and resentment over the disproportionate share of white-collar jobs held by Tamils triggered "time and again the communal riots directed by the have-nots against a nominated 'enemy,' the Tamils, who have been stereotyped as privileged, and about whom the Sinhalese man on the street has been taught to say, 'We have already given them too much'" (56).

The JVP also scapegoated Tamils and helped popularize ideas of Tamils as malicious and stealing what rightfully belongs to the Sinhalese. Although the JVP actively participated in anti-Tamil violence as early as the 1950s, it only became overtly anti-Tamil in the 1970s and 1980s (Perera 1991: 14–5; Tambiah 1996). This reorientation was a reaction to growing Tamil demands for a separate Tamil state and fears that the government was overlooking Sinhalese interests to placate Tamils. As a consequence, the JVP attacked the government and placed it under extreme pressure to play hardball with the Tamils, a situation that only worsened the ethnic-based civil war.

The Competition Mechanism. Many scholars of ethnic violence in Sri Lanka believe high levels of ethnic competition was an influential cause and claim that the relative scarcity of resources in Sri Lanka promoted intense competition. According to Senaratne (1997):

Sri Lanka is a country with scarce resources, a growing population, and a relatively underdeveloped economy. There is intense competition between ethnic groups, and between classes for all manner of resources – land, water, credit, employment, education, urban space, housing, and political power and representation. This competition manifests itself in the market-place, in government departments, between government officials and the public, in schools, in public debates in newspapers, in neighbourhoods, in universities and in numerous other contexts. (21)

Educated individuals, in turn, frequently found themselves at the heart of competition and had the most to gain from vanquishing their competitors, suggesting that the competition mechanism helps explain why educated individuals commonly participated in ethnic violence.

Education heightened ethnic competition in Sri Lanka in two separate ways. First, education placed individuals in more competitive job markets, and the educated therefore had greater incentives to eliminate ethnic competitors. This type of competition is linked to education only indirectly because it was not education per se that promoted competition. Instead, white-collar jobs were very scarce, causing the educated to compete intensively for jobs.

Historically, Tamils possessed a disproportionate share of elite jobs, and anti-Tamil violence was perceived by some Sinhalese participants as a way to eliminate competitors and thereby improve the material condition of the Sinhalese community. Although this mechanism was driven largely by concerns about the collective interests of the entire Sinhalese community, educated individuals also had selective incentives to support and participate in ethnic violence because they received the greatest benefits from the removal of ethnic competitors. Most notably, some Sinhalese white-collar professionals and merchants attacked their Tamil rivals during early incidents of ethnic violence, actions that were likely calculated to benefit themselves individually by eliminating their economic competitors. Indeed, Tambiah (1996) notes that the "middle-level Sinhala entrepreneurs, businessmen, and white-collar workers" had the most to gain from ethnic violence (100). For their part, educated Tamils had even more incentive to participate in the violent separatist movement: they were excluded from state patronage in a country where the public sector was the most important source of white-collar employment, so a Tamil homeland would open up large political and economic opportunities for educated individuals. Alternatively, separatism offered less-educated Tamils few material benefits.

Second, the competition mechanism contributed to ethnic violence more directly, as Sinhalese and Tamils competed over education itself. This competition turned heated and contributed to escalating tensions and animosity because each side viewed education as a finite resource and sought to improve their individual and communal access to it. Education in Sri Lanka has been a source of competition and conflict since colonial times, and this situation has its roots in the educational inequalities that resulted from the three-tiered system of colonial education. Percentage-wise, the English and mixed English-indigenous vernacular schools were only a small segment of all schools in the colony, but they had important consequences on postcolonial ethnic violence because of the inequalities they promoted. Most notably, the elite schools in Colombo were attended by the colony's Westernized elites, with the Christians and Burghers being greatly overrepresented. As Dharmadasa (1992) notes, "English education, as against education in the vernacular languages, conferred on individuals access to lucrative and 'prestigious' occupations," especially the civil service (192–193). And given their English educations, the Christian and Burgher communities ended up dominating the civil service until the 1930s (Samarasinghe 1984: 176). Even as late as 1948, they held more than 21 percent of the positions in the Ceylon Civil Service and made up 55 percent of high-ranking police officers despite comprising only one or two percent of the population (Samarasinghe 1984: 177).

Although less so than the Christian Sri Lankans and the Burghers, the Tamil community also found itself in a relatively advantaged position because of the concentration of missionary schools in the north, a situation causing the overrepresentation of Tamils in secondary and postsecondary education during the British colonial period (Corea 1968: 154; Ryan 1961). This overrepresentation continued after independence, especially within the university programs that offered the greatest chances at mobility: medicine, law, engineering, and the sciences. Despite comprising 10 percent of the total population, 35 percent of university admissions to the science faculties were Tamil in 1970, and their percentages were more than 40 percent in engineering and medicine (C. R. de Silva 1984b: 127).

Whereas the island's Burgher, Christian, and Tamil minorities had disproportionate access to elite education and thereby white-collar employment, the vast majority of schools offered much more limited opportunities. These Sinhalese and Tamil vernacular schools were quite poor in quality and did not impart the necessary skills (especially English) needed to find white-collar employment. Although most Tamils received only vernacular education, the Sinhalese were much more concentrated in this final and lowest tier because of their more limited access to missionary schools, making the numerically dominant ethnic community the most poorly educated and thereby the least capable of securing the coveted white-collar jobs. Such ethnic-based inequalities in education – and thereby white-collar employment – were publicized by Sinhalese politicians and created the impression that Tamils had greater access to high-quality education. When combined with high levels of frustration and aggression caused by both very limited opportunities and the belief that Sinhalese were the rightful but disadvantaged inhabitants of Sri Lanka, this competition influenced some educated Sinhalese to attempt to eliminate Tamil rivals either through policy or violence.

The clearest example of education-induced ethnic competition involved university admissions in the 1970s. The expansion of education and the removal of fees caused an educational explosion, freeing children from nearly all backgrounds to attend school in Sri Lanka, but the number of positions open to student enrollment in the university system remained limited. As a consequence, only a fraction of the students wanting to attend university could actually do so. In 1965, only 20 percent of applicants were admitted to university, and this number declined to only 11 percent in 1969 (de Silva 1984b: 126). In an environment with high levels of ethnic competition over jobs, politics, land, and other resources, competition over university positions quickly gained an ethnic dimension. As de Silva (1997) writes:

Education, especially university education, is a key channel of social mobility in most developing countries and hence the distribution of opportunities for higher education is often regarded as the distribution of future wealth, status and power. In countries like Sri Lanka where university education is available only to a small minority, the competition...becomes...intense. Further problems arise, when in the context of a plural society each ethnic and religious group tends to evaluate the ratio of university admissions obtained by its members as an index of equality of opportunity or of discrimination. (85)

As mentioned previously, Tamils were overrepresented in the most sought-after university programs, and they gained access to these and other university programs through national examinations, with those students having the highest scores accepted into the programs. Such a procedure seems very meritocratic, but vocal factions within the Sinhalese community saw two problems. First, some claimed that Tamil scores were improperly inflated. Because Sinhalese and Tamil students took their exams in different languages, Sinhalese corrected the exams of Sinhalese students, and Tamils corrected the exams of Tamil students. Under these conditions and the overrepresentation of Tamils at the universities, some claimed that the Tamil graders systematically inflated the scores (de Silva 1984: 98). Second, it was a common belief within the Sinhalese community that Tamils had a relative advantage in education because of the privileged position they had gained under British colonialism. Feeling that the educational system was unfairly set against them in these ways, many Sinhalese – in particular the educated youth standing to gain from it – demanded a type of affirmative action that would allocate university positions based on ethnic quotas, thereby allowing Sinhalese to have their "fair" share.

Given pressure from segments of the Sinhalese population who were angered by the underrepresentation of Sinhalese (especially the first JVP revolt in April 1971), the government implemented different admissions formulas, all of which privileged Sinhalese over Tamils (most also privileged rural over urban students, regardless of ethnicity). This policy was first used in 1971 and changed form almost yearly during the 1970s. By playing with admissions, the percentage of Tamils in university plummeted by mid-decade. For example, the percentage of Tamils admitted into the science faculties declined from 35 percent in 1970 to 19 percent in 1975 (de Silva 1986: 263). The percentage losses for engineering, medicine, dental surgery, and agriculture were even greater (de Silva 1984b: 138–140). Following 1975, admissions criteria were changed to reduce the negative impact on Tamil admissions, although the new systems continued to favor Sinhalese students – especially rural Sinhalese students.[7]

---

[7] Sinhalese students in Colombo were actually negatively affected by the policy because the policy favored disadvantaged areas, which were almost all rural. Given the rural base of

Tamils perceived government interference with university admissions as flagrantly discriminatory and advantaging Sinhalese over Tamils in the battle for education, thereby preventing fair competition. In so doing, the policy further strengthened the frustration-aggression mechanism. Simultaneously, it heightened the competition mechanism by placing another obstacle to employment in front of educated Tamils and thereby creating incentives for Tamils to eliminate competitors by forming their own national state. As such, Tamil students were furious and decided to pursue their interests through a new method: by organizing a violent separatist movement.[8] Indeed, it is no coincidence that the period during which Tamil students organized the LTTE (1974–1975) was also the period in which admissions policy most dramatically affected Tamil university admissions (Thangarajah 2002: 182). Demonstrating this link, the admissions issue sparked the organization of the Tamil Students Movement as a means of protesting the policy, and it subsequently splintered into thirty-five different insurgency groups, many of which played an active role in the separatist movement (Gunaratna 1998: 106). De Silva (1986) goes so far as to claim that no issue "did more in radicalizing the politics of the Tamil areas in the north" than university admissions (242): "Nothing has caused more frustration and bitterness among Tamil youth than this, for they regarded it as an iniquitous system deliberately devised to place obstacles before them" (262). The university admissions policy therefore highlights how communal competition can spark discriminatory acts that advantage one community and how discriminatory acts can, in turn, both intensify frustration among the affected community and create incentives for the affected community to eliminate competitors, clearly showing how the competition and frustration-aggression mechanisms interact to promote ethnic violence.

Even after the admissions policy was revised in the late 1970s to increase Tamil admissions, competition over education continued to inflame ethnic rivalries. Tamils were scarred and lost all confidence in Sinhalese politicians. The Sinhalese, in turn, felt that the government had caved in to Tamil pressure by weakening the quota system, allowing Tamils to capture an "unfairly" high number of university seats.

---

the JVP, this element shows how the university policy was used to address the demands of the JVP and attempt to prevent future rebellions.

[8] See de Silva 1984a: 119; de Silva 1984b: 133; de Silva 1984: 100; Jayawardene and Jayawardene 1987: 159; Jayaweera 1990: 68; Manogaran 1987: 127; Sabaratnam 2001: 218; Shastri 1994: 212–213; Tambiah 1986: 17; Wilson 2000: 103.

Discussing this reaction within the Sinhalese community, de Silva (1984) writes:

> Rumours were afloat that the pendulum had swung decisively in favour of the Tamils and that the Sinhalese had been reduced to a minority in terms of admissions to the prestigious science based faculties. One rumour held that few, or indeed, no, Sinhalese students in some major state schools in Colombo, which normally sent numerous students to the university each year, had qualified for admissions in 1978–9. (102–103)

The government appears to have barely avoided Sinhalese-led disturbances in 1978 over the revising of the university admissions policy in favor of Tamils by closing schools and arresting student organizers who were planning a large strike (de Silva 1984: 102–103).

CONCLUSION

This chapter uses Sri Lanka as a case study to explore whether the statistical relationship between ethnic violence and education is driven by the impact of education on ethnic violence. For this, it uses three types of evidence. First, and most elementarily, it analyzes the temporal sequence between educational expansion and ethnic violence and finds that educational expansion preceded ethnic violence between Sinhalese and Tamils. Second, if education contributes to ethnic violence, one would expect that the educated played a vital role in ethnic violence. Although hardly the only actors, I find that educated individuals have historically played important roles framing ethnic grievances, mobilizing the population to pursue ethnic interests, and actively participating in ethnic violence on both sides of the Sinhalese-Tamil divide. Indeed, it seems unlikely that ethnic violence would have occurred with such intensity if educated individuals had not filled these roles. Finally, I explore mechanisms linking education and ethnic violence. Although the causes of violence were complex and multiple, I find that each educational mechanism helps explain why many educated Sri Lankans participated in ethno-nationalist violence, but the frustration-aggression and competition mechanisms appear particularly influential. In an environment with a glut of educated individuals and very few jobs, several educated individuals blamed ethnic rivals for unmet expectations and acted aggressively toward them. This frustration-induced scapegoating was promoted by preexisting ethnic divisions and the fact that powerful elements in Sri Lankan society – including the educational curriculum, student organizations, and politicians – emphasized intercommunal difference and antipathy. In addition, education-based inequalities heightened ethnic competition, and competition for white-collar jobs and limited university spots drove many Tamils to support the LTTE. Conversely, this very competition drove many educated Sinhalese to try to eliminate Tamil competition, either by attacking them or through discriminatory political policy. Overall, the analysis provides evidence that both the frustration-aggression and competition mechanisms are powerful in resource-scarce environments experiencing educational bubbles and strongly reinforce one another. It also shows how political discrimination, ethnic clientelism, and the state's support for ethnic violence against Tamils intensified the frustration-aggression and competition mechanisms.

Thus, by showing a temporal sequence in which ethnic violence followed educational expansion, describing how educated individuals played important roles in ethnic violence, and highlighting mechanisms linking education to ethnic violence, this chapter provides evidence that education contributes to ethnic violence and therefore reinforces the statistical findings of Chapter 3.[9] Yet, as a single case study, it remains uncertain whether the mechanisms are generalizable. For additional insight, I now turn to Cyprus.

[9] Notably, sequence, the role of educated individuals in violence, and the presence of mechanisms linking ethnic violence to education all also offer additional evidence that the statistical relationships highlighted in Chapter 3 run primarily from education to ethnic violence.

5

Education and Ethnic Violence in Cyprus

Cyprus is an island in the eastern Mediterranean the size of Massachusetts and has been a member of the European Union since 2004. Its 800,000 inhabitants are divided into two main ethnic communities who differ along both linguistic and religious lines: Greek (Orthodox) Cypriots, who presently make up more than 75 percent of the population; and Turkish (Muslim) Cypriots, who comprise less than 20 percent of the population. Although recognized internationally as one country, Cyprus has been under the control of two separate authorities since a civil war in 1974: southern Cyprus is inhabited overwhelmingly by Greek Cypriots, and its government is recognized internationally as the legitimate government of all Cyprus; and northern Cyprus is a Turkish-controlled enclave inhabited overwhelmingly by Turkish Cypriots and immigrants from the Turkish mainland. The present ethnic and political divisions of Cyprus are the result of violence that began in 1955 and reached a stalemate after 1974. The violence began as an anticolonial conflict in the 1950s, quickly transformed into intercommunal violence, and finally erupted into an international war that provoked ethnic purges.

This chapter continues to explore the impact of education on ethnic violence through a case study of Cyprus. I begin by providing relevant background material, paying particular attention to the island's history of foreign domination, an ethno-nationalist movement among Greek Cypriots, and Cyprus' history of ethnic violence. This section also explores the sequence between educational expansion and ethnic violence. Next, I describe the country's educational system, explore the educational background of individuals implicated in ethnic violence, and investigate whether the educational mechanisms outlined in Chapter 2 help explain intercommunal violence.

BACKGROUND: FOREIGN DOMINATION, ENOSIS, AND ETHNIC VIOLENCE

A History of Foreign Domination

Cyprus was first inhabited approximately 12,000 years ago. Since then, several subsequent waves of settlement and conquest have followed, with the island passing from one foreign power to another several times. Of all conquerors, four were particularly influential and had considerable bearing on the subsequent violence between the Greek and Turkish Cypriot communities: the Greeks, Byzantines, Ottomans, and British.

Greek rule had a great impact on contemporary Cyprus through large-scale Greek settlement and the assimilation of the indigenous population into the Greek cultural world. It began around 1600 BC and continued until the Assyrians conquered the island in the eighth century BC. Four centuries later, Alexander the Great conquered the island and reincorporated it into the Greek world, where Cyprus remained until falling to the Roman Empire in 58 BC.

In the fourth century AD, the Roman Empire split into eastern and western components, and Cyprus remained part of the eastern empire for seven more centuries. The eastern Roman Empire is better known today as the Byzantine Empire but was frequently referred to as the Empire of the Greeks by its contemporaries. Indeed, it was ruled from Constantinople, inhabited primarily by Greek-speaking peoples, and adopted Greek as its official language. Different from its Roman precursor, Byzantine rule therefore reinforced Cypriot Hellenism. Most notably, the Orthodox Church was introduced to the island during the Byzantine period, and it has been a powerful cultural and political fixture and the center of community life for the majority of the population ever since.

After the Byzantines, Cyprus passed to the Knights of Templar and then the Venetians before being conquered by the Ottomans in 1570. Ottoman rule lasted until 1878, destroyed the island's feudal land system, and transformed the population by bringing thousands of Muslim settlers from the Anatolian mainland. For the Greek Cypriots, Ottoman rule was initially favorable, as the Ottomans – unlike the Venetians who preceded them – did not prosecute Orthodox Christians (Crawshaw 1978: 20). In addition, the Ottoman *millet* system granted religious minorities control over communal affairs by recognizing religious heads as leaders of the community, giving them considerable political powers, and using them as intermediaries between the people and Ottoman officials. Under this system, Orthodox Church officials gained considerable power, so much so that they earned the title "the Ethnarchy" and were described by some as the real rulers of Ottoman Cyprus (Persianis 1978: 3). Indeed, the Church emerged as the "central institutional sphere around which the political, intellectual, and cultural life of Greek Cypriots revolved" (Markides 1977: 5).

Although the *millet* system empowered Orthodox officials and allowed more religious freedom than the Venetians, Orthodox officials were hardly content with Ottoman rule. Because the religious officials were educated in Greece and maintained strong ties with the Greek Orthodox Church, they saw Cyprus as part of a greater Greek civilization. In particular, the Archbishop of Cyprus (the island's top Orthodox official) joined the Society of Friends in the early 1800s, which was organized to fight for Greek independence from Ottoman rule. During the ensuing Greek war of independence, the Ottomans learned that the Archbishop had given financial and moral support to the Greeks and executed him and several other Cypriot Church officials. Although the execution of the island's political and religious elite caused tension and hostility between the Greek Cypriot community and their rulers, the Ottomans continued to use the *millet* system and even allowed the Greek Cypriot community to maintain ties with Greece after the latter's independence from the Ottomans in the 1820s.

Much to the delight of the Orthodox Church officials, the British gained control of Cyprus in 1878 in exchange for a British pledge of support to the Ottomans in their conflict with Russia. The British maintained a system of rule that separated the island's main religious communities and collaborated with each community's religious leaders. Similar to Ottoman rule, however, the early support of Orthodox officials quickly waned. For one thing, the British did not give Orthodox officials the same powers and support that they enjoyed under Ottoman rule. For example, the Ottomans allowed the Orthodox officials to use police to collect taxes, but the British forbid this practice, thereby placing the Church under greater financial duress (Bryant 2004: 16). In addition, the Ottoman-British agreement for the transfer of Cyprus to British hands stipulated that Great Britain pay the Ottomans a yearly tribute, and the British simply extracted it from the Cypriot population. This created a difficult situation lasting until 1920 where Cypriots were double-taxed:

once to pay the Ottoman tribute and once to pay for British rule. Finally, Church officials grew disillusioned with the British because they gave no sign of leaving the island.

Because of these grievances, relations soured, and Greek Cypriot leaders began mobilizing their community against British rule. Ironically, after thousands of years of foreign conquest and domination, their goal was not independence. Instead, the Orthodox officials mobilized the population to pursue enosis, or the union of Cyprus with Greece, a territory from which it had been separated since being snatched from the Byzantine Empire nearly a millennium before. Such mobilization grew dramatically after World War II and was epitomized by a referendum organized by the Orthodox Church to join Cyprus with Greece, during which priests actively encouraged the population to vote for enosis. After the British refused to acknowledge the overwhelmingly pro-enosis results, Church leaders helped organize and finance an armed struggle in pursuit of enosis.

Enosis and EOKA

After Greek independence from the Ottoman Empire in 1829, Greek politics was fixated on the *Megali Idea*, or Great Idea. The Great Idea was an outline of irredentist nationalism seeking to return Greece to its ancient splendor by expanding its borders to include the Greek-speaking population living in adjacent lands. In effect, this new nation would reassemble the Byzantine Empire, making Constantinople the new capital and merging Greece with Crete, Cyprus, the Ionian Islands, Epirus, Macedonia, Smyrna, and Thrace.

The Great Idea was taught in Greek schools and gained a powerful popular base. "From childhood," writes Crawshaw (1978), "the Greek is conditioned in church and school to believe that in the fullness of time all Greek-speaking areas must be united within the frontiers of the Motherland" (18). Popular nationalism, in turn, encouraged the Greek government to pursue the Great Idea, albeit with only limited success: the Greek borders expanded to include Crete, Epirus, southern Macedonia, and Thessaly. After a disastrous war with Turkey in 1919–1922 that saw Greece lose much of the territory it was pledged after the Ottoman defeat in World War I, Greece and Turkey agreed to exchange populations, and more than one million ethnic Greeks moved from Turkish territory to Greece. With this population movement, the underlying drive for territorial expansion weakened, and the Greek government and public pursued the Great Idea with less vigor.

Although originating in Greece, the Great Idea spread and inspired people beyond Greek national borders. In Cyprus, the Orthodox religious leaders accepted it and actively pursued enosis because of their close ties with the Greek Orthodox Church and the fact that nearly all Greek Cypriot Orthodox officials were educated in Greece. Because of the ever-present risk of Ottoman violence, the Orthodox elite in Cyprus did not openly advocate enosis during the final half-century of Ottoman rule. With the arrival of the British, however, Church officials in Cyprus pursued enosis with more and more verve, culminating in a violent anticolonial guerrilla movement organized by EOKA in the 1950s.

EOKA, or the National Organization of Cypriot Struggle, was founded by religious officials, military officers, and professionals, some of whom were Greek nationals still struggling for the Great Idea. The purpose of the group was to organize a guerrilla movement to fight for enosis in the face of British resistance. Although the Church provided important resources and legitimacy to the movement, it was a military operation and therefore was dominated by a military man: General George Grivas, who was born and raised in Cyprus, was educated in Greece, became a Greek national, and worked his way up the ranks within the Greek military.

Grivas realized that a frontal assault on the British would be suicidal and therefore organized a guerrilla-based movement focused on strategic bombings, protests, the dissemination of information, and the assassination of colonial officials, British nationals, and – especially – Greek Cypriots who opposed the movement. As the guerrilla movement developed, EOKA grew into an organization with approximately 25,000 people and three distinct subcomponents. The first, PEKA (the Political Committee of the Cyprus Struggle), was staffed by professionals and the intelligentsia and had four main duties: to coordinate the political struggle, maintain a solid internal front, raise national morale, and fight enemy propaganda (Varnavas 2001: 44). The second was the core of EOKA and consisted of between 100 and 200 combatants who specialized in kidnappings, assassinations, and bombings (Demetriou 2007: 175). Finally, ANE, or the Strong Youth of EOKA, was a student organization that helped organize mass protests and civil disobedience, disseminated information through pamphlets and graffiti, and assisted the combatants. In fact, combatants were usually students who had worked their way up the organizational hierarchy.

EOKA first made its presence felt on April 1, 1955 with a series of bombings of government buildings and infrastructure. Over the next four years, it waged a constant and violent campaign; its members engaged in more than 1,000 armed incidents, detonated nearly 1,500 bombs, and orchestrated hundreds of street demonstrations (Demetriou 2007: 175). Although supported by many Greek Cypriots, EOKA was based on violence and was not afraid to use it to enforce its interests among the Greek Cypriot population. As a consequence, the public generally followed EOKA's commands whether they supported the movement or not. For example, EOKA distributed propaganda threatening any Greek Cypriots attending the English School in Nicosia in 1958. Noting EOKA's murder of many Greek Cypriots for opposing directives, parents removed their students from the school, and the number of Greek Cypriot's attending the school – which had been growing – fell precipitously from 317 to only 21 (Colonial Office 1959).

Ethnic Violence in Cyprus

Although the EOKA movement used considerable violence, it did not purposefully wield it against the Turkish Cypriot population. Many more Greek Cypriots were killed by EOKA than their Turkish compatriots, and Grivas insisted that EOKA avoid attacking Turkish Cypriots. Despite such efforts, the EOKA movement ultimately stirred up intense communal conflict and was a very influential cause of Cyprus' subsequent history of ethnic violence.

The EOKA movement promoted communal conflict by using violence to pursue a national idea at odds with that of the Turkish Cypriots. In fact, Greek Cypriot nationalism seemed to ignore the very existence of Turkish Cypriots, viewing them as illegitimate interlopers (Markides 2001: 5). The 1950s was not the first time that the enosis movement sparked ethnic conflict, however, as demands for enosis had always irked Turkish Cypriots (Bryant 1998b: 280). Between 1882 and 1931, for example, there were twenty separate – albeit minor – incidents of Turkish reprisals against the enosis movement (Crawshaw 1978: 24).

The actions of the British during their battle with EOKA also heightened ethnic tension. Shortly after the movement began, the colonial government quickly realized that EOKA had infiltrated the administration and security forces, a situation that seriously hampered colonial efforts to combat the guerrillas. In reaction to this problem, the colonial officials privileged Turkish Cypriots for government service, and Turkish Cypriots were all too willing to combat EOKA given their disdain for the movement. Simultaneously, EOKA killed several Greek Cypriot police officers for collaborating with the British, causing many Greek Cypriots who did not sympathize with EOKA to leave the force out of fear. With the departure of Greek Cypriots and the employment of more and more Turkish Cypriots, the island's security forces – which countered EOKA violence with its own – quickly became overwhelmingly Turkish, causing Turkish Cypriot police officers and Greek Cypriot members of EOKA to actively fight one another (Copeaux and Mauss-Copeaux 2005: 32; Holland 1998: 60–68). Under these conditions, Greek and Turkish Cypriot communities were effectively at war, and all EOKA had to do to instigate communal conflict was to kill a Turkish Cypriot police officer, something that occurred in 1958 and sparked the island's first bout of ethnic violence (Holland 1998: 216–220).

The 1958 violence occurred in June and July and, according to official statistics, caused the deaths of 109 Cypriots. It also began a process of ethnic segregation whereby Greek and Turkish Cypriots attacked one another in efforts to cleanse their communities. In an attempt to limit violence, the British created the infamous green line in Nicosia, the capital, which allocated the north to Turkish Cypriots and the south to Greek Cypriots.

Although independence occurred in 1960 with very limited ethnic violence, the latter returned in a more intense form in 1963 and 1964 in reaction to proposed constitutional changes that favored the Greek Cypriot community. During the violence, Greek and Turkish Cypriots attacked one another and further segregated their communities to such an extent that Copeaux and Mauss-Copeaux (2005) refer to the process as ethnic cleansing (42). In the process, twenty-eight Turkish Cypriot communities were evacuated because they could not be protected from Greek Cypriot attacks. The end result of the violence was a hypersegregated country, with nearly all of the Turkish Cypriot community living in forty-five ethnic enclaves dispersed throughout the island, covering only 1.5 percent of the territory, and ruled exclusively by Turkish Cypriot authorities (Copeaux and Mauss-Copeaux 2005: 44). From 1964 until 1968, the Turkish Cypriot population did not dare to leave their tiny enclaves, a situation that, according to Volkan (1979), caused them to empathize with caged birds and sparked a fad of keeping parakeets as pets (91–98).

The present ethno-nationalist division of the island – with the Turkish Cypriots controlling the north and the Greek Cypriots controlling the south – resulted from the Turkish military invasion in 1974. The war was sparked by a military coup led by Greek Cypriot nationalists who were collaborating with the military junta in Greece. The coup leaders quickly proclaimed the merger of Cyprus with Greece, a move that prompted the Turkish government's invasion of Cyprus. The Turkish military captured the north of the island and divided Cyprus into its present divisions. The Turkish invasion caused great fear among Greek Cypriots and provoked ethnic purges and counterpurges by civilians, and the violence during the war far exceeded that of the previous bouts of ethnic violence, with approximately 1,000 deaths between 1955 and 1974 but as many as 6,000 during the summer of 1974. In addition, approximately 40 percent of the island's population was rendered internal refugees by the war.

Although the ethno-nationalist violence between Greek and Turkish Cypriot communities often had a spontaneous character, it was dominated by organized elements on both sides. EOKA was the main organization on the Greek side. By 1974, EOKA had been disbanded, but a group of extremist elements of EOKA organized a new group – EOKA-B – that orchestrated the military coup and much of the ethno-nationalist purges during the war. The parallel organization on the Turkish Cypriot side was originally named Volkan, or Volcano, but was eventually renamed TMT, or the Turkish Resistance Organization. It was relatively small, having only 100 members in 1956, and had close ties to the colonial security forces and the Turkish government, the latter of which supplied it with arms (Varnavas 2001: 38). The goals of TMT were to protect the Turkish community and to pursue the partition of the island into Greek and Turkish sections. Toward these ends, TMT copied EOKA's tactics: using violence to discipline its own community, organizing militant youth organizations, and orchestrating murders and bombings (Copeaux and Mauss-Copeaux 2005: 33–34). Both groups also actively promoted communal segregation by organizing communal activities, threatening communal members that interacted with noncommunal members, and attacking rival communal members.

EDUCATION AND ETHNO-NATIONALIST VIOLENCE IN CYPRUS

Most recent analysis of violence in Cyprus recognize the extremely important role played by international actors, including Great Britain, Greece, Turkey, and the United States (Anderson 2008; Holland 1998). Indeed, Cyprus found itself at the center of international intrigue because of Cold War politics, continued hostility between Greece and Turkey, and the desire of Great Britain to retain Cyprus as a colony, all of which combined to promote an unwieldy constitution and British, Greek, and Turkish military presence on the island at independence.

While not disregarding the importance of international factors, domestic conditions also contributed to violence, and ethnic violence in particular. In fact, the enosis movement was arguably the single most important cause of ethno-nationalist violence in Cyprus, as it inspired Greek Cypriots to risk life and limb to incorporate Cyprus into Greece, and their fanaticism and tactics sparked fear within the minority Turkish community, thereby turning an anticolonial struggle into violence between two ethnic communities with competing ideas of nation. Education, in turn, played a very important role within the enosis movement and is therefore implicated in the subsequent ethnic violence. As described later in the chapter, not only were those actors who inspired and led the population to pursue enosis relatively educated, but education contributed to ethno-national violence through several educational mechanisms.

Education in Colonial Cyprus

During the period of Ottoman rule, education in Cyprus was communalized, with Greek and Turkish Cypriots having their own schools. This division was logical because education was hardly secular, being run either by churches or mosques and focusing on religious instruction. After the British took over Cyprus, they left education under the control of local religious leaders for several decades, thereby retaining a communally segregated system of education.

While maintaining the status quo, the British expanded the system of education and made it more accessible to the public. In pursuit of this end, they initially provided grants-in-aid to primary schools and encouraged communities to set up additional schools. After World War I, the colonial government took a much more active role in education, increasing colonial funding and gaining some control over the curricula and staffing of schools. Despite their new formal powers, with few exceptions, the government continued to allow the communities to run their schools as they saw fit. This was especially the case for secondary education but also applied to primary schools despite laws giving the colonial government formal control over them.

With British support and high local demand, the number of Cypriots attending school increased rapidly during the eighty years of British rule. For instance, there were only 5,000 students attending primary school in 1879, but this number rose to 11,000 only six years later and continued to increase to 40,000 by 1917 (Bryant 1998b: 208; Crouzet 1973: 107). Despite this dramatic growth, the largest expansion did not occur until after World War II, with 95 percent of primary-school-aged children regularly attending school by the mid-1950s (Foreign Office 1955). The number of students attending secondary school was considerably lower but still increased rapidly following World War II: there were only 5,000 secondary school children on the island in 1941 but nearly 20,000 by 1955 (Foreign Office 1955). All in all, by 1955, 70 percent of Cypriots aged six to eighteen attended school regularly, a figure on par with several European countries at the time (Lennox-Boyd 1956).[1] Like Sri Lanka, a dramatic educational expansion in Cyprus therefore clearly preceded the onset of severe ethno-nationalist violence in 1958.

The Educated Elite and the Enosis Movement

Scholars of nationalism have long noted that the most active participants in nationalist movements are the intelligentsia (Anderson 1983; Gellner 1983; Smith 1983). Cyprus is no exception. From the beginning, doctors, lawyers, journalists, teachers, church officials, and other professionals played a vital role publicizing the enosis movement and inspiring other Greek Cypriots to pursue it (Bryant 1998b; Loizos 1974: 116–117). According to Markides (1977), enosis originated "in the minds of intellectuals in their attempt to revive Greek-Byzantine civilization" (11). Some showed their willingness to risk their lives for enosis by volunteering to join the Greek army in 1897 to fight a war against the Ottoman Empire (Pollis 1998: 91). Half a century later, nonelites had also begun to support enosis, but the intelligentsia remained the most active element pursuing it. Such support was exemplified by the Association of Greek Cypriot Intellectuals, which championed the enosis cause, going so far as to declare during their 1954 annual meetings that they would intensify efforts and do all in their power to make enosis a reality (Bryant 1998b: 473).

Of all segments of the intelligentsia, three stand out for their pro-enosis efforts. First, members of the literate urban elite strongly supported enosis because they saw it as a way of asserting their identity and protesting the British monopoly of top political and economic positions (McHenry 1981: 82). Journalists were particularly important, as they helped strengthen support for enosis by constantly championing the enosis cause in their editorials and describing union with Greece

---

[1] Cyprus' secondary enrollment rate was 47.1 percent in 1960, compared with 67.4 percent in Great Britain, 56.5 percent in France, 44.8 percent in Germany, 40.6 percent in Portugal, and 37.1 percent in Spain.

as natural, inevitable, and supported by all true Greek Cypriots (Bryant 1998b; Weir 1952: 108–110).[2] Second, teachers were the most important cultural gatekeepers of the Greek Cypriot community and actively supported enosis as a means of protecting and reinvigorating Greek Cypriot culture (McHenry 1981: 82). Finally, the religious elites within the Greek Orthodox Church were arguably the single most important element of the pro-enosis intelligentsia (Markides 1977: 10–11). From Archbishop Kyprianos, who was a member of the Society of Friends that fought for Greek independence from Ottoman rule in the early nineteenth century, to Archbishop Makarios III, who was instrumental in founding and funding the EOKA movement, the leaders of the church have consistently taken it on themselves as a quasi-religious duty to pursue the dream of enosis. As Salih (1968) writes, "The Orthodox Church, under the leadership of the Archbishop, had become the promoter and the symbol of Greek Cypriot nationalism" (40).

Beside simply popularizing a national idea, the educated elites also actively pursued enosis by organizing and perpetrating violence. As mentioned previously, Archbishop Makarios III helped organize the EOKA movement, and the remaining founding members of the organization were also highly educated: two others were high-level church officials, one was a lawyer, two were generals, and two were university professors. Once the movement began, EOKA's political wing, PEKA, continued to include the intelligentsia, including "mayors, lawyers, teachers, the church and the medical profession" (War Office 1959). Among the most notable examples of educated professionals involved in EOKA were a doctor who trained Cypriot university students in Athens to use arms and guerrilla tactics and two teachers who headed the student organizations (OXEN, or Young People's Christian Orthodox Union, and PEON, or Pancyprian National Youth Organization) that recruited and trained many – if not most – of EOKA's combatants (Foley and Scobie 1975: 17; Varnavas 2001: 11).

---

[2] An editorial from the newspaper *Fonti ti Kyprou* in 1900 the supposed failure of a religious official to support enosis provides one notable example:

> The Cypriot people always distinguishes itself by patriotism in the true meaning of the word, patriotism pure, sincere, and brotherly.... They never permit themselves to be used by representatives as the means of their advancement. It is from such signs that it is possible to be certain in saying that the entire orthodox population of the island remains in complete harmony, and no one would dare to be exploited for other reasons, so that a child of Cyprus would not blame his brother for lacking patriotism. In other words, in this question all have lived as brothers, because they have but one goal, one single desire, their physical restoration through enosis with Greece. (Bryant 1998b: 156)

Whereas the previous examples focus on the leadership of EOKA, the educated were also well represented among the mid- and low-level positions within the organization. Analyzing the occupations of incarcerated EOKA combatants, colonial officials cited students as the most common occupation and described how secondary and university students formed the core of the organization (Colonial Office 1955; Colonial Office 1956c). Among those actually employed, colonial officials found that white-collar clerical employees were the largest occupation group of arrested EOKA members and continually highlighted the important roles played by the intelligentsia, especially teachers (Colonial Office 1955; Foreign Office 1955). Supporting colonial claims, Persianis (1978) reviews Cypriot newspapers to compile a list of EOKA members who were arrested between 1955 and 1959 and finds that teachers were the most common profession, with 105 teachers detained or imprisoned (153).[3] He also finds that other members of the intelligentsia were commonly arrested, including thirty lawyers and ten doctors. And, because the educated were found at all levels of EOKA, educated individuals did not simply organize violence but also participated directly in acts of violence. For example, members of EOKA's first "killer" squad were well educated, middle class, and "destined to rise in their chosen careers": one was a law student, two were graduates of a prestigious British college, one was a medical student, and one was a university graduate who held a mid-level position within the colonial administration (Foley and Scobie 1975: 53).

Even more so than EOKA, EOKA-B was dominated by the educated. Unlike EOKA, however, students comprised a very small segment of it. Instead, government employees, other white-collar workers, and professionals were very prevalent, comprising more than 60 percent of those accused and convicted of EOKA-B membership (Markides 1977: 86–121). Markides (1977) points to teachers, lawyers, and church officials – all highly educated – as particularly prone to this violent organization whose actions ultimately led to war and ethnic purges.

Educational Mechanisms

According to Bryant (2004), "It was not until the post–World War II period that Greek nationalism in its Cypriot phase was able to claim popular support for violent revolt; not coincidentally, it was only in the post war period that education could genuinely be claimed to be

---

[3] Bryant (2004) also claims that teachers played a vital role in helping organize the anticolonial student movement (156).

universal" (158). The preceding analysis supports such claims by verifying the sequence linking educational expansion to violence and highlighting the influential roles of educated individuals in ethno-nationalist violence. An analysis of mechanisms linking education and educational expansion to ethno-nationalist violence offers additional support for Bryant's claims.

Similar to Sri Lanka, both the frustration-aggression and competition mechanisms help explain why many educated individuals participated so actively in ethnic violence in Cyprus and why ethnic violence followed a dramatic expansion in education. Considering the first, the frustration-aggression mechanism – while not causing ethnic violence directly – contributed to it by promoting the enosis movement. In colonial Cyprus, as elsewhere, education was very valued because it was a status symbol and a means of social advancement (Bryant 2004: 127; Persianis 1978: 49). The social value of education appears to have been particularly strong in colonial Cyprus, as Greek Cypriots commonly claimed that one became a person through education and viewed education "as a necessary part of one's growth to full humanity" (Bryant 1998b: 127). As a consequence, the educated had very heightened expectations for status and mobility. This can be seen in the refusal of many educated individuals to accept menial jobs. According to Bryant (1998b), educated young men frequently became financial burdens on their family during the British colonial period because they were unwilling to engage in manual labor. "Instead," she writes, "[an educated young man] would grow the fingernails of his pinky fingers long to indicate his more educated status and would spend his days debating politics in the coffeeshops" (211).

The educated had heightened expectations for respect and mobility, but they faced considerable obstacles to social advancement. In combination with the confidence derived from their elevated status as educated individuals, unmet expectations appear to have driven many to participate in the EOKA movement. The lack of white-collar employment was one obstacle that caused grievances among educated Cypriots. There was a high demand for education in colonial Cyprus because of the value Cypriots placed on education. Yet, the Cypriot economy was unable to absorb all school graduates as far back as the turn of the twentieth century, leaving many unemployed (Bryant 1998b: 226; Persianis 1978: 51). The Colonial Report of 1925, for example, exclaimed, "Cyprus can provide only a limited number of professional and business openings and there is no doubt that the needs of the island in secondary education are now more than fully satisfied, and that the future prospects of secondary schools depend on a large extent on improved facilities and increased opportunity for emigration" (Persianis 1978: 51).

In addition to limited employment opportunities, the educated in colonial Cyprus faced considerable impediments to mobility because of active discrimination. Writing in the early twentieth century, Orr (1972: 160–171) notes that educated Cypriots resented British rule because senior administrative posts were reserved for non-Cypriots and because colonial administrators hardly interacted with the locals. He writes:

[A]s soon as the time comes, as come it must, when Cypriots are admitted to important posts under Government, the barrier which now exists between them and the English community will begin to disappear. But so long as it remains, "Enosis" will continue to be the gospel of the educated Cypriot, preached to the peasant, encouraged in the schools, and given daily prominence in all the Greek newspapers. (171)

Despite Orr's warning, colonial officials continued to exclude Cypriots from top administrative posts until the final years of colonialism, which was "a source of deep bitterness" causing secondary school graduates to be "the most militant of the pro-enosis groups" (Barham 1982: 51, 80). For example, low-level clerks facing limited possibilities for mobility within the administration actively participated in the EOKA movement, being the second most common occupation of arrested EOKA members after students. Loizos (1974) also links limited mobility and discrimination to the anticolonial movement in Cyprus, claiming that the treatment of Cypriots as second-class citizens "encouraged protests of all kinds" (117). Even after independence, he (1975) finds that Greek Cypriots with Greek educations were more likely to support extremist parties in favor of enosis because they believed high-status positions were still reserved for individuals with English education (284). Indeed, educated intellectuals – especially Greek-university-trained teachers and lawyers – were among the strongest supporters of EOKA-B because an oversupply of educated elites combined with a growing preference for individuals trained outside of Greece severely limited their economic mobility and caused great frustration (Markides 1977: 97–103).

Along with – and, in fact, interacting with – the frustration-aggression mechanism, education also contributed to ethnic violence in Cyprus through the competition mechanism. For one thing, both anticolonial and anti-Turkish violence were strengthened by potential material and political gains derived from violence. Most notably, the educated elites stood to ascend to top political and economic positions after the withdrawal of the British. Thus, the elimination of British rule was in the material interests of the educated, thereby pushing many to participate actively in the enosis movement. Similarly, because Greek Cypriots trained at Greek universities faced disadvantaged employment opportunities after independence (vis-à-vis Greek Cypriots with degrees from non-Greek universities), many of the former supported EOKA-B, as enosis would transform their disadvantage into an advantage and improve their economic position (Markides 1977: 97–103).

In addition, education sparked competition and conflict over education itself, as conflict between British officials and Greek Cypriot elites over the control of education provided an emotional issue that strengthened the EOKA movement and pushed them to fight for enosis. Despite granting Greek and Turkish Cypriot schools great autonomy during the first fifty years of British rule, their inability to control education caused consternation among colonial officials for two reasons. First, officials were concerned that the extremely nationalistic content of the Greek schools might transform into anti-British sentiments. Second, many officials believed that the curriculum failed to impart necessary skills to the students (Bryant 2004: 126). Given these concerns, the colonial government slowly reformed the educational systems by expanding their formal control over it. Despite these reforms, very little actually changed in Greek Cypriot schools because of colonial inaction (Crouzet 1973: 111–112; Persianis 1978: 170; Weir 1952: 115). For example, despite having the right to control the curriculum of primary schools, the government interfered only limitedly, trying simply to prohibit symbols of Greek nationalism such as the flying of Greek flags and the celebration of Greek national holidays.[4] In the secondary schools, the colonial authorities – despite threats – hardly interfered at all (which allowed primary school students to go to secondary schools to celebrate Greek national holidays). Lamenting this lack of influence, several colonial officials claimed that the government's complete inability to control education was the ultimate cause of EOKA violence. As one writes, "It is, I think, generally accepted that the greatest single cause of the present trouble in Cyprus is the failure of the Colonial Administration (despite the clear warning of the 1931 riots) to institute State control over Greek-Cypriot education, which has remained to a very large extent in the hands of the Orthodox Church and mainland Greeks" (Ward 1956).

---

[4] The colonial government closed most of the island's Greek Cypriot primary schools during periods of the EOKA movement because they flew Greek flags.

The most important reason for the lack of British interference in Greek Cypriot education despite such strong sentiments among colonial officials about the need to do something (as well as the fact that they possessed the formal powers to do so) was the uproar that colonial efforts to influence education caused among the Greek Cypriot community. Indeed, church authorities, teachers, and other elites viewed education as a means of protecting Greek culture and pursuing the enosis dream. In this way, it served both as a symbol of Greek nationalism and as an instrument to pursue it. Any attempt by the colonial government to interfere with education – no matter how trivial – therefore became a *cause célèbre* among the nationalist elites, sparking vindictive editorials, letters of protest, and even mass protests (Crawshaw 1978: 52; Crouzet 1973: 110; Persianis 1978: 171, 176; Weir 1952: 96–119). Most notably, violent protests occurred in Cyprus in 1931, during which thousands of Greek Cypriots took to the streets and even burned to the ground the governor's residence (Crouzet 1973: 110). The major rallying cry behind the violence was allegations that the British were attempting to de-Hellenize the island's youth by usurping control of the educational system (Crouzet 1973: 110). Discussing the 1929 educational laws that motivated the violence, McHenry (1981) claims, "The law outraged the advocates of Enosis and made their opposition to British rule even more adamant" (94). Similarly, EOKA used British interference with Greek Cypriot education as a rallying cry to gain support and mobilize people into action during the 1950s. In one of the many pamphlets that EOKA distributed, for instance, it claimed, "The ruler, being ignorant of the power of endurance of the Greek soul, is perfidiously trying to attack the Greek schools. But, he may rest assured vigorous resistance from all teachers, parents and pupils" (Colonial Office 1956b).

In this way, competition between colonial officials and Greek Cypriot elites over control the educational system reinforced the enosis movement and actually fanned the flames of nationalism. Indeed, the British appear to have made poor decisions in their middling attempts to control education as a means of counteracting the nationalist movement, as such action gave colonial officials little actual power over the schools and sparked a virulent backlash among church and educational officials that only strengthened calls for enosis (Markides 2001: 4).[5]

---

[5] Still, as Kelling (1990) notes, the British walked a difficult tightrope with no evident strategy for success, as too much British interference would instigate Greek Cypriot opposition and too little would encourage enosis (7).

Beside the frustration-aggression and competition mechanisms, the socialization and mobilization mechanisms help explain the link between education and ethnic violence. Indeed, the literature on violence in Cyprus points to each – much more so than the frustration-aggression and competition mechanisms – as influential causes of ethno-nationalist violence.

The Socialization Mechanism. Field Marshall Harding (1956a), the Governor of Cyprus between 1955 and 1957, claimed that schools were the "breeding places for enosis," and a colonial report on secondary education in Cyprus in 1956 claimed:

The Greek secondary schools have been deliberately used as agencies for the political indoctrination of Greek Cypriot youth. The systematic perversion of youthful minds for political purposes has proceeded with callous disregard for the well-being of the children themselves. It has been pushed to lengths which recall the hateful methods of the totalitarian states. (Foreign Office 1956a)

Although Harding's views must be scrutinized given his position as a colonial authority struggling to maintain control in the face of an anticolonial movement, there is strong evidence to support his belief that education actively socialized Greek and Turkish Cypriots to hold strong and incompatible ethno-national identities. In particular, the curriculum, rituals, and activities all strengthened and popularized – but did not create – competing ethno-national identities. Although true for both communities, like the colonial officials, I focus on the Greek Cypriot educational system because of space constraints and its greater relevance to the EOKA movement.

As described previously, education has always been strongly linked to religion in Cyprus. Through the *millet* system, the Ottomans endowed the Orthodox Church with the right to run schools for the Orthodox community, and the British allowed the Orthodox Church to retain its control of the Greek Cypriot educational system. Through schools, the Orthodox Church was able to influence – if not dictate – the curriculum, spirit, and staffing of the schools throughout the period of British colonial period (Bryant 2004: 167; Persianis 1978: 42–3). As a consequence, Greek Cypriot education was hardly secular, teaching religion and reverence for church leaders and stressing that it was the duty of Greek Cypriots to be good Christians. The church also used its might to ensure that the educational system spread the idea of enosis (Foreign Office 1955). Indeed, Persianis (1978) writes, "For the Church the strengthening of national feeling was the major, if not the exclusive, aim of education" (51). As a result, the church used education to shape the national identities of students both because they believed the realization of one's "Greekness" made students better individuals and because they believed enosis was highly desirable for the Greek Cypriot community as a whole (Bryant 1998b; Pollis 1998: 90; Weir 1952: 85).

The pro-enosis bias of Greek Cypriot education can be seen in the curriculum of the schools.[6] The Greek Cypriot schools imported nearly all of their reading material from Greece throughout the period of British rule (Colonial Office 1956a; Persianis 1978: 168; Weir 1952: 115). In fact, most Greek Cypriot secondary schools copied the official curriculum of schools in Greece and were recognized by the Greek government for doing so. As a result, Greek Cypriot students who graduated from these schools were automatically accepted to the Greek university system without having to take any qualifying exams (giving them an advantage over Greek nationals, who needed to pass an exam) (Crouzet 1973: 112–113; Persianis 1978: 46).

Because of the Greek national curriculum, Greek Cypriot schools introduced students to powerful ideas about being part of the Greek nation and imparted a particular Greek perspective by stressing the magnificence of Greek civilization (Education Advisory Committee 1966: 11; Foreign Office 1956a; Tremayne 1958: 106–107). For this, schools focused their curricula on Greek history and literature, religion, and ancient Greek; and this curricula constantly emphasized the Great Idea as a means of making Greece a great nation once again and reuniting Cypriots with their long-lost nation. According to Bryant (2004), the goal of Greek Cypriot secondary education "was the creation of Hellenic citizens who could parse their Ancient Greek verbs, recite Homeric verse, prattle about ancient Greek history, and still be prepared to take an active part in commerce, in the professions, and in the intellectual life of the Greek kingdom that it was believed Cyprus would eventually join" (123–124). Another expert of the Cypriot educational system claims that education "taught the pupils that they were Greeks and should look forward to union with Greece" (Persianis 1978: 17).

An elementary school reader used throughout Cyprus in the 1950s provides one example of the Greek nationalist component of Cypriot education. It includes a speech given by a school headmaster in Greece for a Flag Day celebration, a text overflowing with Greek nationalism and claiming that Cyprus was enslaved by the British who prevented Greek Cypriots from attaining the glory of nationhood with Greece

---

[6] See Bryant 1998a, 1998b, 2004; Hill 1952: 492–493; Orr 1972: 131–132; War Office 1960: 14.

(Foreign Office 1956b).⁷ This and other textbooks also excluded Turkish Cypriots from the moral community both by defining the Greek nation according to language and religion and by describing Turks as the historic archenemies of the Greeks. Offering evidence for the latter, two-thirds of a history textbook used in Greek Cypriot secondary schools focused on wars between Greece and the Ottoman Empire/Turkey (Education Advisory Committee 1966: 11).

Along with the curriculum, the rituals, and extracurricular activities of Greek Cypriot schools also promoted strong Greek ethno-nationalist identities. Despite its separation from Greece for nearly a millennium, Greek Cypriot schools celebrated several Greek national holidays, including Flag Day (which celebrated the Greek flag), Greek Independence Day (from the Ottoman Empire), and Oxi Day (which commemorates Greek Prime Minister Ioannis Metaxas's rejection of the ultimatum made by Mussolini in 1940) (Persianis 1978: 195).⁸ On these holidays, priests led processions of students to local churches for service and then to public gatherings where speeches exhorted students to struggle for their country's liberation and union with Greece (Persianis 1978: 195; Salih 1968: 40). The speech of the Headmaster of Nicosia's Pancyprian Gymnasium during the Flag Day celebration in 1946 provides an example of how these ceremonies heightened one's awareness of being Greek:

"The Greek Flag is the symbol of national unity between the free and the enslaved brothers, the symbol which includes within itself the whole brilliant greatness of the past, the present and the future of the Greek nation. This is why we should never forget that our present and future life is always the result of our past."

---

⁷ The text reads: "The headmaster of the school made a speech more or less as follows:

'Ladies and gentlemen, and my dear children, we have gathered here today in order to honour the sacred emblem of our nation, the glorious Blue and White banner. Every nation has its own flag. This blue and white flag of ours was woven by Glory and embroidered by Liberty. It streams out proudly and proclaims to the ends of the earth the honour of Greece and the heroism of our race.

This flag in the dark years of slavery imparted strength to the gigantic figures of the 1821 revolution. It passed honour and pride into Epirus, Macedonia and Thrace, and streamed over Crete and the islands. And it gathered in an embrace under its renowned folds the martyred and heroic Dodecanese. On this date, under this blue and white flag, with the help of St. Deetrius the Greek Army commanded by King Constantine, liberated the far city of Salonika; and this same flag now waits to be hoisted over Cyprus and Epirus; which are still in slavery.'"

⁸ With the loss of autonomy of the primary schools, they were not allowed to celebrate Greek national holidays, although the secondary schools continued to celebrate them and many primary school students participated in the secondary-school celebrations.

After inviting the public to take a holy oath to the Greek flag, the Headmaster continued:

"The taking of an oath to the national symbol is more imperative for the Cypriot youth than for the free brothers of Greece, who are only invited to preserve the freedom they have obtained. For us matters are different.... Expectations and hopes are not sufficient to obtain our freedom. We need positive work, constant orientation towards our nation's ideals, the preservation of our Greek conscience.... The day which is devoted to the Greek flag must infuse into you, my dear pupils, more Greek spirit, it must make you feel that you are Greeks not only in origin but also in soul, mind and spirit." (Persianis 1978: 195)

Demonstrating the anti-Turkish element of such ceremonies, students at another Flag Day celebration marched carrying Greek flags and chanting "the heads of the Turks must be cut off and their bodies thrown in filth" (Persianis 1978: 172). Importantly, this and other anti-Turkish rituals occurred long before the onset of ethno-nationalist violence in Cyprus.

Whereas holiday rituals helped instill a Greek consciousness in students, students also participated in nationalist ceremonies and perceived nationalist symbols on a daily basis. Students sang the Greek national anthem at school events, and most classrooms were decorated with symbols that reinforced Greek national identities: Greek flags, pictures of the Greek royal family and heroes from the Greek War of Independence, and maps of Greece that – to the dismay of colonial officials – depicted Cyprus as part of Greece instead of the British Empire (Foreign Office 1955; Hill 1952: 492–493; Orr 1972: 131–132). Even after-school activities provided powerful nationalist rituals, with students publicly proclaiming their loyalty to enosis at soccer games, social clubs, reading groups, musical performances, and plays, and even pledging an oath of loyalty to the King of the Hellenes at the Boy Scouts (Bryant 1998a: 62; Bryant 2004: 130). In fact, Governor Storrs described the Greek Cypriot Boy Scouts as a training ground for being Greek and subsequently suspended it.[9]

---

[9] On this, Storrs writes:

All Greek Cypriot troops were under the Greek Constitution (from which Scoutmasters received their warrants and instructions) and made annual returns to the Greek Ministry of Education. The second article of their Scout Law is 'to be faithful to the Fatherland and the laws of the State'. Their flag was the Greek St. George flag, i.e. a broad white cross on a blue ground, with the Scout Fleur-de-Lys in the centre. Each section (or year) received graduate instructions in patriotism, beginning with the respect due to the Greek flag, the 'History of the Greek flag from the most ancient times', 'the constitution of the Greek Nation' and leading up to 'an extended knowledge concerning the political and military organization of the State and the duty of a citizen'. The Greek National hymn had to be learnt by heart. (Persianis 1978: 173)

Besides simply bombarding students with pro-Greek, pro-enosis, and anti-Turkish curricula, ceremonies, and symbols, Greek Cypriot schools also protected students from opposing views (Bryant 1998b: 471). In 1954, for example, the colonial government began publishing an intercommunal periodical for students in an effort to increase Cypriot national unity. Administrators of Greek Cypriot schools quickly mobilized to limit its influence by sending all teachers circulars warning against the periodical's content: "school administrators and teachers are exhorted carefully to consider this serious problem and to protect their schools from this publication, which removes education from its natural ethnic foundation and leads the youth in dangerous paths" (Bryant 1998a: 62). As a consequence, teachers prevented students from reading the material, and the government failed to find an audience for its magazine.

As this last example shows, the ethno-national socialization of Greek Cypriot students depended greatly on the school administrators and teachers and required that both not only actively promote enosis through their interactions with students, but also provide a thoroughly pro-enosis school environment. In colonial Cyprus, teachers and administrators pursued these tasks with great energy for two main reasons. First, Orthodox officials had formal and informal power over educators and pressured them to promote enosis (Bryant 1998b: 257–258; Persianis 1978: 42–43, 145). According to Persianis (1978), teachers were expected to follow the directives of religious authorities and "play the role of priests in Greek schools," and the church exerted considerable pressure on them to assure their active compliance (43). This pressure was based on church influence over school funding, hiring, and disciplinary practices, and the fact that the Orthodox Church was the center of community life and therefore had the power to exclude individuals from the Greek Cypriot community. A letter sent by Archbishop Makarios III to all Greek Cypriot teachers in 1952 clearly highlights the pressure the church exerted on teachers to promote a Greek national consciousness and pro-enosis views among the student body:

Mother Church, following the work of the Greek teachers of the Island with great interest, is particularly glad whenever it realizes that this work is successful.

Unfortunately it has recently noticed with regret that some of the teachers, ignoring the fact that they are the teachers of Greek children do not make the necessary efforts to create Hellenic consciences in their pupils and content themselves with disseminating the knowledge laid down in the curriculum. Sometimes they go so far as to remove [more high-spirited matter] from the Greek [schools] than was removed by the Government curriculum....

We are well aware that teachers, being employees of the Government and completely dependent on the Education Department, which seeks through intimidatory and suppressive methods to create through the teachers good subjects of Her British Majesty, are finding it difficult to fulfill their high mission. But in spite of this every teacher must find the way not to fail in his duty. The complete subjugation of the elementary education of our country aims at dehellenising our children. But we must not allow such a thing to happen. We have a responsibility towards history. (Colonial Office 1952)

The fear of Church retribution helped keep teachers on the path to enosis, but most teachers were already very favorably inclined to the movement, and this is a second reason why they actively pursued enosis in and out of the classroom. Because Greek Cypriot teachers and administrators needed to successfully pass through the educational system themselves, the educational system helped produce teachers and administrators with strong enosis sentiments. Of greater importance, school staff had strong ties with Greece. For one thing, the use of Greek curriculum in Greek Cypriot schools caused philologists to comprise a large segment of all teachers, and these teachers emphasized the value of everything Greek and were self-proclaimed guardians of Hellenism who believed it was their duty to socialize students to support enosis (Markides 1977: 97–98). In fact, philology held such a prestigious position in Greek education that philologists dominated the administration of Greek Cypriot schools (Markides 1977: 98).

In addition, most Greek Cypriot teachers in secondary schools received their university education in Greece because of the absence of a Cypriot university throughout the period of British rule (Markides 1977: 97; Persianis 1978: 216–217). In 1955, for example, three-quarters of qualified secondary-school teachers in Greek Cypriot schools were trained in Greece (Foreign Office 1955). Besides limited educational opportunities, Persianis (1978) suggests that church leaders encouraged study in Greece "so that the historical and intellectual links of Cyprus with Greece could be preserved and the Greek intellectuals of Cyprus could always be expected to look upon Greece for inspiration and guidance" (217). Indeed, Orthodox officials and even school administrators constantly opposed the founding of a university in Cyprus throughout the British colonial period (and even after independence) to maintain the academic link between Greece and Cyprus (Crouzet 1973: 115; Karagiorges 1986: 28; Markides 1977: 98).

One additional reason for the pro-enosis views of administrators and teachers was the nationality of the staff: Greek Cypriot schools were filled with Greek nationals, many of whom had chosen to leave Greece in pursuit of the Great Idea. This situation began during the Ottoman period because of the shortage of educated Greek Cypriots who were qualified to teach. It continued throughout the British period, and large segments of the staff in Greek Cypriot schools were Greek nationals. Even during the final decade of British colonialism, after the dramatic expansion in education allowed more and more Cypriots to become teachers, more than one-quarter of teachers in Greek Cypriot secondary schools were expatriate Greek nationals.[10]

Colonial officials commonly believed that teachers from Greece preached hatred against the British and helped popularize enosis in Cyprus. Although colonial administrators might seem paranoid, it was a well-known policy of Greek nationalists to send Greek teachers "trained in the virulent, anti-Turkish nationalism of Greece" to Cyprus and Anatolia to cultivate the Great Idea (Bryant 1998b: 240). General Grivas, the military leader and mastermind of EOKA, for example, recognized the considerable influence Greek teachers played in instilling his nationalist beliefs. "At the age of eleven," he writes, "I went to live with relatives in Nicosia, where I attended the Pancyprian Gymnasium. Like all the other secondary schools on Cyprus it was staffed by teachers from Greece who brought fresh fervour to our nationalism" (Foley 1965: 3).

Whereas the Greek Cypriot schools were imbued with Greek nationalism during the British colonial period, the Turkish Cypriot schools also helped propagate their Turkish equivalent during the final decades of British rule (Bryant 1998b; Copeaux 2002). Similar to Greek Cypriot schools, most of the reading materials of Turkish Cypriot schools and many of their teachers came from Turkey. After Ataturk's modernizing revolution in Turkey, the schools secularized and taught a curricula dripping with virulent Turkish nationalism, the latter of which popularized the idea of partitioning Cyprus along communal lines and merging the Greek section with Greece and the Turkish section with Turkey.

Thus, education in colonial Cyprus helped disseminate the idea of enosis among the Greek Cypriot population and thereby sparked popular demands and mobilization for the integration of Cyprus into Greece. Simultaneously, Turkish Cypriot schools provided a means for Turkish nationalism to spread to Cyprus after Ataturk's assumption of power. Both educational systems therefore strengthened oppositional national

---

[10] In 1954, 27 percent of secondary-school teachers (116 of 430) were Greek Nationals (Sanuey 1955).

identities, portrayed one another as historic enemies, and promoted ethno-nationalist violence once Greek Cypriots mobilized to pursue their nationalist dreams. As one colonial report lamented, "The present secondary educational system in Cyprus tends to train Greek Cypriots to think of themselves as Greeks and Turkish Cypriots to think of themselves as Turks, and none of them to think of themselves as Cypriots, still less British subjects" (Foreign Office 1955). The presence of strong and oppositional national ideas, in turn, provided a fecund environment for ethno-national violence.

The preceding analysis focuses on the link between education and violence during that late colonial period and overlooks postcolonial Cyprus. Whereas ethnic violence is frequently an asymmetric causal process, with violence creating new conditions that perpetuate it even after the removal of initial causal conditions, the socialization mechanism appears to have contributed to intercommunal divisions and violence in postcolonial Cyprus as well. Karagiorges (1986), for example, concludes that the postcolonial educational system in Cyprus helped undermine the very country it was meant to serve, ultimately promoting ethno-nationalist antagonism and the division of the island into two ethnically segregated components (152).

Whereas the British attempted to exert some control over education during the colonial period, at independence they left both Greek and Turkish Cypriot communities in complete control over their schools, with each community having its own Communal Chamber that – among other things – administered education (Karagiorges 1986: 32). In combination with resentment over communal violence in 1958 (and subsequently in 1963–1964 and 1974), communal control over education made possible biased curricula that strengthened oppositional ethno-nationalist identities. Most importantly, communal control allowed both Greek and Turkish Cypriot schools to strengthen ties with Greece and Turkey and teach curricula stressing Greek and Turkish nationalities instead of a shared Cypriot nationality. Greek and Greek Cypriot officials, for example, collaborated to make the Greek Cypriot schools almost identical to their Greek counterparts, and Greek officials actively pressured Cypriot officials to remove content from the curricula on Cyprus and make Greece the one and only focus (Karagiorges 1986: 37). Indeed, the first Minister of Education was a longtime advocate of enosis, and he proclaimed the dual goals of postcolonial education Hellenization and the union of Greek and Greek Cypriot schools, going so far to proclaim in a speech to the House of Representatives in 1967: "To those who ask what is our educational policy I answer: The educational policy of the Greek mainland is the Cyprus educational policy. Our links with Greece are very close, because we have the same blood, a common language, a common culture. Do we not ask for and do we not fight for Union with Greece?" (Karagiorges 1986: 48).

The relations between Turkish Cypriot educational officials and Turkish officials were even stronger because the latter provided funds and material for Turkish Cypriot education (Karagiorges 1986: 42–44). And after the Turkish conquest of North Cyprus in 1974, Turkish Cypriots attended schools formally controlled by Turkey.

With growing ties between Cypriot schools and their respective "motherlands," Greek and Turkish national symbols held – and continue to hold – a prominent place in Cypriot schools, and the curriculum strengthened opposing and mutually incompatible ideas of nation (Markides 1977: 23). Indeed, a number of analyses of postcolonial education conclude that the curricula and teaching are geared toward heightening national awareness and strengthening divisions between Greek and Turkish Cypriots (Copeaux 2002; Koullapis 2002; Papadakis 2008). Papadakis (2008), for example, analyzes the content of textbooks used in both Greek and Turkish Cypriot schools and concludes that both attempt to construct national communities, describe the other as their natural enemy, and outline the hardships experienced at the hand of the other. The textbooks also provide graphic pictures that promote these ends, with one Turkish Cypriot textbook showing a photo of a Turkish Cypriot distraught and on his knees in front of the unearthed and burned corpses of family members who had been killed by Greek Cypriots in 1974, and a Greek Cypriot textbook showing a Greek Cypriot impaled by a Turk. Papadakis's findings paint a very negative picture of Cypriot education today, suggesting it remains divisive and is a powerful impediment to reconciliation between Greek and Turkish Cypriots.

Similarly, Yashin (2002) describes how the Museum of Barbarism is a common field trip of Turkish Cypriot schools. The museum highlights the many atrocities suffered by Turkish Cypriots at the hands of Greek Cypriots during the ethnic violence of 1963 and 1964, and the field trips are organized to coincide with the actual dates that the violence occurred in order to maximize their emotional impact. The museum is located in the house of a Turkish Cypriot family that was murdered by Greek Cypriots, and the house has been left largely untouched since the murders, with the actual blood of the victims still in the bathtub where they were killed and graphic pictures of the tub filled with the corpses on the wall. Even more, the husband/father of the victims gives the tour personally and provides a detailed and grisly account of the events. The museum fieldtrip is therefore a powerful means of maintaining social distance and strengthening ideas of Greek Cypriots as eternal enemies.

The Mobilization Mechanism. In addition to motivating Cypriots to partake in ethno-nationalist violence through socialization, education also contributed to ethnic violence in a fundamentally different way: by providing the mobilizational resources to organize a large-scale ethno-nationalist movement that subsequently sparked ethnic violence. In particular, the EOKA movement depended greatly on secondary and even primary schools to recruit members, organize activities, and disseminate information.

All histories of the EOKA movement document the vital role of students. Varnavas (2001), for one, claims that they "played the main role in the success of the EOKA struggle" (19). Backing up such claims, the colonial government recorded 149 major acts of violence and disorder by students between August 1, 1954 and January 31, 1956, including a number of marches, violent demonstrations, and bombings (Harding 1956b: 1–13).[11] Among the most notable examples during the 1955–1956 school year were:

1.) A 16 year old Gymnasium pupil was arrested in the street carrying a loaded sub-machine gun in a violin case.
2.) Three pupils of the same school were arrested for planting bombs at the Court House of the Town.
3.) Bombs were thrown from secondary school buildings on a number of occasions. One such attack, made from the building of one of the principal Gymnasia during a schoolboy riot, resulted in the death of one soldier and wounding of another.
4.) The head boy of another Gymnasium was shot dead by Security Forces during a riot in the act of throwing a bomb.
5.) A senior pupil of a Greek commercial school blew himself up with his own bomb while preparing to throw it at a military vehicle.
6.) A demonstration staged by girls of a Greek Cypriot secondary school was used to lure Security Forces into a bomb ambush in a narrow street, which resulted in the death of one soldier and one policeman. (Persianis 1978: 142)

[11] According to colonial records, 4 students were killed, 32 sentenced to whippings, 51 imprisoned, 42 detained, and 576 sentenced to fines between April 1955 and August 1956 (Foreign Office 1957).

Based on its intelligence, the government claimed that three-quarters of all students in their final three years of secondary school were members of the EOKA's student organization (ANE),[12] that the student involvement in the enosis movement was inspired and organized by EOKA, and that all of the island's Greek secondary schools had cells taking order from EOKA leaders (Crawshaw 1978: 108–109; Harding 1956b: 2).

As the previously listed activities highlight, students were not simply implicated in menial activities. In fact, students were extremely involved in the two activities that were arguably the most important for the EOKA-dominated movement. First, they led and formed the overwhelming majority of participants in mass demonstrations in favor of enosis. These protests brought hundreds – if not thousands – of people together to disrupt the government and demonstrate the numerical strength and determination of the enosis movement. Second, students formed the core of EOKA's most violent combatants, the "killers." Students in these positions planned and perpetrated hundreds of bombings and assassinations in an effort to intimidate both the population and the colonial authorities. Teachers, for their part, frequently aided students in both activities. For instance, several teachers trained students to use arms, and others led student protests (Persianis 1978: 143). Considering the former, the heads of the two student/youth organizations that formed the core of EOKA's first members – OXEN and PEON – were teachers (Foley and Scobie 1975: 17; War Office 1959: 8).

Students and teachers were so actively involved in EOKA because – as described previously – the schools were Greek nationalist institutions that legitimized the enosis movement and therefore encouraged participation in EOKA. In addition, schools offered several mobilizational resources that were exploited by EOKA leaders in pursuit of their goals. Most importantly, schools brought together large numbers of individuals and were therefore important places of recruitment. Recruitment efforts, in turn, were facilitated by the fact that the educational system actively pressured students to support enosis. Similarly, schools provided preexisting organizational and communication resources that facilitated recruitment. OXEN and PEON, for example, were active at schools, and Grivas and his officials used the organizations as the basis on which to build EOKA (Crawshaw 1978: 101–102; Foley 1965: 17, 25–29; Varnavas 2001: 11–12; War Office 1959: 8). Schools also offered a safe

---

[12] Persianis (1978) offers a slightly smaller figure, claiming that more than half of Greek Cypriot secondary school students were involved with EOKA (142).

environment to spread EOKA propaganda to large numbers of people and to plan EOKA activities. Considering the first, student members of EOKA distributed countless leaflets and two EOKA-sponsored magazines at schools (Varnavas 2001: 66). The relatively safe environment of schools also allowed EOKA members to use school facilities for other activities beyond spreading propaganda. For instance, schools were used as a temporary shelter for members and as a location for planning EOKA activities (Foley 1965: 48).

Notably, the structure of secondary education provided an additional resource that facilitated both student recruitment and participation. Students had classes only 180 days a year for 5 hours a day. As a consequence, they had the free time to actively participate in both EOKA and the numerous student clubs and associations that were ultimately co-opted by EOKA to recruit members and organize activities (Foreign Office 1955).

Finally, Bryant (2004) describes how Greek Cypriot schools were powerful disciplining institutions that made the students themselves valuable resources. She suggests that high levels of individual and group discipline proved vital to EOKA's guerrilla activities, as students could be trusted with important duties and were willing to risk their lives (156, 166–167). Such discipline was both internally and externally enforced and verged on what is often considered the familial realm. For example, schools enlisted after-school disciplinarians who patrolled public places to enforce school curfews and keep students from misbehaving (Bryant 2004: 166–167). In this way, the schools helped make students the disciplined actors the movement needed.

In all of these ways, schools provided the mobilizational means of both mass protests in the streets and covert operations involving a select group of "killers." Students and teachers therefore did not simply form the core of EOKA and organize and implement EOKA's most important activities because they were motivated. Instead, schools also provided students and teachers with an environment that allowed them to organize and mobilize in pursuit of enosis.

CONCLUSION

Similar to the case study of Sri Lanka in Chapter 4, an analysis of Cyprus provides three types of evidence that education promoted ethnic violence. First, educational expansion directly preceded ethnic violence. Second, many educated individuals played an influential and conspicuous role in the ethno-nationalist movement subsequently leading to ethnic violence. Finally, the chapter highlights different educational mechanisms that link education and ethnic violence. In particular, the Cypriot educational system was ethnically segregated, used ethnically divisive curricula, and incorporated ethno-national symbols and rituals; and all three socialized students in ways that increased divisive and oppositional ethno-national identities. Socialization was particularly influential in colonial Cypriot schools because ethnic communities controlled their own schools. As a consequence, communal authorities holding strong ethno-nationalist interests ran schools, and this allowed them to use schools to disseminate their nationalist views. These efforts proved very successful because the teachers from both communities actively supported the ethno-nationalist message and because of preexisting communal divisions. Thus, the message was effectively taught, and the students were predisposed to accept it. The mobilization mechanism also linked education and ethnic violence: the educational system was a very important mobilizational resource that was exploited to organize a violent ethno-nationalist movement that ultimately sparked severe ethnic violence. Most importantly, schools were prime recruiting grounds for enosis militants. They proved such a fecund source of recruits because they were relatively safe, had large concentrations of individuals, and were full of students subjected to a pro-enosis curriculum. In this way, the socialization mechanism strengthened the mobilization mechanism.

All three types of evidence therefore coincide with the findings of Chapter 4 and offer evidence that education contributed to ethnic violence in influential ways. Both case studies, in turn, provide additional evidence that the statistical relationships highlighted in Chapter 3 run from education to ethnic violence, as the sequence of events, the active participation of educated individuals, and mechanisms all suggest that education promotes ethnic violence.

6

Education and Ethnic Violence in the Palestinian Territories, India, and Sub-Saharan Africa

While providing strong evidence that education can contribute to ethnic violence in influential ways, the findings of the Sri Lankan and Cypriot case studies do not necessarily apply to a larger set of cases. Additional analysis is needed to explore whether the educational mechanisms help explain ethnic violence in a broader array of cases. The case studies in this chapter pursue this objective.

The first case explores ethno-nationalist violence between Palestinians and Israelis but focuses on Palestinian militants. I selected the case because the Palestinian territories strongly fits the statistical findings, as it has very high levels of education relative to its economy and very ineffective political institutions. Moreover, unlike Sri Lanka and Cyprus, data exist on the level of education of Palestinians who were directly involved in violence. I therefore analyze the education of individuals who participated in ethno-nationalist violence against Israelis and explore whether the educational mechanisms shaped their participation.

The second case analyzes ethnic violence in India. Historically, India has experienced very high levels of ethnic violence but does not appear to conform to the statistical analysis, as the average level of Indian education is moderate to low. Yet, India has an educational system that is top-heavy, with a disproportionate amount of resources invested in secondary and postsecondary education and – until recently – very little investment in primary education. As a result, the aggregate educational statistics of India tend to hide a large pool of highly educated individuals, and educated individuals are not easily absorbed into the Indian economy. I therefore explore the impact of educated unemployment on the frustration-aggression and competition mechanisms and check whether

India is a statistical exception that helps prove a general rule. Within India, I focus on the states of Assam and Kerala. I selected Assam because the region has relatively high levels of educated unemployment and has experienced several incidents of ethnic violence. It is therefore an appropriate region to explore whether educated unemployment has promoted ethnic violence in India. Alternatively, Kerala has had low-to-moderate levels of ethnic violence despite having the most advanced educational system in India and experiencing very high levels of educated unemployment. Kerala is therefore an exceptional case within India that offers a check on the previous findings.

Finally, the chapter considers education and ethnic violence in sub-Saharan Africa. The region has relatively low levels of education but relatively high levels of ethnic violence and therefore appears to oppose the findings from the previous chapters. Yet, there is considerable variation in both educational development and ethnic violence within the region, and the analysis explores whether the two are related through both statistical analysis and abbreviated case studies.

ETHNO-NATIONALIST VIOLENCE IN THE PALESTINIAN TERRITORIES AND ISRAEL

Violence between Muslims and Jews in the Palestinian territories and Israel – especially when it involves Muslims attacking Jews – is commonly described by politicians and the media as "terrorism." Given the many violent acts committed by Muslim militants under the guise of jihad, this portrayal might seem merited, yet it overlooks or downplays the fact that Muslim violence against Jews is inherently political in nature and part of an ongoing ethno-nationalist struggle between Jews and Muslims. Violence between Muslims and Jews, in turn, commonly conforms to the definition of ethnic violence. Indeed, many Palestinian Muslims live in Israel, many Jews reside in settlements in the Palestinian territories, and violence that occurs between Muslim and Jewish civilians living in the same country and that is at least partially motivated by ethnic difference is by definition ethnic violence. Moreover, the Palestinian territories remain an Israeli dependency without full self-rule, and Israel annexed parts of the Palestinian territories after 1968 and occupied the remainder of it until the Oslo Accord in 1993, making national boundaries – and thereby distinctions between ethnic and international violence – blurry and subjective.

Possibly because politicians and the media categorize Palestinian militants as deranged and fanatical terrorists, many believe they are deficient in some way. Most relevant to this book, many commonly assume that Palestinian Muslim militants who attack the Israeli state and Jewish civilians are uneducated and act out of ignorance. An empirical analysis of Palestinian Muslim militants, however, paints a very different picture.

The founding figures of Hamas, for example, were well-educated, white-collar professionals (Mishal and Sela 2000: 37). Since then, Hamas leaders have been very successful at recruiting from the more educated segments of Palestinian society. Many of its officials, for example, are university graduates and even professors at Palestinian universities (BBC 2006). They are particularly well represented at the Islamic University, which, in fact, is partially funded by Hamas. After the 2006 elections, sixteen members of the University's faculty, staff, and board of trustees served on the Palestinian Legislative Council for Hamas, making up one-fifth of Hamas's parliamentary representatives. Similarly, thirteen of the twenty-four ministers appointed by Hamas were from either the Islamic University or al-Najah University, another Hamas stronghold (BBC 2006).

These educated officials are not necessarily involved in Hamas' violent activities, as Hamas is a multifaceted organization focusing primarily on politics and the provisioning of social services. An analysis of the backgrounds of individuals directly involved in ethno-nationalist violence, however, provides strong evidence that the perpetrators of violent acts are relatively educated. Pape (2005) analyzes data on sixty-seven suicide attackers in Lebanon and the Palestinian territories/Israel and finds that 54 percent had some postsecondary education, compared with only 7 percent of all Lebanese Shia and 18 percent of all Palestinian males (213). In a more thorough analysis focusing on violence perpetrated by either Hamas and Palestinian Islamic Jihad in the Palestinian territories and Israel, Berrebi (2007) analyzes data on 335 Palestinian militants who were either arrested or killed between 1987 and 2002. He finds that 96 percent had at least a high school education and that 65 percent had postsecondary education. Alternatively, while controlling for age, sex, and religion, the comparable figures for the Palestinian population were only 51 percent and 15 percent, respectively, showing that the militants of these organizations were twice as likely to have completed high school and four times as likely to have postsecondary education (17).[1]

---

[1] The Palestinian territories are not the sole location where Islamic militants are relatively educated. In Pakistan, Islamic militants are also generally much more educated than their peers (Fair 2008: 69; Hussain 2007: 56).

Beside simply being overrepresented among individuals acting violently, surveys also suggest that educated Palestinians are more likely to support the use of violence against Israelis. A 2001 poll of Palestinians in the West Bank and Gaza Strip found that education level is positively related to support for violence. Most notably, educated individuals were more likely to believe that terrorist methods are a legitimate means of achieving political goals and were the strongest supporters of violence against Israelis (Krueger and Maleckova 2003: 127).

Factors Promoting Militancy among Educated Palestinians

The factors affecting why educated Palestinians have a greater risk of becoming ethno-nationalist militants vary from individual to individual and are impossible to document fully. An analysis of the available evidence, however, suggests that three mechanisms have contributed to the overrepresentation of the educated among Palestinian militants who attacked Jews and the Israeli government since the beginning of the first Intifada in 1987: the socialization, frustration-aggression, and mobilization mechanisms.

Socialization. Since the Palestinian Authority gained control over the educational system in 1993, there has been considerable debate over whether the educational curricula in Palestinian schools encourage students to participate in violence against Israel. At the center of the debate was a Center for Monitoring the Impact for Peace report claiming that official school textbooks actively incite anti-Israeli violence. Some agree with the report, but most view it as biased, recognizing that it was written by a Jewish settler living in the West Bank, and that the new Palestinian textbooks are actually less anti-Israeli than the Egyptian and Jordanian textbooks that were used prior to 1993. Many also note that Israeli textbooks are equally guilty of promoting anti-Palestinian sentiments.

Even among critics, however, there is general agreement that Palestinian textbooks – both before and after 1993 – hardly promoted tolerance toward Israelis but contributed to the opposite by emphasizing the hardship and disgrace experienced by Palestinians at the hands of Jewish settlers.[2] Numerous scholars also note that education has helped propagate common ideas of a threatened Palestinian nation and demand

---

[2] See Berrebi 2007: 29; Brown 2001; Burdman 2003: 100–102; Cronin 2004: 97–103; Ichilov 2004: 76–9; Leirvik 2004: 225; Nordbruch 2001.

violence against Israel and Jews.³ Nordbruch (2001), for one, notes that nationalism and national sacrifice are central to the curriculum of primary and secondary schools:

The appeal to defend the Palestinian nation is a central theme in the new textbooks. Even in Arabic lessons, there are numerous texts and exercises that call upon the students to sacrifice their lives. The concept of a threatened Palestinian nation gives the impression that the students too must fight the present threats and dangers. National defense is perceived not only as a struggle against the occupation and other external threats, but also as a struggle for the preservation of Palestinian traditions and values.

Highlighting this message, an eighth-grade textbook includes the following statements:

In your left hand you carried the Koran, And in your right an Arab sword.... Without blood not even one centimeter will be liberated. (Reader and Literary Texts for Eighth Grade #578, p. 102)

My brothers! The oppressors [Israel] have overstepped the boundary. Therefore *Jihad* and sacrifice are a duty.... [A]re we to let them steal its Arab nature[?]... Draw your sword.... [L]et us gather for war with red blood and blazing fire.... Death shall call and the sword shall be crazed from much slaughter.... Oh Palestine, the youth will redeem your land.... (Reader and Literary Texts for Eighth Grade #578, p. 120– 122) (Berrebi 2007: 29)

This emphasis on the Palestinian nation and sacrifice appears equally strong at the university level. In fact, Bruhn (2006) claims that universities played a vital role strengthening the Palestinian ethno-nationalist movement. In the absence of a Palestinian state and in the face of Israeli coercion against any sign of Palestinian nationalism in public, private universities became the primary institutions both linking and representing the nation in the 1970s and 1980s. Paz (2000) makes similar claims but notes that universities were particularly important in the Palestinian territories because of the "Islamic cosmopolitanism" that was originally propagated by the Egyptian-dominated Muslim Brotherhood. Given the social context in which Palestinian students lived, Palestinian universities countered this Islamic nationalism with a more localized ethno-national ideology based on the shared experiences and culture of Palestinians.

---

³ See Abu-Saad and Champagne 2006: 1044; Anabtawi 1986: 57; Bruhn 2006; Paz 2001, 2003.

Besides helping to strengthen ideas of a threatened Palestinian nation, socialization in Palestinian universities also contributes to anti-Israeli sentiments. The universities in the West Bank and Gaza teach curricula and provide activities that remove Israelis from the moral community and actively encourage or even pressure students to participate in violence against Israelis. Jensen (2006) provides an ethnographic study of one university with particularly strong ties to Hamas: the Islamic University of Gaza. He notes that the curriculum of the school promotes strong Muslim identities and depicts Israel as a natural enemy. He also describes how university-sponsored activities pressure students to support anti-Israeli activities.

Education therefore appears to promote anti-Israeli sentiments and to encourage militant action against Israelis. One must not overstate the impact of educational socialization, however, as anti-Israeli sentiments and the glorification of martyrs are widespread throughout Palestinian society given the history of Palestinian-Israeli conflict. Mazawi (1998), for example, finds that the street – and not schools – is the most important location of political socialization in the Palestinian territories. At the very least, however, the socialization mechanism helps reinforce and legitimize preexisting views and sentiments that encourage violence.

Frustration-Aggression. Evidence suggests that the frustration-aggression mechanism also contributes to an overrepresentation of the educated among Palestinian militants committing acts of violence against Israelis. Indeed, the educated are aggrieved because they live in conditions that commonly impede social mobility. Because this hardship is widespread, because of a history of Israeli conquest and occupation, and because Palestinians have experienced severe discrimination and violence at the hands of Jews, the frustration and aggression of many educated individuals target Jews and the Israeli government.

Numerous Palestinians living in the Gaza Strip and the West Bank face extremely difficult living conditions. A 2002 study by scholars at Johns Hopkins University found that 22.5 percent of children below the age of five suffer from either chronic or acute malnutrition (Roy 2004: 386). Economically, the West Bank and Gaza commonly experience negative economic growth, with per capita GDP declining by 14 percent between 1994 and 2005 (World Bank 2009). During the same period, official unemployment rates have fluctuated between 10 percent and 50 percent, and a 2005 report found that 60 percent of Palestinians live below the income poverty line.[4] Finally, the Palestinian territories are among the most violent places in the world, and severe violence affects the lives of nearly all Palestinians. This violence takes many forms, including Israeli military attacks, conflict between Palestinians and Jewish settlers, and internal violence among Palestinians.

The absolute hardships of the less educated are undoubtedly greater than those of more educated Palestinians, but educated Palestinians have greater expectations for mobility and are therefore more likely to be frustrated by their hardships. And these hardships are considerable. For one thing, the violence in the Palestinian territories is widespread and affects people of all educational backgrounds. Similarly, the decrepit condition of the Palestinian economy affects all Palestinians. In fact, Angrist (1995) provides evidence that it has a disproportionate effect on the opportunities and earnings of the educated. He finds that rapid educational expansion and limited economic opportunities combined to cause high levels of educated unemployment and low returns to education in the 1980s and 1990s – the very period of the first Palestinian uprising against Jews and the Israeli government. In 1985, for instance, the unemployment rate was only 2 percent among individuals with less than eleven years of education, 5 percent for individuals with twelve years of education, 13 percent for individuals with between thirteen and fifteen years of education, and 16 percent for individuals with sixteen years or more of education (1068, 1070). Angrist also finds that the wage gap between the educated and less educated shrank throughout the 1980s. Relative to individuals with twelve or fewer years of education, the wage premium of individuals with sixteen or more years of education fell from 41 percent in 1981, to 20 percent in 1986, to only 5 percent in 1989 (1072–1073). An equally dramatic decline occurred among individuals with thirteen to fifteen years of education, showing that the economic well-beings of the educated are greatly affected by economic difficulties. As the Sri Lankan case highlights, such severe economic difficulties among the educated can contribute to frustration, aggression, and – thereby – violence.

Many educated individuals also experience open discrimination at the hands of Israelis. Prior to greater Palestinian self-governance after 1993, the Israeli government denied graduates of Palestinian universities the right to apply for civil service jobs in the occupied territories – a discriminatory policy that spurred animosity against Israel and gave many

---

[4] See World Bank 2009; Qazzaz 2009: 90; Roy 1999: 76; Roy 2004: 379; Sayre 2009: 7.

educated individuals even greater reason to blame Israelis for their economic difficulties. Moreover, Palestinian Muslims living in Israel have very low economic returns on education, and discrimination appears to account for much of the wage gap between Arabs and Jews (Semyonov and Yuchtman-Yaar 1992). Given all of these hardships and grievances against Israel and wide-spread anti-Israeli sentiments, the frustration-aggression mechanism is a logical explanation for the greater participation of the educated in militant activities against Jews and the Israeli government.

Recruitment and Mobilization. Despite relatively widespread anti-Israeli sentiments among Palestinian Muslims, finding individuals to partake in violence against Israelis is not necessarily an easy task. For one thing, many people believe that violence is not an appropriate option. In addition, one cannot openly advertize for recruits given the secretive nature of the activities and the ever-present threat of informants and the Israeli military. Leaders must also have great confidence in their recruits because of the sensitive activities performed by and the knowledge gained by the recruits. Available evidence suggests that mosques are the most common location for militant recruitment, as they provide relatively safe environments in which recruiters can observe the characteristics of individuals and approach those that appear willing to fight for the cause. Another very important location is university campuses.[5] Both Israeli intelligence officers and academic observers, for instance, find that schools serve as a prime recruitment location, with approximately 20 percent of Hamas militants recruited from universities (Levitt 2006: 83, 100–101). All universities are important bases of Hamas support, but some are more important than others, with al-Najah University and the Islamic University topping the list. For example, more than 10 percent of the 415 members of Hamas and Islamic Jihad that Israel deported to Lebanon in December 1992 were either students or employees of Islamic University (Mishal and Sela 2000: 24).

Different factors make universities prime recruiting grounds. Most obviously, universities concentrate thousands of individuals in a small area and therefore provide recruiters with a large pool of candidates. As centers of Palestinian nationalism and privately run institutions with great

---

[5] See Abu-Amr 1993: 14; Abu-Saad and Champagne 2006; Bruhn 2006: 1131; Intelligence and Terrorism Information Center 2004: 1; Levitt 2006; Paz 2000, 2003: 11; Post, Sprinzak, and Denny 2003: 173.

autonomy over academic programs and staffing, they also provide relatively safe environments with a high concentration of sympathetic individuals (Abu-Saad and Champagne 2006: 1044). Given the anti-Israeli curriculum and activities, recruiters can closely monitor students and approach those students supporting violence against Jews and the Israeli government. Similarly, the educated commonly have the skills needed to successfully complete attacks against Israelis, so recruiters are more likely to find individuals with the requisite skills at universities (Benmelech, Berrebi, and Klor 2010).

The numerous student organizations found on university campuses are another factor that make universities prime recruiting grounds for militants. By either co-opting preexisting student organizations or creating their own, militant recruiters are able to interact with students in small groups and learn which ones are sympathetic to the cause. The Islamic Center is one such organization. According to Mishal and Sela (2000), the group had more than 5,000 student members at Islamic University by the early 1990s and "became intensively involved in every facet of the university, from setting the budget to setting the curriculum and appointing the faculty" (24). Islamic Bloc is another student association that is affiliated with and funded by Hamas and is directly involved in militant recruitment (Levitt 2006: 24). The organization is very active at al-Najah University and has produced many of Hamas' most notorious militants, causing some to refer to al-Najah as a training ground for violence.

In addition to simply recruiting members, student associations on Palestinian campuses also serve as organizational resources that increase the capacity of Palestinian militant organizations to coordinate their activities. In fact, Paz (2000) describes how Palestinian universities were the sites where militant anti-Israeli movements began in the mid-1980s and that student organizations provided the critical center for its development. Bruhn (2006) agrees and writes that the "liberation of Palestine was the focus of all student groups" at Palestinian universities (1129). She claims that universities were such strong centers of resistance to Israeli occupation that the Israeli military forcibly closed all universities in 1988 (1131).

EDUCATED UNEMPLOYMENT AND ETHNIC VIOLENCE IN INDIA

Since the early years of British colonial rule, India has had an elitist educational system that severely limits primary education but highly subsidizes secondary and, especially, postsecondary education. In the 1980s, for example, India had among the lowest primary completion rates in the developing world but among the highest rates of postsecondary enrollment (Weiner 1991). Thus, many Indians receive little or no formal education, but many also receive high levels of education. As a consequence of this minimalist but elitist educational system and an economy with limited capacity to provide jobs for the educated, India has had extremely high rates of unemployment among highly educated youths during the past half-century. Indeed, the educated made up 63 percent of all individuals registered as unemployed in the 1990s (Singh 1996: 106).

As elsewhere, unemployment in India has many negative effects on individuals (Parvathamma 1984: 73; Singh, Kumari, and Singh 1992; Singh 1996). Most obviously, it pushes people into poverty, lowers status, and causes enormous stress. These characteristics, in turn, can cause extreme frustration and deviant behavior. For one thing, the educated have great expectations for social advancement. As Jeffrey (2009) notes, Indian students are raised to believe "in a vision of future progress based upon formal education and entry into government employment" but rarely are able to attain these status expectations (195). And, according to Bhattacharya (1982), these unmet expectations threaten social stability. Similarly, Gour (1984) concludes his analysis of student unrest in Bihar by claiming: "It is an admitted fact that the unemployed, whatever their economic conditions, are focal points of tension in society. When unemployment is fuelled by the educated, the situation can become potentially inflammable. In this situation, given the right pre-requisites, there can be an explosion" (119).

Different studies analyzing the psychological state of young Indian adults support these claims. Singh (1996) finds that the educated unemployed are abnormally apathetic and disenchanted and favor "direct political action, lawbreaking, and violent change" (102). In similar analyses, Singh, Kumari, and Singh (1992) find that the educated unemployed have very high levels of hostility; and Chakrapani (1995) provides evidence that the unfulfilled expectations of the educated unemployed promotes radical attitudes and hostility.

A growing number of works find that radicalism and hostility have helped fuel different types of violence, including intercaste violence. Anandhi, Jeyaranjan, and Krishnan (2002) describe how young educated and unemployed Dalits are increasingly assertive and turn to confrontational and violent activities as a means of addressing caste inequalities and discrimination. Similarly, different studies find that unemployment and competition over jobs has increased intercaste conflict and resulted in diverse types of violence, including "murder, assault, sexual harassment, rape, bullying and vandalism" (Jeffrey, Jeffery, and Jeffery 2005: 20; see also Rogers 2008). Describing two specific incidents of intercaste violence, Shah (1987) claims that the combination of high unemployment among the educated and a policy of reserving jobs for lower-caste Hindus sparked intercaste violence.

The literature on communal violence between Hindus and Muslims also highlights the important role played by the educated unemployed. Hansen (1996) investigates why extremist Hindu nationalist parties are gaining strength and highlights the role of frustration over limited employment opportunities. He writes:

To young Hindu men without steady jobs, deprived of a chance to support a family, and thus deprived of an essential part of their manliness, the Muslim other becomes an object of intense hatred: stealing his jobs, stealing his pride as a man, his enjoyment of community and his self-identity. To join the Hindu nationalist bandwagon, to attack Muslim houses and shops, to burn, kill rape and loot, becomes a way of shedding this perceived humiliation, and a way of recuperating masculinity (152-153).

While focusing on limited employment opportunities for all Hindus, he claims that the educated middle-class are most prone to supporting ethnonationalist violence out of frustration over unattained expectations and the risk of losing status (157). Similarly, Jeffrey, Jeffery, and Jeffery (2008) find that some unemployed and educated Hindu men reacted to their hardships by "engaging in hyper-masculine violence, often oriented against Muslim minorities, especially Muslim women" (582). In an authoritative analysis of the rise of Hindu nationalism, Jaffrelot (1996) makes similar claims. He notes that the educated middle-class organized and filled the rank-and-file of the Hindu nationalist movement during its initial phase. Although the movement has increasingly mobilized less-educated Hindus over the years, it is still dominated by educated elements.

On the other side of the communal divide, educated unemployment has contributed to Muslim violence against Hindus. While Hindu perceptions that Muslims impede their advancement appear misguided and driven by frustration and ethno-nationalist fervor, Muslim claims of grievance and hardship are well founded and take a number of forms: police brutality, limited political representation, daily prejudice and discrimination, and poor job prospects. Considering the latter, a 2006 government report found that Muslims are greatly underrepresented among white-collar positions: they hold only 3 percent of positions in the Indian

Administrative Service, 2 percent of positions in the Indian Foreign Service, and 4 percent of positions in the Indian Police Service despite comprising more than 13 percent of the total population (Government of India 2006: 165). Even more than their underrepresentation, the report finds that Muslims are concentrated in low-level positions (167). Different analyses also find that education is positively related to both unemployment and casual labor, resulting in what Das (2008) calls an "education penalty" for Muslims (14; see also M. Das 2002: 177).

One Muslim organization that has used violence against Hindus is the Students Islamic Movement of India, or SIMI. Its parent organization – Jama'at, which was formed in the 1940s – was comprised largely of university students and graduates and attempted to begin an Islamic revolution. SIMI was organized as a subunit of Jama'at in 1977, split from it in 1982, and gained notoriety after using terrorist techniques in 2000. Like Jama'at before it, SIMI is a university-based student organization comprised largely of disaffected, middle-class, and educated Muslims who view their community as deprived (Sikand 2003: 340; *South China Morning Post* 2003; Upadhyay 2003). According to Sikand (2003):

> SIMI's rhetoric served... as a symbolic source of pride, strength and assertion for groups of Indian Muslim students faced otherwise with bleak employment prospects and what they perceived as pervasive anti-Muslim discrimination and general Muslim powerlessness. Many of these students seem also to have been unable to compete with better educated students of other communities and to have suffered from a sense of deprivation and marginality on their university campuses. For such students, the 'Islamic alternative', the slogan of Islam as an answer to all the ills of modern man, provided a powerful symbolic weapon in their struggle against great odds (341).

Another report agrees that SIMI members are very educated and motivated by grievances but pays greater attention to the influence of communal grievances (*South China Morning Post* 2003). It notes that several well-educated militants were economically successful but joined the movement out of a feeling of communal grievance, pinpointing the 2002 Gujarat riots as one particular event that promoted intense animosity and thereby SIMI retribution.

Beside showing how frustration over unemployment and discrimination pushed some educated individuals to participate in ethnic violence, the SIMI example shows that educational institutions also provide important mobilizational resources that can contribute to ethnic violence. Indeed, Indian universities are frequently locations of violence, and SIMI and several other student organizations have been engaged in violent movements (Altbach 1968; Bryjak 1986; Hazary 1987). For example, students organized a movement against attempts to make Hindi the national language in 1965. In Tamil Nadu, the Students' Action Committee coordinated the movement by exploiting their access to mobilizational resources to organize strikes and demonstrations (Altbach 1968: 55). Many of these turned violent, and more than fifty people were killed. More recently, the mobilizational resources of education have been used to help organize violent protests pitting upper- and lower-caste students against one another over affirmative action programs (*The Guardian* 1990; Shah 1987).

Educated Unemployment and Ethnic Violence in Assam

To explore in greater detail the potential link between educated unemployment and ethnic violence in India, I analyze ethnic violence in Assam. Assam is a state in northeastern India with approximately 27 million inhabitants. Geographically, it is the size of Austria and is T-shaped, with a long-horizontal section that follows the Brahmaputra River and a shorter vertical section that is comprised of the Karbi and Cachar hills and the Barak valley. Assam and the other states in northeastern India are connected to the rest of the country by an 18-kilometer-wide corridor wedged between Bangladesh and Bhutan and are quite isolated from the rest of the country both geographically and culturally.

The region is among the most ethnically diverse states in India. According to the 1991 census, there are some 68 languages spoken by the different communities in Assam, and 12 languages are spoken by at least 100,000 people (Baruah 1999: 18–19). The ethnic Assamese – or Asamiyas – constitute the largest ethnic group, with approximately 50 percent of the population. In addition, there are several "tribal" communities living both in the hills and along the plains; and ethnic Bengalis, Nepalis, Marwaris, and others migrated to the region during the past 150 years. Religiously, two-thirds of the population is Hindu and nearly 30 percent of the population is Muslim, with the remainder consisting of animists, Buddhists, and Sikhs.

Assam's economy is primarily agricultural, and the region is one of the world's leading producers of tea. Relative to the rest of India, the state is poor, having a per capita income that is 45 percent lower than the Indian national average (Government of Assam 2003). Alternatively, the state's social development is roughly on par with the rest of India, with a literacy rate of 64 percent (versus 65 percent in all of India) (Government of Assam 2003).

Explosive population growth, the rapid expansion of the educational system at the higher levels, and poor economic opportunities have combined to cause educated underemployment and unemployment to emerge as a severe problem in Assam. Considering the first, Assam has experienced very rapid population growth over the past century as a result of health care improvements and, especially, in-migration. Overall, the population more than tripled between 1901 and 1961 (from 3.7 million to 11.9 million), and it more than doubled between 1961 and 2001 (from 11.9 million to 26.7 million) (IndiaStat 2010). Prior to World War II, very few Assamese received an education, but the number of educated individuals expanded rapidly afterward, especially at the higher levels. For example, the number of university students in Assam increased from 8,601 in 1950 to 45,387 in 1965, and the number of secondary-school students increased from 43,386 to 224,247 during the same period (IndiaStat 2010; Weiner 1978: 111). Thus, the number of students in higher education increased more than fivefold in only fifteen years, and it has continued to expand, albeit at a slower rate. Unfortunately for the growing pool of educated Assamese, there have been very limited white-collar job openings over the past half-century because of an abysmal economy. Indeed, the state's per capita income stagnated after independence, increasing by an average yearly rate of less than 1 percent between 1950 and 1998 (Government of Assam 2003: 25).

Given the growing pool of educated individuals but the failure of the economy to provide opportunities for them, Assam has been afflicted by an educational bubble, causing high levels of educated unemployment and underemployment. According to official statistics, the number of educated unemployed increased from 19,000 in 1969 to 320,000 in 1979 (Chattopadhyay 1990: 171; Hussain 1993: 83). By 1989, this number had increased to more than 550,000, representing 57 percent of all people on the state's unemployment register (Das 1992: 6). In 2004, the official unemployment rate of educated Assamese was 12.7 percent in rural areas and 10.5 percent in urban areas, rates that far exceeded the Indian averages of 6.5 and 7.1 percent, respectively (IndiaStat 2010). Notably, these official statistics are notorious for undercounting the unemployed. A more accurate survey completed by the Assamese Government in 2005, for example, found that 54 percent of the educated between the ages of fifteen and forty were unemployed (Madhab 2005: 31). The same survey, in turn, found that *under*employment was a severe problem for individuals who had jobs: 64 percent of educated individuals with jobs sought alternative or additional work (36).

Ethnic Violence in Assam, 1960–1985. During this period of educational expansion, limited growth, and high educated unemployment, Assam experienced several different bouts of ethnic violence. Although distinct, most have pitted Asamiyas against nonindigenous ethnic communities and were instigated by Asamiyas who attempted to protect their cultural heritage and increase their economic and political power. Such efforts, in turn, have sparked violent autonomy movements among several of the state's indigenous minority communities, who perceive Assamese nationalism as chauvinistic and discriminatory. In the pages that follow, I focus on ethnic violence between 1960 and 1985, a period of intense violence between Asamiyas and nonindigenous minorities.

One of the first serious instances of ethnic violence began in 1960 and pitted Asamiyas against Bengali Hindus. It began when many Asamiyas mobilized to make Assamese the sole state language. The two main protagonists were the Assam Literary Society and various student organizations, including the precursor of the All Assam Students Union (AASU). These initial strikes and protests caused reactionary protests by Bengalis and a back-and-forth exchange of propaganda through the press. By June, organized rallies with thousands of students and protesters occurred throughout the state. Both the rallies and the constant propaganda heightened animosity, and acts of aggression became frequent on both sides, causing a curfew to be proclaimed on June 30. Student agitation continued, prompting the police to open fire on one occasion, killing one Asamiya student and injuring six others. Word quickly spread of the death, and Asamiya protesters reacted by attacking Bengali Hindus (instead of the government forces that killed the student). Such violence, in turn, sparked Bengali counterattacks. During the ensuing violence, 34 people lost their lives and more than 10,000 lost their homes (Goswami 1997: 59).

By 1967, a new issue pitted Asamiyas against minorities: economic inequality. The Food Movement was launched by the AASU under slogans of internal self-sufficiency and self-reliance for the Assamese, but soon was directed against non-Assamese who controlled a disproportionate share of the state's commerce. Throughout large parts of the state between 1967 and 1968, Asamiyas looted and destroyed the property of non-Asamiyas as the police looked on and sometimes assisted. Such attacks, in turn, were followed by a hate campaign focused on the Bengali and Marwari communities. These campaigns used pamphlets, posters, and other media to demand that Bengalis and Marwaris leave Assam and publicly proclaimed "Assam for the Assamese" (Chattopadhyay 1990: 60). After students began a new round of arson in January 1968, the federal government effectively ended the movement by issuing a curfew and deploying the military.

The Language Movement was the next period of ethnic agitation and began in 1972. It started as an academic movement, with demands that Assamese be the official language of university education. Like earlier movements, the AASU and the Assam Literary Society worked together to pursue their interests but were opposed by various Bengali associations. The Academic Council of Gauhati University implemented a compromise that pleased neither side of the language debate. The AASU declared that the decision "endangered the existence of Assam and the Assamese people" and that they would take direct action, and violence between Asamiyas and Bengali Hindus spread throughout the state (Weiner 1978: 119). According to official sources, 33 people were killed in the resulting conflict and 7,000 houses damaged or destroyed (Chattopadhyay 1990: 67).

By the late 1970s, the issue mobilizing the Asamiyas transformed from language to citizenship, and the resulting Assam Movement greatly surpassed all previous movements in terms of ethnic violence. One of the movement's first initiatives was to remove the names of suspected foreigners – mostly Bangladeshis – from the voting list. To press the issue, the AASU organized six days of mass civil disobedience, with more than 100,000 participants on the final day. Soon, the movement began to beat and drive away immigrant jobseekers and needed only a spark to turn violent. This occurred in early December 1979, when police shot and killed a student, causing communal violence to spread throughout the state and claiming 1,000 lives during the first year of the conflict.

The conflict continued until 1985, but the most violent period occurred during a two-week period in February 1983 and witnessed the deaths of more than 7,000 people. The immediate cause of violent upsurge was the federal government's decision to hold elections in Assam despite the fact that the AASU stated it would impede the election if the government refused to remove the names of Bangladeshi immigrants from the voting list. The government refused to budge, and, true to their word, the students organized a massive demonstration and attempted to stop the election by any means, including by burning more than 1,600 bridges to stop the election officials from reaching their sights. When Assamese agitators coercively confronted Bengalis and other ethnic minorities who tried to vote, violence erupted. In the most horrific incident, known as the Nellie massacre, 10,000 tribal minorities and a few Asamiyas raided multiple villages and killed 1,500 people – mostly Bengali Muslim immigrants – during an eight-hour period of bloody mayhem (Chattopadhyay 1990: 85). Along with deaths, intimidation occurred on a daily basis, and arson and bombings became common events. According to one count, 18,514 houses were burnt between 1978 and 1983 (Chattopadhyay 1990: 85).

One fact evident in the history of violence in Assam is that the AASU was the single most important force mobilizing the population to pursue and protect ethnic objectives.[6] Indeed, the AASU mobilized the population to promote Assamese as the sole state language in the early 1960s,[7] to highlight the relative poverty of Asamiyas versus different immigrant communities in the late 1960s, to demand that Assamese be the only language of higher education in the early 1970s, and to expel recent immigrants and remove their names from the voting lists during the Assam Movement in the late 1970s and early 1980s. According to Baruah (1994), "the explosion of micro-nationalist politics in Assam coincided with the founding and consolidation of this organization" (667).

The AASU is one of the largest associations in Assam. Its members are overwhelmingly students, primarily at the university level, and the organization is controlled by students at Gauhati University, many of whom have made careers as students because of an inability to find a job . Officially, the AASU protects and pursues student interests in Assam, regardless of ethnicity. In reality, its members are overwhelmingly Asamiya, and the association has actively pursued an agenda of ethnic nationalism that pushes the state government to support the interests of Asamiyas. This was particularly the case in the 1960s, 1970s, and 1980s.

The AASU's power and influence comes from its ability to spearhead ethno-nationalist movements. By effectively spreading information at the university, through the press, and through its organizational structure, the AASU is able to disseminate its views and organize demonstrations and strikes. These activities contributed to ethnic violence by heightening Assamese nationalism, villainizing non-Assamese, and bringing thousands of aggrieved Asamiyas together at one time, the latter of which almost inevitably led to violence.

Although the AASU's greatest contribution to ethnic violence has been popularizing intercommunal antipathy and organizing ethno-nationalist

---

[6] See Baruah 1986, 1994; Chhabra 1992: 65–9; Dasgupta 1997: 353–4; Deka 1996; Phukan 2005: 13.
[7] The AASU was not founded until 1967, but its parent organization was an influential organizer of the movement to make Assamese the official language in 1960–1961.

movements that eventually erupted into violence, many of the organization's members were not above direct participation in ethnic violence. Despite the AASU's public claims of nonviolence, it has openly encouraged violence on several occasions, and many of its members helped organize and participate in episodes of ethnic violence, including the Nellie massacre of 1,500 Muslim Bengalis (Ahmad 1984: 66; Kimura 2003: 231–232). For its violent activities, the AASU had a militant wing, the *Sweccha Sevak Bahini* (SSB), "a well-organised para-military force" that was created in 1980 to identify foreigners and had as many as 15,000 volunteers throughout Assam (Ahmad 1984: 135–136, 138). It quickly became an instrument of coercion and played an important direct role in ethnic violence during the Assam Movement. According to one source:

SSB men are trained... to organize a sustained underground movement, to operate firearms, to plan and conduct raids on immigrant areas, to cut off communications to vital spots by burning bridges, snapping telephone lines and setting up road blocks, and to man an efficient communications system that relies on squads of 'bicycle telegraph' men who carry SSB and AASU diktats to the remotest villages. (Ahmad 1984: 137)

Beside the SSB, a violent separatist organization, ULFA, first emerged as a militant wing of the AASU, although it has subsequently severed ties with its parent organization.

Because only a minority of Assamese is able to attend university, the members of the AASU are among the most educated in Assam, and many educated individuals are therefore implicated in the region's history of ethnic violence. One must also recognize that AASU members were not the only educated individuals implicated in the ethno-nationalist violence, as the various Assamese ethnic movements incorporated diverse elements of the Asamiya elite. As Baruah (1986) remarks, the leaders of the movements are the most educated segment of Assamese society: "literary societies, cultural associations, newspapers, magazines and school and colleges, apart from the leadership role of the All Assam Students Union" (1194). Similarly, Goswami (1997) concludes that the working class and peasantry were overwhelmingly passive, but that educated individuals were the main protagonists in the state's history of ethnic violence (115–116).

The Frustration-Aggression and Competition Mechanisms and Ethnic Violence in Assam. The frustration-aggression mechanism helped motivate AASU members and other educated Asamiyas to participate in the ethno-national movements. In Hussain's (1993) words, "The rising expectations... started crumbling by the end of the sixties. The popular expectations of the Asamiyas did not find satiation in post-colonial Assam; instead they were disappointed, deceived and alienated" (96). Many, in turn, focused their frustration and anger on ethnic others (Goswami 1997: 91–107). One reason for ethnic scapegoating was that non-Assamese Indians held a disproportionate share of elite positions. Weiner and Katzenstein (1981), for example, find that only 54 percent of the individuals holding white-collar positions were born in Assam (107). The nonnatives generally came from Calcutta, Mumbai, and other more developed regions of the country and were hired by large Indian companies with head offices outside Assam (Das 1982: 233–234). And of those actually born in Assam, only 48 percent were Asamiyas, meaning that Asamiyas controlled only a quarter of all white-collar positions in the state (Weiner and Katzenstein 1981: 98, 108).[8]

Along with the frustration-aggression mechanism, the competition mechanism helped motivate educated Asamiyas to participate in ethnic violence. In particular, job scarcity caused intense competition for jobs, strong ethnic identities caused people to pay close attention to whether their community received its fair share of elite jobs, and ethnic competition for jobs led to attempts to eliminate communal rivals. University students, in particular, were well aware of their bleak job prospects and found themselves in intense competition for jobs. Consequently, they actively sought to eliminate ethnic competitors through restrictive policy and coercion. Through interviews with AASU students involved in the Assam Movement, for example, Samir Das (2002) finds that "it was the craving for jobs, primarily government ones... that charged their emotions and temped them to join the movement" (139).

Although the poor economic prospects of the educated promoted the frustration-aggression and competition mechanisms, ethnic inequalities strengthened both mechanisms even further by heightening ideas of competition and helping focus frustration on relatively advantaged ethnic communities. Indeed, among Assamese intellectuals, it is popular knowledge that educated unemployment and ethnic inequalities combined to spark middle-class chauvinism and xenophobia.[9] In particular, the AASU and other educated Asamiyas berated Bengali Hindus as interlopers who

---

[8] Similarly, a government Employment Review Committee in 1973 found that Assamese was the mother tongue of only 35 percent of employees in a sample of industries, and this number declined even further among top-level positions (Sarmah 1999: 46).

[9] See Boruah 1980; Chattopadhyay 1990: 4–5, 193; Das 1982: 233–234; Gohain 1973: 12; Goswami 1997; Guha 1980; Kumar 1990: 49–50; Sarmah 1999: 49–51; Singh 1984: 67–68.

stole jobs rightfully belonging to ethnic Assamese (Barua 1978: 71; Weiner 1978). "For the aspiring Assamese middle class," writes Weiner (1978), "it was the Bengali Hindus who stood as its obstacle to economic advancement" (111).

Throughout the colonial period, Bengali Hindus moved to Assam and dominated the administration because of their superior education and experience.[10] Moreover, the British used Bengali as the official language of Assam until 1874, a move that limited the opportunities of Asamiyas, favored Bengalis, and struck fear of cultural annihilation into the hearts of the Asamiya intelligentsia. Because of their superior education, Bengali Hindus also dominated high-status professional occupations, such as doctors and lawyers (Chattopadhyay 1990: 43). Asamiyas therefore saw them as stealing their political power and taking the best jobs, causing deep resentment that persists to date (Barua 1978: 71; Kumar 1990: 49–50). This antipathy, in turn, caused educated Asamiyas to focus much of their frustration and aggression on Bengali Hindus, making the latter common scapegoats. Importantly, the socialization mechanism also helped focus the frustration-aggression mechanism on Bengali Hindus, as the curriculum had a strong Asamiya bias and described the Bengali Hindus as interlopers who – through their collaboration with the British – imposed their language and usurped jobs and resources.

The scapegoating of Bengali Hindus was particularly evident during the two language movements in 1960–1961 and 1972 and the Food Movement in 1968. At the same time, all three movements attempted to eliminate Bengali Hindu competitors and therefore also highlight the importance of the competition mechanism: the movement in 1960–1961 attempted to make Assamese the sole state language, thereby giving Asamiyas advantages over Bengalis for public employment; the Asamiyas sought an educational and economic advantage in 1972 by making Assamese the sole language of education (thereby eliminating Bengali) and by opposing the construction of a separate university using Bengali as the language of instruction; and the Food Movement sought to remove Bengali Hindus and other ethnic minorities from Assam to expand the economic opportunities of Asamiyas.

The Assam Movement (1979–1984) differed from the previous movements because the movement did not focus aggression on Bengali Hindus and was less instrumental, as it generally sought to evict poor Bangladeshi migrants who did not directly compete with educated Asamiyas for jobs. Still, the movement was facilitated by the competition mechanism, as

[10] See Barua 1978: 70–71; Chattopadhyay 1990: 13, 43; Kar 1975; Weiner 1978: 283.

educated Asamiyas stood to gain materially from the elimination of rivals (S. Das 2002: 139). Also, Bangladeshi migrants – although not much of an economic threat to the educated Asamiyas – threatened the political power of the Asamiyas. The frustration-aggression mechanism also contributed to the movement, as frustration continued to scapegoat non-Asamiyas, this time focusing on Bengali Muslims instead of Bengali Hindus. Finally, and likely of greatest importance, individual-level grievances and interests were hardly the sole motivational drive of the AASU for this and other movements. Instead, the AASU saw itself as the "custodian of Assamese civil society," and its members were strongly motivated by communal interests and grievances (Baruah 1994: 668). They therefore mobilized the movements in an effort to protect and pursue the interests of their community, not simply themselves.

Notably, educated non-Asamiyas also contributed to ethnic violence in important ways, and the clash between competing ethnic movements fueled some of the worst incidents of ethnic violence. Educated Bengali Hindus, in particular, competed with Asamiyas for jobs and were extremely frustrated by what they viewed as chauvinistic movements that pursued anti-Bengali policies and attacked Bengali Hindus. Because of this motivation, Bengali students formed the core of reactive ethnic movements in the 1960s and 1970s that confronted the Asamiya movements and, in so doing, helped ratchet up the violence (Bhattacharjee 2002).

The Mobilization Mechanism and Ethnic Violence in Assam. While the frustration-aggression and competition mechanisms help explain why many educated individuals were motivated to participate in violent movements, the movements' success depended greatly on the mobilizational resources of the educated. As elsewhere, institutions of higher education in Assam brought thousands of students together, thereby facilitating the organization of movements. Moreover, the AASU had access to communication technologies and the media and was thereby able to effectively publicize their position both on campus and beyond. Most importantly, the AASU was capable of mobilizing a militant ethnic movement because it had an "extraordinary organizational base" (Baruah 1994: 667). Its organizational structure reached down to most villages and allowed the students to make collective decisions and coordinate tens of thousands of people throughout the state (Chhabra 1992: 66). As Das (1982) describes:

The AASU has organized a grassroot movement in towns and villages. Every college and high school has its own Students' Union. The 35-member AASU executive body has representatives from seven districts.... They have an extremely interesting and effective method of decision making and implementation of decisions. The executive body discusses the strategy, coordinates with AAGSP [Assam Popular Struggle Association, a political party with strong ties to the AASU] and passes the decisions on to local leaders for implementation. (66)

Although mobilizational resources were concentrated in the hands of the educated, such resources did not simply engage the educated, as the success of the AASU-led movements – especially the Assam Movement – depended on the engagement of less-educated individuals as well. Similarly, the violence that erupted during the various movements was commonly committed by individuals with limited education. The Nellie massacre, for example, was carried out primarily by poor non-Asamiya villagers with little education. The villagers, in turn, were motivated by reasons that were different from those that motivated AASU members – mainly, growing land scarcity caused by Bangladeshi immigration. In this way, one cannot view the various ethno-nationalist movements as simply comprised of the educated and motivated by educational mechanisms. Instead, extensive mobilizational resources allowed movement leaders to engage other less-educated participants motivated by other factors. Yet, if the AASU did not organize the movements, the Nellie massacre and other acts of violence committed by the less educated in all likelihood would have been less severe and might never have occurred at all, as the movements framed grievances, provided an opening for less-educated individuals to address their grievances, and actually encouraged and assisted the less-educated in these endeavors.

Kerala: A Negative Case

Whereas Assam provides evidence that educational bubbles promote ethnic violence, the region in India with the highest levels of education and among the highest official levels of educated unemployment – Kerala – has experienced low-to-moderate levels of ethnic violence relative to the rest of the subcontinent. What makes this case even more exceptional is its diversity, with large Muslim and Christian populations alongside a slim and divided Hindu majority. In this section, I explore why such an educated, diverse, and poor region has had relatively limited ethnic violence.

Since the early 1900s, Kerala has had among the most educated population in India, and the educational gap between Kerala and all other Indian states remains large. Besides investing more resources in education, Kerala has differed from other Indian states because, historically, it focused educational spending on primary education and actively encouraged female education (Nair 1981). As a consequence of these policies, not only do more children – especially girls – begin school in Kerala relative to the rest of India, but many more complete primary school. A survey from 1975, for example, found that 82 percent of all children who began primary school completed the fifth grade in Kerala, but the figure was only 26 percent for the rest of India (Weiner 1991: 175). Largely because of the region's greater success at the primary level, Kerala has had a literacy rate that is far superior to the Indian average. In 1971, the state's literacy rate was 60 percent compared to an all India average of only 29 percent (Nair 1981: 64). Today, the literacy rate is 95 percent in Kerala.

Kerala's educational success occurred despite a poor economy. Until the 1990s, the region consistently had a per capita GDP below the Indian average. Although its per capita income has increased at a faster rate than the national average since the early 1990s and is presently slightly greater than the all-Indian average, economic opportunities remain very limited. Indeed, as a result of a phenomenal educational system and a poor economy, Kerala's greatest export is people, who migrate to other parts of India and throughout the world (especially the Middle East), and much of the growth in the Keralan economy in recent years is simply the result of growing remittances. The main reason so many people leave Kerala to find work is that there are very few economic opportunities in the state. This is especially the case for educated Malayalis (individuals from Kerala), who suffer very high levels of unemployment. In 2004–2005, 22 percent of educated Malayalis in rural Kerala were unemployed, and 24 percent of educated Malayalis in urban Kerala were unemployed (IndiaStat 2010). This rate is even higher than in Assam and well above the national averages of 6.5 percent and 7.1 percent.

Diverse factors help explain why Kerala has experienced moderate to low levels of ethnic violence despite its high rates of educated unemployment. One must recognize, for example, that educated unemployment is a relatively new problem in Kerala. Although secondary and postsecondary education have gradually expanded over the past half-century and are presently widespread, historically Kerala had only moderate levels of education at the higher levels because – different from nearly all Indian states – its government focused on expanding primary education. As a consequence, educated unemployment was more limited in Kerala than elsewhere, as most individuals stopped their schooling after completing the primary level. And although educational expansion at the upper levels has caused educated unemployment to become a much more severe problem more recently, the widespread emigration of educated Malayalis to other regions helps to reduce its impact on frustration and competition.

Of greater interest to this analysis, Kerala has very effective political institutions that help limit ethnic violence in different ways, and the case therefore provides strong evidence that the impact of education on ethnic violence depends on politics. Effective political institutions, for example, allow the government to quell ethnic violence and maintain peaceful social relations. Along these lines, Wilkinson (2004) describes how state officials actively and effectively contain ethnic violence as soon as – or even before – it begins. As a consequence, deaths caused by ethnic violence are relatively few, and most deaths have actually been caused by police officers attempting to break up episodes of violence.

The Keralan government has effectively limited ethnic violence because it has both the means and the will to do so. Considering the first, Kerala is commonly recognized as having an extremely effective regional state that has not only been able to promote human development but has consistently enforced the highest level of rule of law in India (Debroy, Bhandari, and Banik 2003; Heller 1999: 83–84; Sandbrook, Edelman, Heller, and Teichman 2007). High organizational capacity, in turn, gives the government the means to contain ethnic violence. If politicians did not desire the containment of ethnic violence, however, state capacity would not limit ethnic violence and could actually be used to instigate it. Malayali politicians have actively sought to limit ethnic violence for different reasons. For one, no individual party is able to have a super majority in Kerala, making coalition governments that span multiple ethnic communities a necessity (Wilkinson 2004). In addition, and likely more importantly, Kerala's political system is much less ethnicized than elsewhere in India. Although ethnicity is still important, class and caste overlap and have been the main basis of political mobilization and competition over the past century (Menon 1994; Varshney 2002). As a consequence, the Bharatiya Janata Party (BJP) and other more radical ethno-nationalist organizations have attracted only limited support and remain weak, and most parties actively seek support from all ethnic communities.

Limited ethnic-based political mobilization is rooted in the region's particular history of class formation. Until the early 1900s, Kerala had among the strongest caste system in India, with many Malayalis being not only untouchable but unseeable. This powerful caste system caused very high levels of discrimination against lower-caste Hindus and extreme caste-based inequalities. By the early 20th century, the caste system contributed to three movements dominated by lower-caste Hindus: an anticolonial movement, a caste reform movement, and an agrarian reform movement. As Sandbrook et al. (2007) describe, the confluence of all three provided an opportunity for the Communist Party of India (CPI) to mobilize a broad segment of society and thereby kick-start the process of class formation (77–78). First voted into power in 1956, the CPI has been voted in and out of power since 1956 and has maintained a powerful labor movement ever since (Heller 1999). The main political rival of labor is the Congress Party, which is supported primarily by the upper-class/caste Hindus and Christians and pays considerably more attention to class than ethnicity.

Other historical factors have also helped limit political ethnicization. Kerala was never formally conquered and ruled by the Mughols, and Malayali Hindus therefore lack historical memories of domination and humiliation at the hands of Muslim invaders. Varshney (2002) also notes that Muslims, Hindus, and Christians in Kerala live among one another and interact with each other regularly, a factor that helps reduce intercommunal misunderstandings and prejudices. Similarly, Narayanan (1972) notes that historically the different communities have rarely competed with one another and actually participated in symbiotic relations. Finally, Singh (2010) finds that the Keralan subnational identity is very powerful and forges a strong collective identity among all religious communities. One factor that promotes a powerful Keralan identity is the fact that nearly all Malayalis speak the same language: Malayalam.

The considerable organizational capacity and relatively non-ethnicized character of Keralan political institutions, in turn, allow them to limit ethnic violence in another way: by allowing individuals and communities to address their grievances through formal political channels. Indeed, Kerala has the most vibrant democratic system in India, a system that goes down to the grassroots level, engages large segments of the population, and respects human rights. Thus, when minority ethnic communities have been attacked, the minority leaders have demanded that their community restrain from retaliation and address their grievances through formal channels. As Varshney (2002) writes, "Violence... is not how [Hindus and Muslims in Kerala] express their differences. Institutionalized channels of politics are the arenas of contestation" (131).[11]

---

[11] Along these same lines, class violence has diminished markedly over the past three decades because the government has institutionalized an effective means of labor arbitration (Heller 1999; Sandbrook et al. 2007: 73).

Kerala therefore shows that high levels of education in the face of scarce resources do not necessarily cause ethnic violence. For one thing, the frustration and aggression of the educated unemployed can be directed toward nonethnic rivals, with the overlapping cleavage of class and caste being the dominant cleavage in Kerala.[12] As a result, Keralan politics are relatively unethnicized, and class/party-based political violence is more common than ethnic violence. In Assam, class is also an important cleavage, but ethnicity easily trumps it as the most important division. Second, an effective government in Kerala limits all types of violence by stepping in and stopping them. As a consequence, ethnic violence – even though occurring regularly – has always been contained before the level of violence spiralled out of control. Such intervention, in turn, is promoted by both high levels of government capacity and the relatively low levels of political ethnicization. Finally, because the state government actively engages the population, is not ethnic-based, and provides an effective means of redress, individuals commonly address ethnic grievances through formal politics instead of taking things into their own hands. The contrast with Assam along these lines is again insightful, as the Assamese government promoted ethnic violence by failing to suppress violence against non-Assamese and by actually providing the violent movements with moral and material support at different times (Horowitz 2001: 357, 360). As a consequence, minorities had no trust in the state government and were more likely to take issues into their own hands instead of trying to address them through formal political channels, a situation that increased violence even more.

EDUCATION AND ETHNIC VIOLENCE IN AFRICA

Ethnic violence occurs in all corners of the world, but some of the most severe cases in recent history took place in sub-Saharan Africa. Levels of education in Africa, however, are quite low, suggesting that the relationship between education and ethnic violence does not hold for the continent. This might very well be the case, as a number of factors affect ethnic violence and the statistical results of Chapter 3 suggest that education only explains part of the variation of ethnic violence. Still, the impact of education cannot be dismissed completely. Most notably,

---

[12] In addition, Halliburton (1995) notes that Kerala has exceptionally high levels of suicide and finds that frustration over unemployment helps explain elevated suicide rates among the educated. In this way, some educated Malayalis appear to turn their frustration and aggression on themselves.

Africa parallels India in that many countries have a mismatch between their educational and economic systems. As a consequence, unemployment among the educated is a severe problem, and – as the previous cases suggest – such unemployment might contribute to ethnic violence through the frustration-aggression and competition mechanisms. Moreover, it is quite possible that many of the educational systems in sub-Saharan Africa are ethnicized and contribute to ethnic violence through the socialization mechanism. And if education helps motivate violence in these ways, its mobilizational resources can also help mobilize it.

Education and Ethnic Violence in Africa: A Statistical Analysis

One initial means of testing whether education contributes to ethnic violence in sub-Saharan Africa is to simply rerun the statistical analyses from Chapter 3 using the set of sub-Saharan African countries. Because the control variables for colonial heritage, communist heritage, and mountainous territory have little variation within sub-Saharan Africa, I exclude them from the model in order to save degrees of freedom. Despite fewer independent variables, the set of cases is quite small, and the analysis potentially suffers from limited degrees of freedom. As a consequence, the findings are less likely to be statistically significant, but they still offer some insight into the relationship between ethnic violence and education in sub-Saharan Africa.

Table 6.1 presents the results, with the first model using secondary completion rate as the focal independent variable, the second model using average years of education as the focal independent variable, and the third model using secondary enrollment rate as the focal independent variable. A quick glance shows that none of the education variables are significantly related to ethnic violence, a finding that is not terribly surprising given the limited degrees of freedom. If one considers the coefficients more closely, however, they are all positive and quite large. Indeed, the coefficients from Table 6.1 are equal to or greater than the coefficients in the models of Chapter 3. Although inconclusive, a cross-national analysis of sub-Saharan Africa therefore suggests that education might help explain variation in ethnic violence.

Colonialism, Education, and Ethnic Violence in Africa

Table 6.2 lists the level of ethnic violence by former colonizer for the three main colonizers of sub-Saharan Africa. The data are on a seven-point

TABLE 6.1. *Random-Effects Models of the Determinants of Ethnic Violence, Sub-Saharan Africa*

Regressors	Secondary Completion	Avg. Years of Education	Secondary Enroll. Rate
Education	0.086	0.341	0.023
	(0.067)	(0.211)	(0.016)
Political Discrimination	0.494***	0.509***	0.537***
	(0.127)	(0.130)	(0.110)
Fractionalization	0.079	0.182	−0.282
	(0.268)	(0.273)	(0.273)
Population (logged)	0.187	0.177	0.270
	(0.214)	(0.234)	(0.176)
Democracy	−0.055	−0.058	−0.048
	(0.039)	(0.040)	(0.036)
GDP (logged)	−0.590	−0.576	−0.506
	(0.401)	(0.404)	(0.351)
% Population between 15–24	10.966	−2.786	−14.211
	(29.425)	(32.313)	(25.390)
1970s	−0.366	−0.233	−0.485
	(0.567)	(0.617)	(0.479)
1980s	−0.667	−0.618	−0.788
	(0.582)	(0.631)	(0.518)
1990s	1.493**	1.650**	1.095*
	(0.633)	(0.682)	(0.573)
Constant	−0.999	1.059	2.078
	(6.585)	(7.403)	(5.954)
Observations	86	82	125
Number of Countries	28	27	39
R-squared (Overall)	0.488	0.495	0.395

Standard errors in parentheses
* p. < .10, ** p < .05, *** p < .01

scale, ranging from 0 = no ethnic violence to 6 = communal warfare. The table suggests that former British colonies had considerably higher levels of ethnic violence during the 1980s and 1990s than former French colonies but that former Belgian colonies had the highest levels of all.

TABLE 6.2. *Ethnic Violence by Colonial Power, 1980–1999*

French Colonies	British Colonies	Belgian Colonies
1980s: 0.23	1980s: 1.13	1980s: 1.67
1990s: 1.85	1990s: 2.56	1990s: 5.67

Blanton, Mason, and Athow (2001) use multivariate statistical methods to explore colonial variation in ethnic violence in sub-Saharan Africa, although they only consider former British colonies and former French Colonies. They find that former British colonies had a greater risk of ethnic violence than former French colonies in the 1980s and 1990s and conclude that the relationship between colonial power and ethnic violence is driven by differences in how the colonizers affected intercommunal competition and the mobilizational resources of ethnic communities. Because education shapes both competition and mobilizational resources, it is possible that education helps explain different colonial legacies of ethnic violence in sub-Saharan Africa.

Although educational institutions differed considerably within empires, the colonial powers generally established educational institutions in sub-Saharan Africa that differed from those of other colonial powers in many ways. The French educational system tended to be much more limited than the educational systems in former British and Belgian colonies. One reason was the powerful place of secularism in French political ideology (especially following the Dreyfus affair) and, concomitantly, the extreme secularism of the educational system back in France (Gifford and Weiskel 1971: 674). As a consequence, the French did not depend on missionaries for the provisioning of education in Africa and actually attempted to limit their influence as much as possible (Woodberry 2004: 26). In British and Belgian colonies, on the other hand, missionaries played a very influential role in education and were arguably the most important providers of education. Indeed, Woodberry (2004) finds that missionaries provided 90 percent of education in colonial Africa. Consequently, although less subjected to proselytizing missionaries, French colonial subjects also had less access to education.

The second factor that limited educational outlays in French colonial Africa was that French officials emphasized the use of French instead of vernacular languages. This, in turn, limited the size of the educational system by decreasing the number of qualified teachers and increasing the cost of education. Moreover, educational reforms after World War II focused on making colonial education equivalent to education back in France, which not only reinforced the use of French but placed emphasis on quality instead of quantity (Gifford and Weiskel 1971: 694). Alternatively, the British and Belgian administrations did not attempt to follow national curricula and encouraged the use of local languages, at least at the primary level. This latter strategy lowered the price of education and thereby created more educational opportunities.

TABLE 6.3. *Educational and Economic Development in Sub-Saharan Africa, 2007*

Former French Colonies

Country	Education Index	Economic Index
Benin	0.445	0.430
Burkina Faso	0.301	0.404
CAR	0.419	0.328
Chad	0.334	0.449
Congo	0.736	0.594
Cote D'Ivoire	0.450	0.472
Gabon	0.834	0.838
Guinea	0.361	0.406
Mali	0.331	0.398
Mauritania	0.541	0.494
Niger	0.282	0.307
Senegal	0.417	0.469
Togo	0.534	0.345
Zambia	0.682	0.435
Total	0.460	0.456

Former British Colonies

Country	Education Index	Economic Index
Botswana	0.788	0.820
Gambia	0.439	0.418
Ghana	0.622	0.432
Kenya	0.690	0.457
Lesotho	0.753	0.457
Malawi	0.685	0.339
Nigeria	0.657	0.497
Sierra Leone	0.282	0.307
South Africa	0.843	0.765
Sudan	0.539	0.507
Swaziland	0.731	0.646
Tanzania	0.673	0.416
Uganda	0.698	0.394
Total	0.649	0.492

Former Belgian Colonies

Country	Education Index	Economic Index
Burundi	0.559	0.205
D. R. Congo	0.608	0.182
Rwanda	0.607	0.360
Total	0.591	0.249

Source: United Nations 2009.

Noting these educational differences, Cogneau (2003) analyzes whether French and British colonialism are associated with different levels of education at both independence and afterward. While controlling for different factors, he finds that former British colonies had significantly higher levels of literacy and years of education at independence. In turn, he finds that these educational differences have increased since independence, suggesting that colonialism established different educational trajectories. At the same time, Cogneau (2003) uses survey data from three former French colonies and two former British colonies and finds that educated individuals in the former British colonies generally find themselves in much more economically competitive situations and receive much more limited returns on their educations. His findings therefore provide evidence

Education and Ethnic Violence

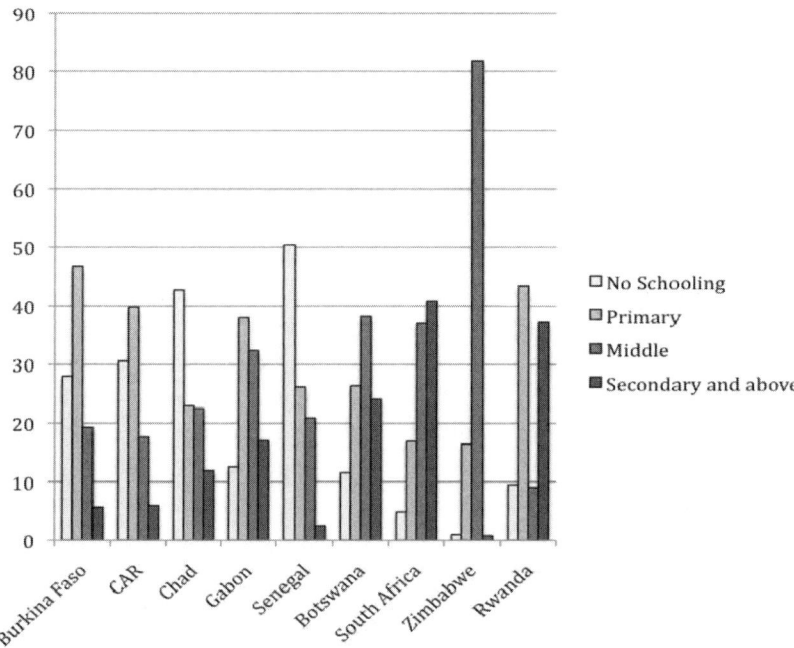

FIGURE 6.1. Percent of Total Unemployed by Educational Level among Select African Countries, 1993–2006. *Source:* International Labour Organization 2010.

that educated unemployment and underemployment are greater in British Africa relative to French Africa and are largely the result of colonial legacies.

Table 6.3 and Figure 6.1 provide additional insight into differences in education and educated unemployment in former British and French colonies in sub-Saharan Africa. They also include former Belgian colonies, which, as noted previously, had educational systems that were more similar to those in former British colonies in terms of educational opportunities and had particularly high levels of ethnic violence. Table 6.3 lists the United Nations indices for education and economic development. These indices are standardized, range from 0 to 1, and are used to gauge a country's relative level of development. The table shows that former French colonies have levels of education and economic development that are on par with one another: the average education index score is 0.460, and the average economic index score is 0.456. Alternatively, although the former British colonies have levels of economic development that are similar to those of former French colonies, their average level of education is considerably greater than the average of former French colonies (0.649

versus 0.460). Thus, former British colonies have a greater mismatch between the educational and economic systems, with considerably higher levels of education relative to economic development. If one considers the three former Belgian colonies, their levels of education are similar to those of former British colonies, but their levels of economic development are considerably lower, showing an even greater mismatch between the economy and the educational system.

Figure 6.1 shows the distribution of unemployment by education level for five former French colonies (Burkina Faso, Central African Republic, Chad, Gabon, and Senegal), three former British colonies (Botswana, South Africa, and Zimbabwe), and one former Belgian colony (Rwanda). Notably, data on unemployment by educational level are very limited for sub-Saharan Africa and are only available for these nine former French, British, and Belgian colonies.[13] The figure categorizes the unemployed by their educational level and shows each educational category's percentage of the total unemployed.

The figure shows that colonial heritage is related to educated unemployment. For the five former French colonies, the unemployed are concentrated among individuals with either primary education or no schooling. The three former British colonies, on the other hand, have much greater unemployment among individuals with secondary education and, especially, middle-school education. Finally, Rwanda has a more bifurcated distribution, with unemployment concentrated among individuals with either primary or secondary education. The figure therefore offers evidence that former British and Belgian colonies have many more educated and unemployed individuals than former French colonies, something one would expect if education contributed to the higher levels of ethnic violence in former British and Belgian colonies.

Additional evidence about the impact of education on ethnic violence in British and French Africa comes from surveys that provide insight into ethnic identification and competition. Bannon, Miguel, and Posner (2004) use survey data from eight former British colonies in sub-Saharan Africa (and Namibia, a former German and South African colony) to explore how competition affects ethnic identification. They find that it has strong and positive effects but that it has a particularly strong impact on ethnic identification among the more educated (although not necessarily the

---

[13] The data for all countries are from the late twentieth and early twenty-first centuries, with the earliest year being 1993 and the latest being 2006. When a country has data available for multiple years, I select the year closest to 2000.

most educated). Alternatively, Bossuroy (2006) uses survey data from seven former French colonies in Africa and finds that ethnic identification decreases significantly and consistently with educational attainment. One notable similarity between the findings of Bannon, Miguel, and Posner (2004) and Bossoroy (2006), however, is that unemployment significantly increases ethnic identification. One can interpret these findings in different ways, but it is quite possible that competition promotes ethnic identification and scapegoating and that the educated in former British colonies find themselves in very competitive situations whereas the educated in former French colonies have much more limited competition for jobs and resources because of a smaller pool of educated job seekers.

Friedman, Kremer, Miguel, and Thorton (2011) offer an insightful study that combines elements of these survey analyses and explores the impact of education on frustration, violence, and identity. They analyze one former British colony – Kenya – and compare girls who won scholarships to attend school with girls who were not awarded scholarships. They find that the girls who did not win scholarships and subsequently did not attend school were 30 percent more likely to claim that their ethnic identity was *not* important, suggesting that education strengthened ethnic identity. Moreover, the girls who won scholarships and subsequently attended school ended up being more frustrated by their lack of opportunities and were much more likely to support political violence, and the authors conclude that the former likely promoted the latter.

So far, the evidence presented in this section suggests that former British colonies have superior levels of education relative to former French colonies and that this difference helps explain the higher levels of ethnic violence among former British colonies. Specifically, it offers evidence that educated unemployment is worse in former British colonies, thereby promoting ethnic violence through both the frustration-aggression and competition mechanisms. To further explore the impact of education on ethnic violence in former British and French colonies, it is useful to consider the histories of education, educational bubbles, and ethnic violence in particular countries. I briefly consider two former French colonies – Burkina Faso and Benin – and one former British colony – Nigeria

Burkina Faso. Burkina Faso is located in West Africa and is one of the poorest countries in the world. In turn, it also has one of the least educated populations. In fact, data from Table 6.2 suggest that the country's educational system is underdeveloped relative to its economy. In 2007, its combined gross enrollment ratio in education (32.8 percent) and its adult literacy rate (28.7 percent) were among the lowest in the world (United Nations 2009: 173). The population of Burkina Faso is quite diverse, and the country has more than a dozen distinct ethnic communities who speak different languages. Of these, the Mossi, who comprise approximately 50 percent of the population, are the largest. Religiously, the country's population is also diverse, with 50 percent Muslim, 10 percent Christian, and 40 percent belonging to diverse indigenous faiths. Despite this diversity, the country has experienced very peaceful ethnic relations over the past half-century.[14] Minorities At Risk, for example, does not recognize any Burkinabe community as at risk of ethnic violence.

All the reasons for relatively peaceful ethnic relations cannot be overviewed here, but one factor is limited competition between ethnic communities. Such limited competition is evident in the lack of ethnic mobilization for political support. As Englebert (1998) emphasizes, politics in Burkina Faso is not ethnicized. Similarly, Basedau and Stroh (2009) use survey data and find that the Burkinabe political system has very low levels of ethnicization, with 86 percent of respondents supporting parties with weak ethnic platforms. Finally, despite economic inequalities, there has been little ethnic mobilization over economic issues.

Low levels of education, in turn, appear to have contributed to limited ethnic mobilization. Most notably, despite severe economic difficulties, economic competition among the educated is limited because of the small pool of educated job seekers. At independence, for example, the primary enrollment rate was less than 6 percent, and the literacy rate was only 3 percent (Lavoie 2008: 63). As a consequence, there were not enough educated Burkinabe to fill the white-collar jobs that were available. Very slow improvements in education and a focus on primary education, in turn, have kept educated unemployment in check, and limited competition over jobs and frustration over limited mobility has helped impede ethnic mobilization and scapegoating.

Nigeria. The comparison of Burkina Faso and Nigeria highlights a stark contrast. Unlike Burkina Faso, ethnicity was the major basis of mobilization in Nigeria both during the independence transition and afterward. Whereas several factors undoubtedly account for this difference, high

---

[14] Recently, there have been incidents of violence between farmers and nomads with different ethnicities, but the focus of the violence has been land instead of ethnicity.

levels of competition and frustration among the educated appear influential. Indeed, several works on ethnic violence in Nigeria during the 1950s and 1960s note that education promoted ethnic violence through the competition and frustration-aggression mechanisms.

During the colonial period, Nigeria was divided into three administrative units that largely coincided with different ethnic groupings – the Yoruba in the southwest, the Igbo in the southeast, and the Hausa-Fulani in the north. These administrative units were autonomous from one another and only merged during the final years of colonialism. Because of high levels of conversion to Christianity, the Yoruba and especially the Igbo developed relatively advanced educational systems during British colonialism, with the Igbos the most educationally advanced of the three major ethnic communities at Nigerian independence, followed closely by the Yoruba (Abernethy 1969: 262–265). The Hausa-Fulani, on the other hand, had very low levels of education because of an extremely indirect form of rule that limited both government and missionary provisioning of education. In 1965, the enrollment in secondary schools was 110,000 in southern Nigeria and only 10,000 in northern Nigeria (Abernethy 1969: 265). Similarly, the primary enrollment rate was nearly universal in eastern Nigeria at independence but was only 10 percent in the north (Curle 1973: 89).

Unfortunately for educated Nigerians, there were very limited opportunities for employment in the 1950s and 1960s because of a weak economy, and rates of unemployment among the educated were high (Abernethy 1969: 206; Callaway 1963). Because of particularly limited economic opportunities in the southeast, many educated Igbos moved to other regions of Nigeria and soon became a conspicuous minority holding desirable positions. This situation, in turn, caused fear and resentment of the Igbo among the Yoruba and, especially, the Hausa-Fulani (Abernethy 1969: 253–277; Diamond 1983: 471–472; Paden 1971). As a result, northerners commonly discriminated against Igbos in an effort to protect their own community. Such sentiments and discrimination only intensified as the British prepared Nigeria for independence by expanding and Africanizing the civil service, a process that provided advantaged opportunities for Igbos because of their superior education. Recognizing the relatively advantaged position of Igbos, a prominent Hausa-Fulani leader declared that ethnic competition for civil service jobs was "a matter of life and death to us" and one that warranted violence in pursuit of Hausa-Fulani interests (Abernethy 1969: 264).

Given the strength of resentment against Igbo educational superiority and competition for elite jobs, Igbos living in the north became the targets of ethnic riots in the 1940s, 1950s, and 1960s, with up to 30,000 killed and one million internally displaced during the 1966 riots alone (Abernethy 1969: 266–267; Paden 1971; Young 1976: 472). This was particularly evident in the ethnic purges against Igbos in 1966. In January 1966, a military coup lead primarily by Igbos successfully toppled a northern-dominated government. Four months later, the new military government declared the unification of the civil service, a move that placed northerners in direct competition with southerners for government jobs and thereby severely jeopardized their ability to work in the civil service. Shortly after the unification of the civil service was announced, Hausa-Fulani college and secondary school students organized demonstrations in Kano that escalated into deadly anti-Igbo pogroms (Paden 1971: 134). Paden (1971), in turn, notes that economic competition and frustration over perceived injustices motivated several educated individuals to demonstrate against the Igbos.[15]

Benin. A comparison of Burkina Faso and Nigeria therefore highlights how educational differences appear to have contributed to their different histories of intercommunal relations, as Nigeria suffered from an educational bubble whereas Burkina Faso suffered from a lack of educated individuals. Still, one might argue that British colonial heritage contributed to ethnic competition to a greater extent than French colonial heritage and that ethnic competition – not education – explains the differences in ethnic violence. Yet, French colonialism promoted greater ethnic competition and divisions in some colonies, and these countries – like other former French colonies – generally have low levels of education relative to former British colonies. Such cases therefore allow one to test whether low levels of education helped contain ethnic violence even in ethnically charged environments.

Benin – a former French colony and western neighbor of Nigeria – is a notable example of a former French colony with high levels of ethnic competition but low levels of education. It parallels Nigeria's political system in many ways. Most notably, it is ethnicized and regionalized, with

---

[15] A similar situation occurred in Burma, where missionary education targeted the Karens but avoided ethnic Burmans. The Burmans subsequently attacked the Karens over the latter's greater mobility and thereby sparked a separatist movement led by Karen educated elites.

forty-six ethnic communities and three main ethno-regional blocks (Allen 1988; Basedau and Stroh 2009; Magnusson 2005). In the 1960s and 1970s, extreme ethnic competition contributed to half a dozen coups and nearly sparked a civil war between different factions (Allen 1988; Houngnikpo 2001: 117–131). The ethnicization of politics was also linked to an indirect system of colonial rule, regional inequalities between the coastal south and the northern interior, and ethnic imbalances in the colonial military and administration (Allen 1988; Houngnikpo 2001). Despite these similarities with Nigeria, ethnic violence has been very limited and almost always occurred at the government level through coups and purges. As a consequence, violence among civilians has been very rare, a situation similar to Burkina Faso but starkly different from Nigeria.[16]

One notable factor that helps explain the country's divergence with Nigeria and similarity to Burkina Faso in terms of ethnic violence is limited economic competition among the educated. Indeed, like Burkina Faso, education has been so limited that the government was able to guarantee government jobs for the educated up until the mid-1980s (Allen 1988; Magnusson 2005: 81). This contrasts greatly with Nigeria, where higher levels of education created a severe shortage of white-collar jobs as early as the 1940s and 1950s and intense zero-sum competition for them. As a consequence, competition and frustration were much more limited among the educated in Benin, a situation that impeded ethnic scapegoating and helped prevent ethnic violence. This environment, in turn, allowed the government of Mathieu Kérékou to implement left-leaning and nationalist policy that successfully reduced ethnic tensions and ethnic-based political competition (Dickovick 2008).

Even in 2001, more than a decade after a severe financial crisis forced the government to limit the size of the public service, unemployment rates were quite low in Cotonou, the Beninois capital, at 5.5 percent (Brilleau, Roubaud, and Torelli 2004: 17). The expansion of education and the scaling back of the public sector has taken its toll on the educated, however, as unemployment in Cotonou was positively related to education level in 2001, with the unemployment rate going from 2.4 percent among individuals with no education and continuously increasing to a peak of 12.9 percent among individuals with postsecondary education (Brilleau, Roubaud, and Torelli 2004: 18). And, Brilleau, Roubaud, and Torelli (2004) find that it is becoming a problem in other former French colonies

---

[16] Minorities at Risk does not recognize any ethnic community in Benin that is at risk of ethnic violence.

as well. Notably, it was the worst in Abidjan, the capital of Cote d'Ivoire, with more than 20 percent of individuals with postsecondary education being unemployed in 2001. One year later, in 2002, an ethnic-based civil war erupted, and one of the many factors causing the violence was economic difficulties and the belief that ethno-nationalist others were unfairly taking the jobs of pure-blooded Ivoirites. Thus, while unemployment among the educated has not been a problem in French Africa historically, it is increasingly becoming one and might have violent consequences.

Education, Socialization, and Ethnic Violence in Rwanda

Whereas the frustration-aggression and competition mechanisms help explain different levels of ethnic violence among former French and British colonies in sub-Saharan Africa, the socialization mechanism might also account for some of the difference. The French educational systems generally taught in French and emphasized the national community in the curricula. Alternatively, the educational systems in former British colonies usually taught in multiple vernaculars. Vernacular education allowed more people to attend school and helped maintain local cultures, but it also helped strengthen ethnic identities by segregating students linguistically, creating linguistic competition, and using curricula that focused on the local ethnic community instead of the greater national community.[17]

Along with former British colonies, scholars offer evidence that the socialization mechanism contributed to ethnic violence in the former Belgian colonies of Burundi, Congo, and Rwanda. Analyses of colonial Congo find that vernacular education heightened both ethnic divisions and intercommunal competition, especially in an environment with limited economic opportunities (Jewsiewicki 1991; Roberts 1991). Similarly, several scholars find that education in Rwanda strengthened ethnic divisions and intercommunal antipathy and thereby contributed to severe ethnic violence in both the 1960s and the 1990s.[18] The case differs from the Congo, however, because both Hutus and Tutsis speak the same language, so vernacular education was not an issue. Instead, colonial officials and missionaries believed Tutsis were genetically superior to Hutus

---

[17] See Harries 1991; Ranger 1991; Vail 1991: 11–12; Vail and White 1991.
[18] See Des Forges 1969; Gasanabo 2006; Linden 1977; Mamdani 2001; Mbonimana 1978, 1995; Walker-Keleher 2006.

and therefore segregated schools ethnically and taught a curricula proclaiming Tutsi superiority. In addition to the socialization mechanism, this argument also notes the influence of the frustration-aggression and competition mechanisms, although I only focus on the socialization mechanism here.

As part of the indirect system of colonial domination, the Belgian administration designated Tutsis – formerly an elite status community – as a race of relatively recent and racially superior migrants to Rwanda and declared them the natural rulers of Hutus. Colonial officials and missionaries strongly believed in the racial division between Tutsi and Hutu and rationalized it by combining eugenics with religion: they believed that Tutsis were descendants of Ham, Noah's damned son, whereas Hutus were miscreants completely outside of God's chosen community (Mamdani 2001; Mbonimana 1978). The colonizers, in turn, helped institutionalize this racialization in different ways, among the most important being a census that categorized individuals as either Tutsi or Hutu based on their physical appearance, their political status, and the number of cattle they owned. Of greater relevance to this book, they also helped institutionalize the Hutu-Tutsi cleavage through education.

Nearly all schools in colonial Rwanda were controlled by Catholic missionaries, and they implemented a biased system of education that greatly favored Tutsis. Indeed, the Catholic missionaries were overtly pro-Tutsi and anti-Hutu and strongly criticized the colonial government whenever it gave administrative positions to Hutus, believing that such positions should be reserved for the more civilized and superior Tutsis. Beginning in 1925, missionaries began restricting education to Tutsis, causing the great majority of students to be Tutsi despite the fact that Tutsis were only a small minority of the population (Linden 1977; Mbonimana 1978; Mbonimana 1995). In addition to communal restrictions, the missionary schools taught a curriculum declaring Tutsis racially superior to Hutus and the rightful rulers of Rwanda. Both the ethnic segregation of schools and the teaching of ethnically biased material continued until World War II, after which time the educational opportunities of Hutus expanded very rapidly (Linden 1977).

With the expansion of education among Hutus, a growing number of educated Hutus became frustrated over discrimination and inequalities, and many of them organized and led the Hutu Revolution between 1959 and 1961. The movement overthrew the system of Tutsi dominance and resulted in the deaths of tens of thousands of Tutsis and the exile of tens of thousands of others. In the aftermath, the Rwandan educational system continued to emphasize the racial difference between Hutus and Tutsis yet substituted an ideology of Tutsi malevolence for the old ideology of Tutsi superiority. In particular, schools now taught that Tutsis were evil and ruthless interlopers who invaded and conquered Hutus, and they declared Hutus the only true Rwandans (Gasanabo 2006; Walker-Keleher 2006: 41). Even more, teachers frequently ridiculed Tutsis in class to highlight their "otherness" and inferiority, and schools formally discriminated against Tutsis by creating strict racial quotas that limited their enrollment (Gasanabo 2006; Walker-Keleher 2006: 44). In this way, the postcolonial educational system emphasized the difference between Hutus and Tutsis, declared that Tutsis were outside the moral community, blamed Tutsis for Hutu hardships, and thereby helped legitimize the subsequent genocide of Rwandan Tutsis (Gasanabo 2006; Walker-Keleher 2006). As a report of an international conference on education and the Rwandan genocide declared, "Instead of trying to eradicate ignorance among the people, a system of propaganda and incitement to ethnic and regional hatred was established by making clever use of that ignorance" (quoted in Gasanabo 2006: 371). The socialization mechanism therefore appears to help explain Verwimp's (2005) findings showing that individuals who participated in the genocide were, on average, considerably more educated than individuals who did not.

CONCLUSION

This chapter analyzes additional cases to explore whether the educational mechanisms described in Chapter 2 and highlighted in the Sri Lankan and Cypriot case studies can be applied to a larger set of cases. The analysis supports the findings of the previous chapters but also offers new insight. I selected the Palestinian territories because it strongly conforms to the statistical findings in Chapter 3 and because data exist on the educational levels of militant Palestinians. The data show that educated Palestinians are greatly overrepresented among those participating in ethno-nationalist violence. The educational mechanisms, in turn, help explain the active participation of educated individuals in ethno-nationalist violence.

I selected India because its elitist educational system produces a large oversupply of educated individuals who are not easily absorbed by the economy. It therefore offers an opportunity to explore the impact of educational bubbles on ethnic violence. Through a review of the literature on India and an analysis of ethnic violence in Assam, the Indian case offers evidence that unemployment among the educated motivates ethnic violence through both the frustration-aggression and competition mechanisms and that this motivation pushes educated individuals to exploit their mobilizational resources to organize violent ethnic movements. The Indian case study also considers Kerala, a state in India that has experienced only limited ethnic violence despite very high levels of educated unemployment. I find that the state's effective political institutions helped limit ethnic violence by containing ethnic violence and allowing ethnic communities to pursue grievances through formal political channels. In addition, class/caste – not ethnicity – is the most politicized cleavage in Kerala. As a consequence, extreme ethno-nationalist organizations have received only limited support, politicians and officials respect and pursue the interests of all ethnic communities, and ethnic-based discrimination and grievances are limited.

The final section of the chapter analyzes sub-Saharan Africa, a region that does not appear to support the findings of the previous chapters because it has relatively high levels of ethnic violence but relatively low levels of education. Yet, colonial heritage, educated unemployment, and ethnic violence are all related, and education helps explain variation in ethnic violence in the region. Moreover, educational socialization appears to have promoted ethnic violence in some African countries. Thus, although not the most important cause of ethnic violence in sub-Saharan Africa, education still appears to affect it.

7

Education and Ethno-Nationalist Conflict in Canada and Germany

While providing evidence that education contributes to ethnic violence, the statistical findings of Chapter 3 suggest that education does not promote violence in all environments, pointing to the scarcity of resources and ineffective political institutions as influential factors that interact with education to promote ethnic violence. Most of the qualitative case studies in previous chapters analyze ethnic violence in countries characterized by scarce resources and relatively ineffective political institutions. The sole exception is Kerala, which is relatively poor but has effective political institutions, and the case offers insight into how effective political institutions interact with education to limit ethnic violence.

In this chapter, I continue to explore whether and how scope conditions shape the impact of education on ethnic violence, focusing on both effective political institutions and resource availability. The first case study analyzes the Quebec separatist movement in Canada. This ethno-nationalist movement had the potential to turn violent (and did in a few instances) but has been overwhelmingly peaceful. I begin the case study by exploring whether education contributed to the separatist movement in any way. Next, I investigate whether any factors directly and indirectly related to its economy and political institutions help explain why the separatist movement did not turn violent. The second case study analyzes Germany. Instead of simply considering contemporary Germany, however, the case study compares contemporary Germany with Germany in the 1920s and 1930s, focusing on the Nazi and neo-Nazi movements and the ethno-nationalist violence committed by each. The analysis describes how the educated were overrepresented among the supporters of the Nazis but underrepresented among the supporters of the neo-Nazis and investigates whether the different economic and political contexts help explain this difference.

ETHNO-NATIONALISM AND CONFLICT IN CANADA

Canada has multiple divisions on which ethnic violence could possibly occur. First, there are indigenous Canadians whose ancestors settled in Canada thousands of years ago and nonindigenous Canadians whose progenitors settled in Canada over the last 400 years. Similarly, Canada is an immigrant country, and nearly 20 percent of its present population was born outside of Canada. In addition to indigenous and European Canadians, large numbers of recent immigrants came from Asia, the Caribbean, Latin America, and Africa, making the country very racially diverse. Finally, Canada is a multinational state. Most notably, and of particular interest to this chapter, Canada was settled by both French and British colonists, and historically French and British nationalism competed with one another on Canadian soil. Today, the Canadian government officially endorses a more inclusive multiculturalism that celebrates the diversity of Canada, but French Canadian nationalism continues. Since the 1950s, the latter has morphed into a regionally based Quebec nationalism.

Present-day Canada was born from conflict between the French and the British, as New France – with its 70,000 French settlers – was conquered by the British during the Seven Years' War (1754–1763). Generally speaking, the British let French Canadians maintain their culture and lifestyles, with English colonists settling in the Atlantic provinces, Ontario, and eventually the western provinces, leaving Quebec primarily to French Canadians. There were exceptions to this rule, however. For one, French Canadians residing outside of Quebec lived alongside a growing number of British settlers, and their cultural autonomy was much more limited than French Canadians living in Quebec. In fact, they faced concerted efforts to assimilate them into Anglophone Canada. There was also a strong British presence in parts of Quebec. Most importantly, Montreal was the economic hub of the new British colony and maintained this position until being eclipsed by Toronto in the second half of the twentieth century. Many Anglophone Canadians lived in Montreal and dominated its financial and business institutions. Also, many loyalists from the American colonies moved north to the Eastern Townships of Quebec after the American Revolutionary War, causing the emergence of several Anglophone communities just east of Montreal. The Anglophone population of Quebec peaked at 25 percent in 1861, a number that has decreased steadily over the years to less than 10 percent today.

Although allowing French Canadians to maintain their culture in Quebec, the English not only dominated the economy but also the politics of Quebec, a situation causing tension to emerge between British and French Canadians and resulting in rebellion in 1837–1838. In reality, there were multiple rebellions during this period (one in Lower Canada, or present-day Ontario, and one in Upper Canada, or present-day Quebec) and the rebellion in Quebec included both Anglophone and Francophone Canadians who were dissatisfied with the concentration of economic and political power within the hands of a relatively small group of elites. Still, many French Canadians participating in the rebellion were motivated by the lack of French Canadians among the elites and a nationalistic desire for greater political autonomy. The rebellion, in turn, had major implications for French-English relations, as the colonial government saw French Canadian nationalism as the root cause of the conflict and recommended a policy of merging Upper and Lower Canada and assimilating French Canadians into British-dominated Canada. Because of the conflict that such measures would have sparked, the assimilation policy was never implemented, and the French Canadian community in Quebec retained considerable autonomy. Even so, the threat of assimilation raised fears among French Canadians for years to come.

In the aftermath of the rebellion, the distribution of political power in Quebec transformed, as the liberal elites – whose power had been increasing but who led the rebellion – found themselves in a more marginalized position while the political power of the Catholic Church increased. The church was the center of cultural life among French Canadians and held considerable power prior to the rebellion. The clergy had opposed the rebellion because of the anticlerical position of the rebel leaders, a situation that caused growing collaboration between church officials and the British colonial government. The collaborative arrangement between the British colonial government and the Catholic Church hardly made the church the only power in French Canadian communities, but it forced French Canadian politicians to respect the church's interests and acknowledge its local influence over the community.

The church retained its quasi-hegemonic influence until the midtwentieth century. The main cause of its eventual demise was the major economic transformations that began in the late nineteenth century and accelerated rapidly during and after World War II. In Quebec, these changes primarily involved rapid industrialization, which, in turn, caused the province to quickly transform from primarily rural to mainly urban. Because of these changes, the influence of the Catholic Church over French Canadians was drastically reduced, and the liberal elites ascended to power once again. Like the rebels in 1837, they were primarily from educated middle-class professions, resented the economic dominance of Anglophones, saw the Church as an outdated authority, and sought to modernize Quebec.

This group gained political power in Quebec in 1960 with the election of the Liberal government of Jean Lesage. With it, the conservative nationalism propagated by the Catholic Church – which emphasized the need to protect the French Canadian community, the centrality of the church, and French communal autonomy within a united Canada – lost prominence and was replaced by liberal nationalism and neo-nationalism. Liberal nationalism emphasized liberal tenets and economic and political modernization within the Canadian Confederation. Alternatively, neo-nationalism emphasized the need to modernize through the expansion of economic and political autonomy. In so doing, neo-nationalism changed the borders of nation by demarcating the community not according to the French-speaking population but provincial borders: those living within Quebec.

The proponents of neo-nationalism formed the core of the emerging Quebecois separatist movement. The movement maintained the Catholic Church's conservative nationalist goal of protecting French Canadian/Quebecois culture but took a very secular position emphasizing the need for Quebecois to become *maîtres chez nous*, or their own masters, by using the government to take greater control of the Quebecois economy and direct the economy to benefit the Quebecois (McRoberts and Posgate 1980: 105–9). Underlying this desire was a belief that Quebec was an internal colony whose economy was controlled by Anglophone Canadians and Americans, both of whom exploited the labor and resources of Quebec and withdrew their profits from the region. Notably, there was a reality backing this belief, as industry and finance in Quebec were dominated by Anglophone Canadians and Americans.

Although rumblings of a separatist movement have been around since the Rebellion of 1837–8, it was not until the 1960s that the movement emerged as an organized and powerful political force. Two of the earliest and most influential separatist organizations were the *Rassemblement pour l'Indépendance Nationale* (RIN), formed in 1960, and the *Ralliement National* (RN), formed in 1965. Both eventually became political parties pursuing Quebec independence, with RN pursuing more conservative nationalism whereas RIN pursued neo-nationalist ideas. In 1967, René Lévesque, who was a popular minister in the Liberal government of Jean Lesage, resigned and formed a new party seeking Quebec separatism. In 1968, it merged with the RN and changed its name from the *Mouvement Souveraineté-Association* to the *Parti Québécois* (PQ). One month later, the RIN dissolved itself, and its leaders urged members to join the PQ. From that point on, the PQ has been the dominant actor behind the separatist movement.

The PQ is a provincial party and has been a powerful force in Quebecois politics since its formation. When leading the provincial government, the PQ has held two referenda for Quebec sovereignty, both of which lost (the second, in 1995, by only a percentage point). The party has also implemented diverse policy within its nationalist agenda, most of which have tried to strengthen the position of the French language within Quebec. The most notable of these was Bill 101, which was passed in 1977 shortly after the PQ formed its first government. Among other measures, the bill required tests of proficiency in French for admission into the professions, made French the sole official language of the provincial administration, required that businesses with fifty or more employees use French as the main language within the office, required that all public signs and advertisement were in French, and restricted access to public English schools to children whose parents were nonimmigrants and schooled in English (thereby effectively barring immigrants and French-speaking Quebecois from publicly funded English schools).

The nationalist movement has been quite peaceful and has only sparked limited violence. One violent episode broke out in St. Léonard, a suburb of Montreal, on September 10, 1969 over the language of education. The neighborhood had a large Italian immigrant population, and this group organized bilingual schools (in English and French). In 1968, the Francophone-dominated school board forbid bilingual education and only offered French education, causing anger among the Italian community.[1] Thus, when a nationalist organization promoting the use of French in schools organized a march through St. Léonard, a brawl erupted, but no one was killed or seriously injured.

The greatest and most deadly ethno-nationalist violence in Quebec was perpetrated by the *Front de la Libération du Québec*, or FLQ, and other affiliated organizations. The FLQ was a Marxist and nationalist

---

[1] Ironically, the Catholic Church, which ran the French education school system until 1964, forbid immigrants from attending their schools (Stevenson 2006: 359–360).

organization formed in 1963 and employed terrorist methods in an attempt to promote independence and revolutionary economic reforms. It was organized in small cells, experienced rapid turnover because of arrests, and likely never had more than 200 members at any time. The group organized approximately 100 bombings of locals that symbolized Anglophone business, the Anglophone community, and the Federal government. These bombings sought symbolic destruction, not deaths, although FLQ killed seven people. The group gained international attention in 1970, when it kidnapped James Richard Cross, the British Trade Commissioner, and Pierre Laporte, the Minister of Labour and Vice-Premiere of Quebec, subsequently killing Laporte.

Education and the Quebec Independence Movement

From its very beginning and continuing to this day, the Quebec nationalist movement has been dominated by the educated elite (although the party has increasingly gained a mass following). For example, intellectuals and professionals dominate both the party's leadership positions and membership. Similarly, intellectuals form the core of nationalist organizations and play a very important role popularizing a nationalist ideology favoring independence (Pinard and Kowalchuk forthcoming). In addition, several quantitative analyses of PQ electoral support show that educated individuals vote for the PQ in disproportionate numbers.[2] Pinard and Kowalchuk (forthcoming) provide the most thorough analysis to date and find that educated individuals are much more likely to vote for the PQ but that this support depends on occupation: educated public sector employees of the federal government and educated workers within the private sector are less likely to support the PQ, but intellectuals and public-sector employees at the provincial level are the strongest supporters of the PQ.

Intellectuals have played a very important role publicizing and legitimizing the nationalist cause. For this, they use the media and public gatherings to spread their views. Indeed, most public intellectuals in Quebec are supporters of the separatist movements, and they very rarely speak out openly against the movement. Although employees of the provincial public sector do not have as high a profile as the intellectuals, they are much larger in numbers – constituting nearly 25 percent of the employed population in the province in 1990 – and are among the most active

---

[2] See Cuneo and Curtis 1974; Hamilton and Pinard 1976; McRoberts and Posgate 1980.

supporters of independence. Indeed, such was the power of separatists in the provincial administration that Robert Bourassa, a Liberal premier of Quebec, believed it was sabotaging his policy and attempted to circumvent the administration through political appointments (Milner 1978). Additional evidence of their influential participation in the separatist movement comes from their activity in unions. Although unions were initially opposed to separation, they have become increasingly nationalistic (Gagnon and Montcalm 1990: 85–89; Guntzel 2000). This growing strength has been linked to granting public-sector employees the right to unionize in 1965, a move that allowed this group to gain a strong position among the leadership of the *Fédération des Travailleurs et Travailleuses du Québec*, the *Confédération des Syndicats Nationaux*, and the *Centrale des Syndicats du Québec*, three powerful unions that became bastions of nationalism by the late 1960s (Guntzel 2000; Milner 1978: 98).

In line with the active involvement of many educated individuals in the separatist movement, the separatist movement only became a powerful force in Quebecois society after the educational system expanded dramatically and produced an increasingly large number of educated individuals. Although educational expansion was a central priority of the Liberal government that came to power in 1960, such expansion actually preceded Lesage's election by a decade and a half. Indeed, per capita expenditure on education in constant dollars increased from a measly $3.85 in 1945 to $23.28 by the time Lesage came to power in 1960. By 1970, it had risen to $89.83, a level of per capita spending more than twenty-three times greater than just twenty-five years earlier (Latouche 1974). This expansion is evident in enrollment rates as well. The first area to expand was elementary education, and its student body expanded by 25 percent annually during the final years of the 1940s (Behiels 1985: 152). A similar but slightly later expansion occurred in secondary and postsecondary education. In 1952, only 4 percent of Francophones of secondary-school age (thirteen- to twenty-year-olds) attended school (Behiels 1985: 168). Shortly thereafter, however, public secondary schools were constructed throughout the province, and the government began to subsidize private schools (Behiels 1985: 170; Linteau, Durocher, Robert, and Ricard 1991: 245). Through these efforts, the number of secondary-school students skyrocketed throughout the 1950s. This trend continued during the following decades, with the percentage of fifteen-year-olds attending secondary school increasing from 66 percent in 1961 to 94 percent in 1971. Similarly, the number of twenty-year-olds attending postsecondary school rose from 6 percent in 1961 to 16 percent in 1971 (Dufour and

Amyot 1972: 496). In absolute numbers, there were, on average, less than 2,000 Francophone graduates from Quebec universities per year between 1956 and 1965, but the average rose to more than 4,000 between 1966 and 1970 and surpassed 15,000 in 1983 (Linteau, Durocher, Robert, and Ricard 1991: 488).

The educated appear to have given disproportionate support to the separatist movement for several reasons. For one, there was a generational effect, with the youth being both more likely to be educated (given educational expansion) and to support the separatist movement (Pinard and Kowalchuk forthcoming). Second, independence was often more in the economic, political, and social interests of the educated. Public-sector provincial employees, for example, appear to have supported independence disproportionately, in part because it was in their personal interests and because they believed it would be best for Quebec.[3] Considering the latter, the public sector has been very active in promoting state economic management in an effort to modernize Quebec and improve the economic position of Francophone Quebecois. They saw the federal government as simply getting in their way and therefore pursued independence as a means of gaining full, unimpeded control. Similarly, independence would place more power and resources at the hands of the public sector and would promote even further public sector expansion, thereby increasing the economic opportunities of educated Francophones. One notable example was the purchase of private businesses by the government, which resulted in the business leaders changing from private and Anglophone to public and Francophone. As Breton (1964) emphasizes, the Quebecois public has gained little beside pride through the creation of these public enterprises, but the middle-class administrators who have taken them over gained enormously.

Independence is also in the interests of Quebecois intellectuals, who are consistently the occupational group most strongly supporting the PQ. Their livelihoods and cultural capital depend on the French language, and they therefore feel threatened living in a country with a large Anglophone majority. More importantly, many view themselves as guardians of Quebecois culture and see independence as a means of protecting and reasserting it (Pinard and Kowalchuk forthcoming). Alternatively, the educated whose livelihoods would be hampered by Quebec separatism – the business elite and federal public-sector employees – are strongly

---

[3] See Behiels 1985: 44; Breton 1964; Gagnon and Montcalm 1990: 68; Heintzman 1983: 39; McRoberts 1975.

underrepresented among the PQ base of public support (Pinard and Kowalchuk forthcoming).

Other analyses also recognize that selective and collective incentives help explain support for the separatist movement among the educated but place equal or greater emphasis on the frustration of educated Francophones over their limited economic opportunities. In particular, the Francophones in Quebec have historically been significantly underrepresented in both the public sector at the federal level and elite positions within the private sector. Indeed, the opportunities of the Francophone population in business and the federal administration were quite limited in the 1950s and 1960s, and studies find that Anglophones held top positions and earned considerably more than Francophones. Based on data from the 1970 Census, for example, a bilingual Anglophone male earned between 11 percent to 13 percent more than a bilingual Francophone male (Shapiro and Stelcner 1987: 98). Among unilingual males, in turn, Anglophones earned between 21 percent and 25 percent more than their Francophone counterparts (Shapiro and Stelcner 1987: 98). Most notably, the earning differentials went up with education level, meaning that educated Francophones experienced a greater gap in income than less educated Francophones (Shapiro and Stelcner 1987: 100).

Coinciding with these findings, a survey from 1970–1971 found that, among Francophone Quebecois, perceptions of inequality increased significantly with education level: educated individuals were more likely to believe that linguistic inequalities are real and that Francophones face disadvantages in the labor market. The data also show that Francophones with more education were more likely to report having experienced discrimination in the workplace and that educated individuals were much more likely to say that something needed to be done to address linguistic-based inequality (Laczko 1987). The data therefore support several more qualitative analyses finding that frustration over limited mobility and Anglophone dominance has promoted support for the separatist movement among educated Francophones.[4] It also helps explain why a major nationalist goal has been government interference in the economy to improve the position of Francophone Quebecois.

Notably, frustration over limited mobility also motivated members of the FLQ to pursue independence through violence. Pierre Vallières, an FLQ intellectual, proclaimed the Francophone Quebecois the white "niggers" of North America and described independence as the only

---

[4] See Clift 1982: 22; Gagnon and Montcalm 1990: 9; Guindon 1964: 155; McRoberts 1975; McRoberts and Posgate 1980: 119–121.

means for them to attain their rightful status. The educated comprised a very large segment of the FLQ, especially the educated youth. Indeed, several FLQ members were university students (and at least one was a university professor), the FLQ had a militant cell at the University of Quebec at Montreal, and the group received considerable support from university student bodies (Bédard 1998; Cardin 1990: 25). Considering the latter, the FLQ successfully drew large numbers of students – as many as 3,000 – to its rallies on campuses, causing Secretary of State Gerard Pelletier to proclaim that the FLQ's base of support was in intellectual circles and among students (Bédard 1998: 67, 86–87, 112–13). Such was the support and participation of university students in the organization that the Quebecois educational system was subsequently blamed for having socialized students to support a radical and violent separatist organization (Bédard 1998: 170–71; Trottier 1982: 15).

Blaming the educational system for the rise of the FLQ has been severely critiqued, and such claims about the socializing role of education are largely unsubstantiated. Still, the potential influence of education cannot be disregarded. Quebecois universities and CEGEPs (roughly equivalent to American community colleges) were hot beds of student radicalism in the 1960s and early 1970s. In addition, Francophone teachers are among the strongest supporters of the PQ, and the main teacher's union was openly and staunchly Marxist and nationalistic by the late 1960s. Finally, analyses of textbooks provide evidence that the curriculum in Francophone schools helped strengthen Quebecois national identities by describing the English as historical enemies, overlooking the rest of Canada, and emphasizing the need to struggle for the survival of the French Canadian nation.[5] Based on a textual analysis of textbooks used in French secondary schools in Quebec, for example, the National History Project concludes, "The interpretations tend to become bitter, resentful and vindictive, with frequent references, in somewhat belligerent terms, to resistance and, in the economic field at least, to revenge" (Hodgetts 1968: 33).

The Impediments of Ethno-Nationalist Violence in Quebec

Although the ethno-nationalist movement in Quebec was overwhelmingly nonviolent, a more violent outcome was undoubtedly possible. Indeed, a number of the educational mechanisms were present in Quebec, and

---

[5] See Coleman 1984: 56–7; Cook 1967; Hodgetts 1968; Lebrun et al. 2002; Trudel and Jain 1970.

ethno-nationalist violence occurred in a few instances, raising the question: Why did ethnic violence remain limited and restricted to a small group of radicals?

One notable characteristic among the separatist movement is the general absence of radicalism (excluding the FLQ), and this absence helps explain why the ethno-nationalist movement remained nonviolent. One factor, in turn, that limited the movement's radicalism was economic prosperity. Specifically, opportunities for social mobility limited the economic grievances of the educated and thereby mitigated the frustration-aggression mechanism. Moreover, available jobs and resources greatly reduced competition for white-collar jobs, thereby weakening the competition mechanism.

Despite periods of economic slowdown, post–World War II Canada (including Quebec) has experienced steady growth, and it presently has among the highest living standards in the world: its UNDP Human Development Index was ranked fourth in the world in 2009. Moreover, Canada has moderate to low levels of inequality and a relatively effective social safety net, suggesting that resources are available to most Canadians. Within this prosperous environment, the educated are particularly well off. Contrary to Sri Lanka, India, and the Palestinian territories, education has been strongly and negatively related to unemployment in Quebec (and Canada more broadly), meaning that the educated are well *under*represented among the unemployed, and well-paying white-collar jobs are relatively numerous (Government of Quebec 2010). Even in 1982, during a particularly difficult period of economic slowdown that affected the educated and less educated alike, the unemployment rate of individuals in Quebec aged twenty-five and older with eight or fewer years of education was 13.6 percent, but this rate declined steadily and consistently to only 5.8 percent among individuals with university diplomas (Fortin 1984: 434). Thus, resources were readily available in Quebec, and the educated had superior access to them, a situation that limited both the economic grievances and competition of the educated. In this way, the economic environment of Quebec weakened the frustration-aggression and competition mechanisms.

The wavering support of university students for the FLQ provides evidence that opportunities for mobility help impede violence caused by the competition and frustration-aggression mechanisms. As noted previously, many students supported the FLQ at the beginning of the October Crisis (as demonstrated by membership and participation in demonstrations). Yet, once the Canadian government enacted the War Measures Act in

1970 in reaction to the FLQ's kidnappings, the government clamped down on students, and student support dried up within a matter of days. Bédard (1998) points to two main reasons for their rapid disengagement. First, the eventual death of Pierre Laporte at the hands of his FLQ captors repulsed students, showing that they were unwilling to go to such lengths to gain independence and that they lacked extremely powerful grievances (Bédard 1998: 188). Second, continued support of the FLQ posed potential dangers to the students because the government was now arresting people with only indirect ties to the FLQ (Bédard 1998: 187). And because students had great potential for mobility and risked it by joining a militant movement, they chose to disassociate themselves from it. Thus, government forces keeping surveillance over students a month after the War Measures Act was declared concluded that student radicalism had disappeared: "Students are concerned now about their examinations and are not in the mood for extracurricular meetings" (Bédard 1998: 171).

The relatively deprived position of the Francophone community in Quebec has also improved markedly during the post–World War II period and thereby limited grievances that drive the frustration-aggression mechanism and increased the costs of ethnic violence. For instance, although significant earnings differentials existed between Francophone and Anglophone Quebecois as late as 1970, these differentials had already improved by that time and virtually disappeared by 1980 (Shapiro and Stelcner 1987). Even more, while the educated Francophones were most affected by inequality in 1970, by 1991, the economic returns of education were actually greater among Francophones (Lian and Matthews 1998). Similarly, Vaillancourt, Lemay, and Vaillancourt (2007) find that the economic returns of knowing French have steadily increased in Quebec since 1970 whereas the economic returns of knowing English have declined. They also find that the percentage of firms owned by Francophones increased from 47 percent of total in 1961 to 67 percent in 2003. Thus, not only has the economic situation of Francophones in Quebec improved in absolute terms, it has also improved greatly relative to Anglophones, and both limited the radicalism of the nationalist movement. Along these lines, Stevenson (2006) describes how the improved economic position of Quebecois nationalists caused the movement to become increasingly moderate: "By the mid-1970s, Quebec nationalists were becoming older and more affluent than they had been during the Quiet Revolution, and they had more to lose than before from economic uncertainty, disorder, and violence" (306).

Besides the general availability of resources and the improving economic situation of the Quebecois, the case also provides evidence that education did not promote ethnic violence because effective political institutions limited the strength of the educational mechanisms. Specifically, the capacity of the state to implement policy, its aversion to using violence against its citizens, and the ability of people to address grievances through formal politics all helped limit the grievances of the educated and thereby weakened the frustration-aggression mechanism.

Effective governments are capable of regulating social relations and implementing policy through nonviolent means, and state repression and violence against ethnic minorities commonly instigates ethnic violence. The Canadian state – at all levels – used very little coercion in dealing with the separatist movement and therefore did not push the educated to participate in violence through its own violent methods. Indeed, the Canadian state refrained from using violence against the separatist movement even when a few separatists chose to use violence against the Canadian government, and this helped contain the radicalism of the movement. The state's relative nonviolence was caused, in part, by its high capacities to provide services and regulate social relations, which limited its need to use coercion. In addition, Canada has a strong democratic regime that respects the rights of its population and would lose legitimacy if it resorted to open violence against its citizens.

An example that highlights the limited use of violence most clearly is, somewhat ironically, the enactment of the War Measures Act by the Trudeau government in 1970 after the FLQ's kidnapping of Cross and Laporte. After the declaration, the Canadian military had a strong presence in Quebec, and 497 people were incarcerated (of whom 62 were eventually charged and 32 refused bail). Many subsequent scholars of Quebec politics have noted that this coercion was excessive given the actual threat posed by the FLQ and ultimately strengthened the separatist movement because force was used against Quebecois. Even though these claims appear valid, the fact that the Act was only declared after the premier of Quebec and mayor of Montreal demanded it shows how weary the federal government was of using coercion. In addition, the fact that nearly all of those detained were quickly released, that the act was only used temporarily, and that the police and military did not beat or kill anyone all helped contain radicalism. In other countries with less effective governments, state coercion would have posed a much greater risk of turning violent because of a greater willingness to resort to violence and because of the ineffectiveness of government.

The fact that neither the provincial government nor the federal government formally discriminated against Francophone Canadians in the post–World War II period also limited the strength of grievances among educated Quebecois. Several recent works find that formal discrimination designates individuals as subordinate and outside the political community and is therefore an important source of ethno-nationalist violence. In Quebec, the lack of formal political discrimination therefore deterred violence. Even more, political reforms actually sought to increase the presence of Francophones in both the public and private sector, a policy that directly benefited Francophone Quebecois in general and educated Francophones in particular.

Notably, the groups facing the most formal political discrimination in Quebec are Allophones (individuals with a language other than French or English) and, especially, Anglophones. The Anglophones view English – one of the two official languages of Canada – as being a second-rate language in Quebec given that French is the sole official language of the province and that several laws limit the use of English in schools, the provincial government and public service, and businesses. Some interpret such policy as placing Anglophones in a subordinate economic position, as they have limited opportunities in the large and highly paid public sector and have higher unemployment rates than Francophones. In combination with these factors, a sentiment of lost privilege and a fear of what is to come (with or without Quebec independence) has caused considerable consternation among the Anglophone community of Quebec.

Despite this frustration, there has been little Anglophone mobilization for two main reasons. First, despite relative changes, the Anglophone community remains privileged and continues to hold considerable economic power within the province. Second, for those who view the pro-French linguistic policy of the provincial government as a grave and unacceptable grievance, flight is a much more attractive option than fight. Indeed, Toronto has eclipsed Montreal as the economic hub of Canada, Alberta has been booming over the past three decades, and English is the dominant language in both regions, causing a number of Anglophones to move out of the province in search of greener pastures elsewhere.

Finally, yet likely of greatest importance, effective governance has limited ethnic violence in Quebec by providing a clear means for disgruntled actors to address their grievances through formal political channels. As a consequence, educated separatists and the separatist movement in general have been able to successfully address their grievances through nonviolent ways. Most notably, the federal system of government in Canada allowed Francophone Quebecois to control provincial politics. Because the provincial government has considerable powers, this allowed the Quebecois to implement policy to address ethno-national grievances. Bill 101, with its efforts to improve and protect the use of French in the public and private sectors as well as in public education, is a notable example. In this way, most Francophones desiring change have sought to do so peacefully through formal politics, not violence. As a consequence, the leaders of the separatist movement – although sympathizing with the FLQ – spoke out strongly and unequivocally against the organization's use of violence.

Alongside provincial politics, the federal government has also proved an effective means of addressing ethno-nationalist grievances. In fact, without a central government willing to address grievances, a federated system of government can actually strengthen intercommunal antagonisms and ethno-nationalist movements by increasing conflict between the center and those regions dominated by ethnic minorities. Although there is inherently a tug-of-war between all provinces and the federal government over the division of power, and despite the fact that this competition has been greatest between the federal government and Quebec given that latter's much more assertive attempts to increase autonomy, the federal government has consistently attempted to accommodate Quebecois nationalism. Examples include treating Quebec fairly (other provinces might say giving Quebec an unfair advantage) with equalization payments between the federal and provincial governments, making a concerted effort to increase the place of French within the Federal government, and allowing the deputies of a separatist party (the *Bloc Québécois*) to participate fully in a national parliament that the separatists would like to see fail.

Like the War Measures Act, an example that strengthened the nationalist movement provides evidence supporting this point. The Meech Lake Accord, which was a set of failed amendments to the Constitution of Canada, strengthened the separatist movement by – at least in the eyes of many Quebecois – demonstrating the inability of Quebec to pursue its interests at the federal level. The accord nearly passed (needing a unanimous vote from the ten provincial premiers) but failed at the last minute because the premiers of Manitoba and, especially, Newfoundland and Labrador had reservations about legislation that would, in their eyes as well as their constituencies, greatly privilege Quebec over all other provinces. The main issues concerned measures recognizing Quebec as a distinct society and giving Quebec alone a constitutional veto – two issues that many Quebecois saw as an absolute bare minimum for acceptance. While the failure to accept these amendments caused great anger among many within Quebec and was successfully used by the PQ to gain electoral support, the overall process showed a considerable effort by the federal government and most other provincial governments to accommodate Quebec interests. The failure of these efforts, in turn, provoked resentment but hardly enough to incite violence.

The importance of the ability to address grievances through formal political channels is also highlighted in comparison to other countries. Both Tamils and Palestinians, for example, turned to violence when there were no formal political channels for them to pursue their communal interests. Similarly, Catholic support for the Irish Republican Army (IRA) in Northern Ireland was sizable, in part, because Protestant Unionists dominated the Northern Ireland Assembly since 1922 and effectively prevented Catholics from addressing grievances over electoral gerrymandering and glass ceilings. In turn, violence in Northern Ireland greatly diminished after 1998 once Catholics faced the new prospects of sharing power and forming a government.

Thus, an analysis of the Quebec separatist movement shows that the educational mechanisms strengthened the movement but failed to promote a violent ethno-nationalist movement because they did not sufficiently radicalize supporters. For one thing, there is a relative bounty of resources in Canada, and the economic and social conditions of Francophone Quebecois continuously and rapidly improved – both absolutely and relatively – after World War II. The availability of resources, in turn, limited both the competition and frustration-aggression mechanisms. In addition, the government was very effective and helped limit the motivations of the educated to participate in violence by implementing nondiscriminatory policy (and policy that actually privileged Francophones), regulating social relations and the separatist movement in nonviolent ways, and providing the educated with formal and nonviolent means of addressing grievances. Although these factors did not impede the separatist movement (in fact, the movement strengthened until the mid-1990s), they limited communal grievances, weakened the strength of the frustration-aggression mechanism, and thereby greatly constrained the use of violent methods in pursuit of ethno-nationalism.

GERMANY, EDUCATION, AND ETHNO-NATIONALIST VIOLENCE

Like Canada, contemporary Germany also possesses a resource-rich environment and effective political institutions and has experienced very limited ethnic violence over the past half-century. The most notable examples of ethnic violence pitted neo-Nazis against immigrants. This violence peaked in the early 1990s but even at that time remained quite minor. In the 1920s and 1930s, however, the Nazi ethno-nationalist movement received much greater public support and – by capturing the German state – committed arguably the worst ethno-national atrocities the world has ever experienced. Relative to contemporary Canada and Germany, interwar Germany experienced severe economic hardship and an ineffective and unstable government. A comparative analysis of interwar and contemporary Germany therefore provides insight into whether wealth and governance account for the different levels of ethnic violence in interwar and contemporary Germany.

The Nazi Party and Education

The National Socialist German Workers' Party (NSDAP), better known as the Nazi party, was founded in 1919 and ruled Germany under Hitler from 1933 until his military defeat in 1945. The party was an ultranationalist organization that used brute coercion whenever necessary to pursue its objectives. The most notorious component of its nationalist program was the protection of Aryan racial purity by excluding and eliminating non-Aryans. Although the Nazis preached the inferiority of Roma, Slavs, and others, anti-Semitism was the most important element of exclusionary Nazi nationalism.[6] In pursuit of its racist objectives, the Nazi party committed among the most heinous and systematic killings the world has ever seen. The party directed the killings of between five and six million Jews, an equal number of Russian POWs, approximately two million ethnic Poles, and 200,000 to 500,000 Roma.

Given such a grizzly record, a number of analyses explore the factors that allowed the Nazis to assume power and use the state to pursue official policies of ethnic discrimination and annihilation. These works investigate who voted for the Nazis, who the members of the Nazi party were, and the background of party elites. Some information on education is available, but educational attainment is usually lacking, and the literature focuses on the class and occupation of Nazi supporters. Despite this problem, the education of Nazi supporters can be inferred from data on occupation, as the two are usually strongly related. In fact, this relationship was particularly strong in pre-Nazi Germany, as all education beyond the primary level prepared students for the professions.[7]

---

[6] See Goldhagen 1996; Mosse 1964: 294–311; Wegner 2002; Weiss 2003.
[7] See Jarausch 1985; Paulsen 1906; Ringer 1967; Speier 1986; Weber 1921.

Despite popular claims that the Nazis came to power on the back of the lower middle class (see Lipset 1963: 131–148), there is presently a general consensus that members of all social classes supported the Nazis but that middle- and upper-class Germans were their strongest supporters.[8] As Muhlberger (2003) concludes in a recent analysis of the bases of Nazi support, "It was the support from established social circles, from the elite, which was significantly over-represented in both the membership and – especially – the leadership of the Nazi Movement" (80).

Data on who voted for the Nazis provides some insight into the bases of Nazi support. In an early analysis, Hamilton (1982) finds that electoral support was strongest in upper-class districts, moderate in middle-class districts, and weakest in lower-class districts. In Germany's two largest cities, for instance, the relationship between the percent of a district's population that was *not* working class is very strongly and positively related to support for the Nazis: 0.75 in Berlin and 0.74 in Hamburg (83, 112). Similarly, he ranks each of the cities' districts according to their SES level and their support for the Nazis and finds that the Spearman's r between the two rankings is 0.73 for Berlin and 0.79 for Hamburg (83, 112). In more recent studies using more extensive data, Falter (1988, 1990, 1991) arrives at a similar conclusion, providing evidence that Nazi supporters had mixed backgrounds but that the middle and upper classes gave disproportionate support and that Nazi voters tended to switch allegiance from more conservative parties traditionally serving the educated elites.[9]

If one turns from electoral support to party membership, one finds the same pattern, as the upper class is easily the most overrepresented segment of German society (Kater 1983; Muhlberger 2003). As shown in Figures 7.1 and 7.2, lower-class members were very underrepresented among Nazi Party members in 1923 and among new Nazi Party members in 1933 despite the active efforts of Nazi elites to gain support among the workers. Alternatively, middle-class members were overrepresented, and the upper class – and thereby the most educated members of German society – was heavily overrepresented. In 1923, for example, upper-class membership was 325 percent greater than expected given its share of the population. This situation continued in 1933, as the upper

---

[8] See Brustein 1996; Kater 1983; Mommsen 1996: 318; Muhlberger 1991: 207–208; 2003; Nicholls 2000; Stackelberg 2009; Zeigler 1989. For older studies that arrive at this same conclusion through nonstatistical methods, see Lebovics 1969; Lichtenberger 1937; Mosse 1964.

[9] See also Childers 1983.

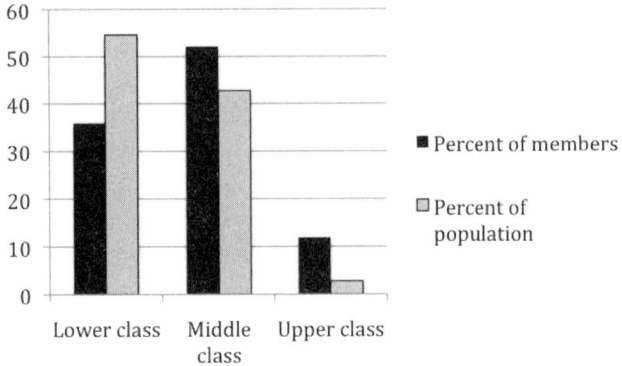

FIGURE 7.1. Class and Nazi Party membership, 1923.

class was overrepresented among new Nazi party members by 335 percent. Considering the more specific occupations that require high levels of education, Nazi membership was very strong among teachers, students, lawyers, engineers, academics, and doctors (Kater 1983: 242–243).

Whereas education is associated with Nazi electoral support and party membership, it was the officials within the party that directed party policy bent on the murder of non-Aryans. Even more than those individuals who voted for the Nazis or who were members of the party, Nazi officials were very well educated (Kater 1983; Muhlberger 2003).

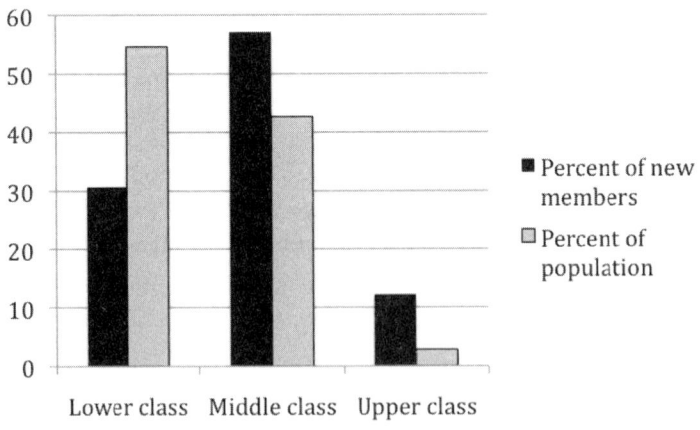

FIGURE 7.2. Class of new Nazi Party members, 1933.

Education and Ethno-Nationalist Conflict

For example, upper-class Germans were overrepresented among gauleiters – the regional heads of the Nazi party – by a factor of 15 both before and after the Nazi's rise to power, and educated middle-class occupations were also well overrepresented among gauleiters, civil servants being the most notable example (Kater 1983: 256–257). Even if one looks at the SS-Totenkopfverbände (SS-TV), the notorious organization running the concentration camps, members were very well educated. One third of the SS-TV came from upper-class backgrounds despite that fact that the upper class comprised only 2.8 percent of the population (Ziegler 1989: 132). In particular, university students, doctors, and academics – among the most educated people in Nazi Germany – were the most overrepresented. Of the remainder of the SS-TV, the majority was middle-class, white-collar workers and therefore relatively well educated.

Notably, data exist on the education level of members of all branches of the SS, and one can therefore not only gain more direct insight into the education of Nazi supporters, but also into the extent to which class and education coincide. As expected given their class position, SS personnel were generally much more educated than the general population, with one quarter of SS members having a university education at a time when only a tiny fraction of the German population completed its secondary education (Zeigler 1989: 115).[10] Similarly, one-third of the officers in the *Einsatzgruppen*, the notorious paramilitary branch charged with the actual implementation of "the final solution," held university degrees (Weiss 2003: 54). Mann (2000) takes a large sample of presumed Nazi war criminals and has similar findings: nearly 40 percent were university graduates.

Indirect evidence about the education levels of Nazis and their supporters can also be gained by analyzing the membership of associations with similar outlooks and concerns as the Nazis. Among the most obvious candidates are the numerous patriotic societies that proliferated throughout pre-Nazi Germany beginning in the 1890s. Like the Nazis, these associations were right-wing and ultranationalist, encouraged German geopolitical expansion and belligerence, had a racial view of the German nation, were anti-Semitic, and focused great attention on purifying and strengthening the German nation (Eley 1980; Mosse 1964: 219–233).

---

[10] In 1930, directly following a period of rapid university expansion, only 2 Germans per 1,000 were enrolled in university. Windolf (1997) finds that the university enrollment rate for men was around 2 percent prior to World War I but fluctuated between 2 percent and 4 percent during the interwar period (4).

Eley (1980) also notes that they purposefully attempted to incorporate nonelites into their ranks to increase the popularity of the nationalist movement, something that the Nazis copied with much greater success (332, 360–361).

Chickering (1984) analyzes the educational background of the local leaders of six of the largest patriotic associations – the Pan-German League, the Colonial Society, the Navy League, the School Association, the Eastern Marches Society, and the Language Association – and finds that they were extremely well educated, with nearly 70 percent having university education and nearly 30 percent possessing doctorates (Chickering 1984: 314).[11] He also analyzes the educational attainment of one patriotic society's long-term activists (the Pan-German League) and finds that the long-term activists were actually better educated than its local leaders, with 76 percent having university education and 34 percent possessing a doctorate (317). Interestingly, Chickering also compares the educational background of patriotic society members with that of its main associational rival – the German Peace Society, a renowned association promoting international peace, democracy, and multiculturalism and claiming several Nobel Laureates among its membership. Although the Peace Society's local leaders were very well educated relative to the German population in general (45 percent had university education and 13.5 percent had a doctorate), their average education levels were only half that of the patriotic societies (Chickering 1984: 314).

A final means of insight into who supported the Nazis involves delineating who assisted Hitler during his rise to power. Several members of the industrial, political, and military elites – all very educated – played instrumental roles in multiple ways: a few elite industrialists willingly financed the Nazi party once it emerged as a viable party, rival politicians invited the Nazis into a power-sharing arrangement, the judiciary allowed the Nazis to disregard the constitution and violently remove all opponents once Hitler had risen to the Chancellorship, and the military and civil service accepted Nazi rule and willingly followed Nazi commands (Geary 1983; Mommsen 1996). Had any one of these elite groups acted differently and refused to collaborate with and support a party that was openly violent, possessed clear autocratic tendencies, and preached ethnic cleansing, it is very likely that the Nazis never would have gained

---

[11] These organizations were all right-wing nationalist organizations that preached military expansion. For more information on them, see Eley 1980.

control of the German state. With tacit or open support from all, however, Hitler was able to successfully rise to power (Mommsen 1996).

The Conservative party, which was made up of Germany's educated elite, provides an example. The party played a particularly important role in Hitler's rise to power by inviting Hitler to become Chancellor under a power-sharing arrangement. Less directly but of equal importance, it helped pave the way for the Nazis through its successful propagation and legitimization of an ultranationalist and anti-Semitic ideology, which it began preaching years before the Nazi party was even founded (Mosse 1964: 237–253; Weiss 1996: 112–127). Given the Conservative party's ultranationalist and anti-Semitic views, it is hardly surprising that the party elites willingly collaborated with the Nazis.

The Causes of Nazi Support among the Educated

In his analysis of the social origins of Nazi Germany, Mommsen (1996) recognizes the privileged backgrounds of Nazi supporters and marvels: "What seems most remarkable in this context was the vulnerability of the educated bourgeoisie to National Socialist propaganda" (344). Although he does not explore why so many of the educated supported the Nazis, numerous works provide insight into this question. The literature commonly points to the socialization, frustration-aggression, competition, and mobilization mechanisms.

The Socialization Mechanism. Several historians describe how education socialized students to support divisive nationalism and anti-Semitism.[12] Indeed, evidence suggests that support for divisive nationalism and anti-Semitism were considerably higher among the nonworking classes, especially among the educated elites (Mosse 1964; Steinmetz 1997: 343–344; Weiss 1996; 2003: 18). This literature suggests that schooling contributed to both nationalism and anti-Semitism through direct socialization in schools and by giving individuals access to a flourishing popular literature on German nationalism, anti-Semitism, and racial hygiene.

After coming to power, the Nazis reformed the educational system to place racial hygiene and anti-Semitism squarely in the curriculum of primary, secondary, and university education; and it is commonly

---

[12] See Jarausch 1982, 1983; Mommsen 1996: 304; Mosse 1964; Steinberg 1977; Weiss 1996.

accepted that educational socialization under the Nazis helped legitimize and encourage the subsequent genocide (Blackburn 1985; Gallagher 2004; Wegner 2002). Indeed, Hitler (1925/1971) transformed education in pursuit of a goal he described years earlier in *Mein Kampf*, writing that the ultimate purpose of education "must be to burn the racial sense and racial feeling into the instinct and the intellect, the heart and brain of youth entrusted to it. No boy or girl must leave school without having been led to an ultimate realization of the necessity and essence of blood purity" (427). Still, Hitler's educational policy cannot be singled out as a reason why the educated supported the Nazis in disproportionate numbers for the simple fact that such Nazi policies were only implemented after the Nazis came to power. If one looks at the pre-Nazi educational system, however, it too socialized students in ways that promoted sympathy and support for Hitler, suggesting that Hitler simply increased the ultranationalist and anti-Semitic content of German education.

Since the unification of Germany, schools were controlled by the government and taught extremely nationalistic curricula that focused on race as the defining element of the German nation.[13] Even this was not sufficient for many German nationalists, however, so various patriotic societies lobbied to increase the nationalist content of the educational system and either rewrote or produced their own textbooks (Eley 1980: 170). In his content analysis of pre-Nazi German textbooks, Weymar (1961) offers evidence that the educational curricula were dripping with right-wing nationalism. Similarly, Weiss (1996) claims that textbooks and lectures at both universities and secondary schools preached and legitimized the doctrine of Aryan racial superiority to such an extent that it gained cliché status (130). He therefore concludes, "We would not be so surprised that a highly educated nation spawned the Nazis if we looked at the reading lists and textbooks in the schools that preceded them" (Weiss 2003: 32). Indeed, Alexander and Parker (1929), who analyzed the German educational system four years before Hitler became Chancellor, described race-based nationalism as a central component of secondary education and gave ominous warnings about the potential consequences:

> The essential aim of the school as it is now conceived, is to fire youth with enthusiasm for service to the race, and to make each generation conscious that its fate is indissolubly linked with the fate of its people – with their joys and sorrows, their successes and failures. Grave danger may lie in this conception of education for it might lead to national arrogance or to imperialistic greed for power. (291)

[13] See Jarausch 1978; Moss 1964; Samuel and Thomas 1949: 71–82; Weiss 1996, 2003.

Mosse (1964) focuses on the volkish curriculum of schools and concludes that socialization in schools contributed to a more specific form of racist nationalism: anti-Semitism. Volkish nationalism was a common and powerful element of the pre-Nazi educational curricula. It claimed that Germans shared a transcendental essence that "was fused to man's innermost nature, and represented the source of his creativity, his depth of feeling, his individuality, and his unity with other members of the Volk" (Mosse 1964: 4). It also focused on Jews as the antithesis of the German volk and effectively dehumanized them: "Not only was the essential nature of the Jews incompatible with the inner character of the German Volk, but their national religion made them an irreconcilable foreign element on German soil" (38).

Besides the formal curricula, schools socialized students to be nationalistic and anti-Semitic in additional ways. For one thing, schools were frequently locations of formal discrimination against Jews. Most notably, fraternities and other educational associations commonly forbid Jews from gaining membership (Mosse 1964: 156, 268). Moreover, many teachers actively harassed and humiliated their Jewish students (Weiss 1996: 130). Confronted with such discrimination and harassment, a Jewish journal began publishing a list of schools that were not openly anti-Semitic (Mosse 1964: 268).

Besides direct socialization at schools, the educated were more acquainted with nationalistic and anti-Semitic views because they devoured a prolific literature on these topics. Such works include the writings of Heinrich von Treitschke, the preeminent nationalist historian whose books lined the shelves of any respectable German family and who coined the expression "the Jews are our misfortune"; Theodor Fritsch, whose *Handbook of Anti-Semitism* appeared in thirty-seven different editions between 1896 and 1914; Julius Langbehn and Paul de Lagarde, both of whom wrote best-selling books berating the Jews as a national menace; and H. S. Chamberlain, who wrote best sellers describing the history of mankind as the struggle between Aryans and Jews. Considering the latter three, Weiss (2003) notes,

Chamberlain, Lagarde, and Langbehn, unlike many anti-Semites in the West, did not write for the ignorant, the uneducated, or the powerless. Their admirers came from the highest ranks of German society, including the Kaiser, his military officers, and the aristocracy. Countless schoolteachers and academics were avid readers, as were members of German student organizations, middle-class youth movements, the Pan German League, the Agrarian Bund, the German Conservative party, and leaders of a variety of anti-Semitic movements. (35)

The Frustration-Aggression and Competition Mechanisms. Similar to Sri Lanka, both the frustration-aggression and competition mechanisms interacted to increase support for the Nazis among the educated. In particular, severe economic depression increased competition between ethnic Germans and Jews, economic hardship and the decline of Germany as an international power promoted immense frustration, and the resulting aggression was directed against Jewish competitors.

Many scholars provide evidence that extreme hardship pushed Germans to support the Nazis. Economic hardship affected all Germans, but there is evidence that its effects on Nazi support depended on class and educational background. Falter (1986), for example, finds that white-collar unemployment was positively related to electoral support of the Nazis, but blue-collar unemployment was negatively related to it, suggesting that economic hardship drove the more educated to support the Nazis but actually drove the less educated away from the party (see also Geary 1987).

Three factors help explain this divergence. First, the educated classes were generally very fearful of socialists and turned to the ideological right in an effort to overcome their economic problems. Alternatively, the less-educated working class was more likely to support the socialists.

Second, the educated were more willing to support radical parties because of their high expectations, which caused them to experience enormous frustration in the face of hardship.[14] Highlighting this view, Weiss (1996) claims that individuals were more likely to support the Nazis when they "failed to maintain their status through educational success" (135). Education appears to have played such an important role in sparking frustration and aggression because it was quite possibly the preeminent means of receiving respect, privilege, and a high-paying job in pre-Nazi Germany.[15] Indeed, *Bildung*, an ideology proclaiming education as the most important source of cultivation and social worth, held a hegemonic position in the German education system (Hahn 1998: 1–18; Jarausch 1982; Ringer 1967). As a consequence, the educated had high expectations and self-confidence, two factors increasing the chances of being frustrated by immobility and acting out against anyone believed to limit their mobility.

---

[14] See Bracher 1970: 157; Jarausch 1985, 1986: 109–110; Kater 1983; Lebovics 1969; Mommsen 1996; Stackelberg 2009: 21–23.

[15] See Jarausch 1982, 1985, 1986; Paulsen 1906; Ringer 1967; Speier 1986: 98; Weber 1921.

In Germany during the 1920s and 1930s, the educated faced both absolute and relative hardship. On an absolute level, the economic crises of the 1920s and 1930s prevented many educated individuals from finding any sort of employment, with the unemployment rate of university graduates hovering between 11 percent and 14 percent (Windolf 1997: 74). Of the remainder, many accepted positions that were well below their educational qualifications. In the late 1920s and early 1930s, for example, 40 percent of university graduates in the postal service and 80 percent of university graduates in the book industry were underemployed (Windolf 1997: 76). Even the educated who were lucky enough to have elite jobs saw their wages decline relative to the less educated because the salaries of the elites were not adjusted to keep pace with the hyperinflation to the same extent as those of the nonelites. Jarausch (1985), for example, finds that the wage ratio of high-level and mid-to-low-level officials in Prussia declined from 5:1 before World War I to only 2:1 in the mid-1920s (385).

The third factor that helps explain why the educated unemployed were disproportionately drawn to the Nazis was heightened economic competition with Jews, which caused them to focus much of their frustration and aggression on Jews. Indeed, Jews held many mid- and high-level positions and were frequently scapegoated for unfairly taking jobs from "real" Germans.[16] As a consequence, the elimination of Jewish competitors was in the economic interests of non-Jewish Germans. Describing anti-Semitism among the middle class, Kater (1984) claims that "the great majority of non-organized, unauthorized and populist actions against the Jews after 1933 originated with 'Aryan' businessmen of the petite bourgeoisie. Their aim was to eradicate the Jewish competition once and for all" (154). Similarly, Jarausch (1985, 1986) describes how Jews were well overrepresented in the professions and how professionals commonly blamed the Jews for their hardships. The Nazis, in turn, emphasized economic elements of anti-Semitism between 1925 and 1933 in an effort to attract societal support, and Brustein (1996) provides evidence that those individuals who supported the Nazis most had occupations that would benefit from the Nazi party's nationalist and anti-Semitic policy. Brustein (2003) also notes that anti-Semitism in Germany was strongly linked to the national economy, with decreases in anti-Semitic sentiments

---

[16] See Brustein 2003: 209; Fritzsche 1998: 157; Jarausch 1985, 1986; Kandel 1935: 5–6, 95–96; Kater 1983: 67–68, 110–111; Speier 1986; Weiss 1996: 134.

during expansionary periods and increases during periods of hardship and heightened competition for jobs (205).

The Mobilization Mechanism. A final general reason for relatively high support for the Nazis among the educated was their greater risk of being mobilized. This point deals directly with the mobilization mechanism, although it is slightly different from the examples presented in previous chapters. Instead of simply exploiting the mobilizational resources of schools and universities, the Nazis co-opted and replaced upper- and middle-class associations and thereby engaged the educated in the Nazi movement relatively easily and rapidly.[17]

The Nazis proved very astute at exploiting diverse associations for support, including professional, patriotic, youth, and student associations. One reason for the Nazi's relative success at this is simply that – more than any other party – they actively strove to organize, infiltrate, and co-opt associations. Such efforts, in turn, were facilitated by the fact that many associations shared the Nazi platform of divisive nationalism, hatred of the Weimar regime, and anti-Semitism, causing some to choose to affiliate themselves with the Nazis without any external prodding (Muhlberger 2003: 57). By providing the Nazis with a place of recruitment and mobilization, associations helped propel Hitler into power on the back of educated and socially active Germans. As Berman (1997) famously recognizes, the Nazi party made a concerted effort to attract middle-class Germans and take over their numerous and varied civil societal associations. Koshar (1990), on the other hand, notes the stronger support for the Nazis among the "educated and well-off classes" and suggests that the Nazis were more dependent on their associations then middle-class associations (39).

Nazi Support among University Students and Medical Doctors

A review of the literature on Nazi Germany therefore suggests that all four of the mechanisms described in Chapter 2 help explain why educated Germans supported the Nazis in such strong numbers. Still, many factors pushed Germans to support the Nazis, and historians recognize that the educated middle and upper class were a diverse group, making it difficult to generalize about specific causes of Nazi support.

---

[17] See Fritzsche 1990: 12, 77–78, 91, 105; Jarausch 1985: 391; Koshar 1990; Mommsen 1996: 343–345; Muhlberger 2003: 57; Speier 1986: 153–155; Weiss 1996: 112–127.

Moreover, past analyses focus on class instead of education level, two characteristics that are strongly related yet distinct. In an effort to address both issues, I now analyze the determinants of Nazi support among two occupations with members who were clearly among the most educated Germans and also among the very strongest supporters of the Nazis: university students and doctors.

University students were among the first Germans to actively support the Nazi party. By 1930, some 30,000 students out of a total university population of 125,000 were members of the National Socialist German Students' Association (Proctor 1988: 69, 158). Such was the power of Nazi students that they were able to dominate student councils and university politics even before Hitler came to power in 1933, and they played an active role in the Nazi party before Hitler's ascendency to the Chancellorship (Steinberg 1977: 72). One reason for their fatal attraction to the Nazis was their rampant anti-Semitism. Along these lines, Hamilton (1982) notes that the "student associations formed what was probably the leading center of anti-Semitism in the entire nation" (349), and Mosse (1964) claims that university students actually criticized Hitler after he became Chancellor for "lacking the correct and proper amount of anti-Semitic feeling" (194).

Doctors also proved very susceptible to the Nazis: 45 percent of doctors joined the Nazi Party, 31 percent joined the National Socialist German Physicians' League, 26 percent joined the storm-troopers (SA), and 7 percent joined the SS (Kater 2002: 80). Notably, all of these membership rates are among the highest – possibly the highest – of any single occupational group (Kater 1989: 59). Indeed, nearly half of all SS members with a university education studied medicine at university, and one study finds that more than half of male medical students between 1933 and 1942 were members of either the SS or SA (Arminger 1984: 25; Ziegler 1989: 104–105, 115–116). In giving this support, some 400 doctors directly participated in crimes against humanity (Kater 1989: 222). Overall, doctors were so active in the Nazi party that Gallagher (1990) claims that "the Nazi administration was as close as the world has come to being a medical state: a government run in accordance with 'doctor's orders'" (191).

Educational socialization appears to have placed both doctors and students at risk of supporting the Nazis. As described previously, schools preached a divisive nationalism that socialized university students in ways that increased their support of the Nazi party (Jarausch 1978, 1982; Mosse 1964). Indeed, the German university was a bastion of nationalism during the Weimar period, and anti-Semitism was an important element of educational socialization, something that helps explain the rampant anti-Semitism found at universities (Jarausch 1982 Mommsen 1996: 304). Doctors, in particular, spent as much of their lives at university as any elite occupational group and were hardly immune to this influence (Kater 1983: 28). In fact, racial hygiene, or eugenics, was an extremely popular subdiscipline within medicine, and Proctor (1988) finds that it "had become a scientific orthodoxy in the German medical community" before the Nazis rose to power (38). Through its racist views or Aryan superiority and Jewish inferiority, several experts find that eugenics gave considerable legitimacy to anti-Semitism and facilitated Nazi recruitment of doctors.[18]

Another reason both doctors and students supported the Nazis in such large numbers was self-interest, as it had the potential to benefit their careers and job prospects. For one thing, Nazi membership opened doors after 1933, creating incentives for professionals to support the party even if they did not support the party's ideals. These incentives were present after the Nazi ascendancy, but different incentives existed even before 1933, which helps explain why both students and doctors were strong supporters of the Nazis before that date. In particular, the Nazi platform of anti-Semitism offered potential economic benefits to non-Jewish students and doctors alike.

Jews held a disproportionate share of positions within both the medical field and among the university student body. In pre-Nazi Prussia, there were nearly sixteen times as many Jews as Protestants attending university on a per-capita basis; throughout Germany, they comprised nearly 6 percent of the university student population in 1914 despite making up only 1 percent of the total population (Jarausch 1984: 312; Kandel 1970: 95–96; Weiss 1996: 134). In addition, Jews held a growing share of professional jobs, which were greatly desired by university students, making competition all the more acute (Mosse 1964: 269). The most notable of these professions was medicine. They constituted 16 percent of German doctors in 1900, and the percentage of Jewish doctors was as high as 40 percent in larger cities (Kater 1987: 35).

In combination with the overrepresentation of Jews in universities and medicine, the very perilous economic position of students and doctors during the 1920s and 1930s promoted powerful ideas of competition with Jews. More than any other group, students were severely

---

[18] See Baumslag 2005: 35–7; Gallagher 2004: 1–2; Kater 1986: 162–164; Kater 1987: 40; Kater 1989: 111–112; Mosse 1964: 302–303; Nicholls 2000: 87; Proctor 1988: 38; Proctor 1994: 39–40; Schmidt 2007: 31–33; Weyers 1998: 153, 169;.

affected by the economic crisis because few companies were making new hires (Giles 1978: 162). As a consequence, the unemployment rate among school leavers was extremely high. The situation was not much better among doctors, many of whom found themselves either unemployed or without enough revenue to support themselves, let alone their families.[19] Whereas the poor economic situation in Germany was an important cause of their hardship, additional factors worsened the lot of doctors. For one, the socialization of medicine limited the wages doctors could earn. In addition, there was a glut of doctors. Indeed, the number of doctors graduating from university increased throughout the 1800s, creating a large surplus by the 1920s and 1930s (Jarausch 1982: 32; Kater 1986: 148). As a consequence, the government set restrictions on and then reduced the number of clients a doctor could have. They also forced recent graduates to complete a three-year, unpaid internship before beginning work as a doctor (Kater 1986: 53; Kater 1989: 12–13). Due to these economic conditions, as many as half of all German doctors were living below the poverty line in 1929 (Weyers 1998: 34). As the economic crisis worsened in the 1930s, a doctors association claimed that this number had risen to 70 percent and that 10 percent of German doctors were starving (Proctor 1988: 156–157; Weyers 1998: 35).

Thus, Jews were overrepresented among doctors and among the university student body, and both doctors and university students faced extremely limited opportunities, causing the elimination of Jews to serve the economic interests of non-Jewish doctors and students. Along these lines, non-Jewish doctors believed Jews were "taking jobs that 'Germans' might have assumed" (Proctor 1988: 145–146). Similarly, students viewed Jews as competitors and sought to remove them. Nazi student leaders, in turn, gained considerable support by demanding the restriction of Jewish student enrollment and the removal of Jewish professionals (Kater 1989: 1969; Mommsen 1996: 304–305).

Although competition appears to have promoted anti-Semitism among students and doctors, it cannot explain two things. First, it provides little insight into why Jews were designated as unworthy competitors. In this way, the mechanism seems influential only when combined with preexisting anti-Semitism, something the socialization mechanism helped promote. Second, competition does not appear to motivate individuals to participate in or support overt violence by itself, as it needs to be combined

---

[19] See Feldman 1993: 532; Gallagher 1990: 191: Kater 1986, 1989; Proctor 1988: 156–157.

with powerful emotions. The frustration-aggression mechanisms, in turn, contribute to just this.

Scholars of Nazi Germany place considerable weight on the frustration-aggression mechanism as a cause of strong Nazi support among students and doctors.[20] Both university students and doctors shared very high expectations for economic mobility and prestige. The common feeling of privilege and merit was the result of the elitist origins of German universities, the elite background of university students and doctors, and the past mobility and status of university students and doctors.[21] Unfortunately, expectations for status and mobility proved difficult, if not impossible, to attain in the 1920s and 1930s because of a rapidly expanding pool of university graduates and doctors and severe economic problems.[22] Given this hardship and their considerable expectations for social mobility, numerous scholars describe how university students became very frustrated with the economic and political order and turned to the Nazis as a means of expressing their discontent and working to overthrow the system.[23] They therefore point to frustration as the primary motivating factor driving students to radicalism. Economic hardship also frustrated doctors immensely, and – like the students – they directed their frustration against the government, who they blamed for socializing medicine and pauperizing doctors. Many doctors also blamed Jews for unfairly stealing their jobs and made or supported emotional appeals to remove them from the medical practice.[24] "In their efforts to oust Jewish colleagues from the profession," writes Kater (1984), "Gentile medical students and doctors stopped short of nothing" (151).

Whereas the socialization, competition, and frustration-aggression mechanisms combined to motivate many students and doctors to support

---

[20] See Giles 1983: 64; Kandel 1970: 95–96; Kater 1983: 27–28; Lebovics 1969: 45; Mosse 1964: 193; Steinberg 1977: 36, 121, 176; Weber 1986: 57.
[21] See Jarausch 1978: 624–625; 1982; Mommsen 1996: 313; Paulsen 1906; Ringer 1967; Speier 1986: 98; Weber 1921.
[22] There was an enormous expansion of the German university system in the late 1800s, and this expansion continued and even accelerated in the 1920s and 1930s (Jarausch 1982). During the first three decades of the twentieth century, for example, university enrollment tripled, creating a much larger pool of educated candidates for jobs (Steinberg 1977: 5, 23). While this increased competition for jobs in its own right, the number of available white-collar jobs declined in absolute numbers because of the severe economic problems of the 1920s and 1930s.
[23] See Giles 1983: 64; Kandel 1970: 95–96; Kater 1983: 27–28; Lebovics 1969: 45; Mosse 1964: 193; Steinberg 1977: 36, 121, 176; Weber 1986: 57.
[24] See Kater 1985: 690; Proctor 1988: 145–146; Proctor 1994: 40; Weiss 1996: 131; Weyers 1998: 35;.

the Nazis, students and doctors also participated in associations that were either co-opted by or formed under the supervision of the Nazi party, and this is a final reason why university students and doctors were overrepresented among Nazi supporters. Considering university students, German universities were full of nationalist associations and fraternities prior to the 1930s, and the Nazi party quickly infiltrated several university organizations both through party efforts and through the independent work of sympathetic students, thereby giving the Nazis a powerful organizational base and making university students the first powerful base of Nazi supporters.[25] This infiltration was facilitated by the nationalistic character of the student body as well as the fact that most student associations were traditionalist, right-leaning, and highly anti-Semitic (Jarausch 1984: 313–314). In turn, a Nazi student organization (the National Socialist German Students' Association) was formed, brought many of the pro-Nazi elements under one roof, and quickly became the dominant political force on German campuses.

Similarly, the Nazis were able to gain the support of doctors relatively easily and rapidly through medical associations. Doctors were very active in civic and professional associations, and the Nazi party used these associations to gain influence over and mobilize doctors (Kater 1989: 20; Mommsen 1996: 344). Most notably, the Nazis encouraged doctors to create a medical association with direct ties to the Nazis – the National Socialist German Physicians' League (NSAB). The NSAB proved very successful and soon eclipsed all other medical associations to become the dominant professional association for doctors. According to Weyers (1998), the NSAB's successful growth depended on Nazis skillfully infiltrated and absorbed "traditional physicians' organizations into the party's own physicians' league" (47). Indeed, Kater (1986) goes so far as to claim that "[t]he NSAB acted as a catalyst for the social and organizational bonding between the Nazi Party and the upper bourgeoisie" (171).

Nazis and Neo-Nazis: Similarities and Differences

In contemporary Germany, the divisive and racist nationalism exploited and popularized by the Nazis continues in the form of neo-Nazi violence. The neo-Nazi movement began to grow in the mid-1980s and peaked

---

[25] See Bracher 1970: 166; Giles 1983: 58–9; Jarausch 1982: 402, 421; Mommsen 1996: 344; Weber 1986: 57–63.

in the early 1990. At its height in 1992, there were more than 2,600 acts of right-wing violence and aggression reported to the police (Kurthen, Bergmann, and Erb 1997: 8). Of these, 9 percent were arson; 12 percent were attacks of individuals; and the remainder included robbery, property damage, and harassment (Kurthen, Bergmann, and Erb 1997: 17). Coinciding with this aggression, support for right-wing parties and extremist organizations expanded and peaked in the early 1990s, with nearly 42,000 Germans joining at least one such organization or party in 1992 (Kurthen, Bergmann, and Erb 1997: 8).

The neo-Nazi movement has many key similarities with the Nazi movement. Most notably, their major political goal is the legalization of the NSDAP (Skrypietz 1994: 135–136). Empirical analyses also find that participants share ethno-cultural and racist ideas of German superiority and are ultranationalist, xenophobic, and anti-Semitic (Schubarth 1997: 144). Neo-Nazis also openly embrace violence as a means of promoting their beliefs. Because of the Nazi annihilation of Jews and, concomitantly, their small numbers in contemporary Germany, Jews have not been the focus of neo-Nazi violence despite the movement's open and active anti-Semitism (Bergmann 1997: 34). Instead, immigrants have been their preferred targets (Anderson 1995: 42).

Although the message and goals of past Nazis and present neo-Nazis are similar, there are important differences between the two. First, and most notably, support for the neo-Nazi movement and acts of violence committed by it are minuscule relative to Nazi-era support and atrocities. Moreover, there is growing evidence that the basis of social support for each movement differed considerably. Several analyses find that neo-Nazi support – measured either by actual involvement in the movement or by anti-Semitic and xenophobic attitudes – is rooted among individuals with lower levels of education.[26] The comparison of the Nazi and neo-Nazi movements therefore raises two questions: Why has support for racist and divisive nationalism diminished in post–World War II Germany? What caused the historic transformation in support for violent ethnonationalism among educated Germans?

The statistical analysis in Chapter 3 and the subsequent case studies all provide evidence that economic hardship promotes ethnic violence, and the economic situation in Germany at the height of the neo-Nazi movement was enormously better than in the 1920s and 1930s. In addition, Germany had emerged as a global economic and political power by

---

[26] See Bergmann 1997: 32; Kurthen 1997: 54; Steinmetz 1997; Weil 1997: 125–127.

the 1990s. As a result, Germans had far fewer individual and national grievances and were therefore less likely to embrace nationalist ideology that scapegoated ethnic or national "others." One notable exception to this is the former East Germany, where individuals faced much more precarious livelihoods prior to and after unification. Not coincidentally, Germans from the former East Germany were also more likely to participate in the neo-Nazi movement.

Along with former East Germans, the segment of the population that was most insecure during the late 1980s and early 1990s was the less-educated lower classes that were increasingly squeezed by growing international competition, the destruction of the "moral economy," and competition with immigrants for employment (Kurthen 1997: 55; Steinmetz 1997). As a consequence of this hardship, Kurthen (1997) claims that the ranks of neo-Nazi supporters were filled with "lower-class members who are threatened by economic and social change" (55). Supporting these claims, education level and unemployment rates are negatively related in Germany. In 2005, for example, the overall German unemployment rate was 12.4 percent, but the rate declined with education level and was only 6.2 percent among individuals with university degrees (Nuñez and Livanos 2010: 478). Moreover, those jobs that were available to the less educated were increasingly nonunionized and low-paid. Notably, despite having low levels of education relative to their peers, the less educated generally have relatively high levels of education relative to their parents. In this way, the composition and motives of the neo-Nazi movement seem to support Bourdieu's (1984) claims that the lower classes will become increasingly frustrated with the expansion of education in affluent Western societies because their education credentials will always be relatively low, thereby trapping the lower classes in marginal positions at the same time that their education has increased their expectations for advancement (144).

Governance also helps explain differences between the Nazi and neo-Nazi movements. Specifically, Germany presently has a very effective government that has gained the respect and confidence of most of the German public (Conradt 1980; Oswald 1999: 102). As a consequence, grievances are usually addressed through formal political channels. Alternatively, the governments of the Weimar Republic lacked public support because they were perceived as imposed by and following the interests of foreign powers and proved highly unstable and dysfunctional (Mommsen 1996). These conditions caused educated Germans to increasingly remove themselves from the formal political arena, to look out for their particular interests, and to address their grievances through informal channels (Berman 1997). It also appears to have pushed many educated Germans to scapegoat the government as a cause of Germany's political crisis and to support extremist elements preaching the need for the overthrow of the Republic and create an autocratic government possessing the power to make Germany great once again. In his comparative analysis of anti-Semitism in Europe between 1870 and the 1930s, Brustein (2003) even finds that acute political instability promoted anti-Semitism by pushing individuals to look for ethnic scapegoats (277–278).

Finally, socialization in German schools since World War II was very different from that occurring both under and before the Nazis. After World War II, educational officials removed divisive nationalism and anti-Semitism from the curricula. In fact, schools – especially at more advanced levels – covered material highly critical of Nazi atrocities and explicitly attempted to decrease prejudice and intolerance and promote democratic values (Brusten 1997; Oswald 1999: 100). A comparative study of political socialization in schools, in turn, found that German teachers actively encouraged students to be open-minded and that German students were extremely strong supporters of democracy (Torney, Oppenheim, and Farnen 1975). Moreover, analyses of the determinants of growing support for democracy and liberal values in Germany point to socialization – including educational socialization – as an important cause (Conradt 1980: 256–258). Thus, the orientation of educational socialization transformed dramatically after the war, and this radical divergence helps explain why the educated were relatively strong supporters of the Nazis and why the less educated were more likely to support the neo-Nazis fifty years later.

8

Education and Ethnic Violence

Conclusions and Implications

Throughout this book, I explore the impact of education on ethnic violence. Using a mixed-methods design that combines cross-national statistics with comparative-historical analysis, I provide consistent evidence that education contributes to ethnic violence. First, the statistical analysis finds that education increases the risk of ethnic violence, especially in environments with ethnic diversity, resource scarcity, and ineffective political institutions. The statistical analysis also offers evidence that the relationship between education and ethnic violence is not driven by the impact of ethnic violence on educational expansion. Next, through a comparative-historical analysis using pattern matching, process tracing, and narrative comparison, I highlight sequences showing that educational expansion precedes ethnic violence, provide evidence that educated individuals commonly organize ethnically violent movements and actively participate in violence, and highlight mechanisms linking education and ethnic violence. The comparative-historical analysis therefore reinforces the findings of the statistical analysis and offers important new insight that helps explain why education is positively related to ethnic violence. All in all, the findings suggest that popular beliefs about the impact of education on peace and tolerance are one-sided and must be reconsidered.

The analysis highlights four mechanisms through which education can contribute to ethnic violence. Through the mechanisms, education shapes both the motivations and capacities of individuals to organize and participate in violent ethnic movements. Through the socialization mechanism, education shapes how people perceive themselves, others, and the appropriateness of relations with ethnic others. The analysis fails to support strong constructivist views suggesting that educational socialization can construct identities from scratch and create intercommunal animosity when none existed previously. Instead, I find that education can strengthen, legitimize, and popularize preexisting views and divisions, and that these effects – while less influential than the strong constructivist position claims – still contribute to ethnic violence. Second, I find that education increases the expectations and assertiveness of individuals. Thus, in environments that offer limited opportunities for the educated to meet their expectations, they are at a heightened risk of frustration and aggression. Third, education can place individuals at a heightened risk of intercommunal competition. Competition is often intense for white-collar jobs and political power, and the educated compete for both. As a consequence, the educated are more likely to use violence as a means of eliminating ethnic rivals. More directly, people commonly compete over access to schools and control of the curriculum. The mobilization mechanism is the fourth and final mechanism linking education and ethnic violence. I find that education provides several resources that individuals commonly use to mobilize ethnic violence.

The importance of each mechanism varies from case to case, but multiple mechanisms contributed to ethnic violence in all cases analyzed in this book. In fact, the comparative-historical analysis provides evidence that all mechanisms commonly interact with and reinforce one another. And because of the multisided impact of education and the synergistic complementarity of the educational mechanisms, this book shows that education can have powerful effects on ethnic violence.

The two educational mechanisms with the greatest interdependence are the frustration-aggression and competition mechanisms. In fact, they are so interrelated in some of the case studies that it is difficult to separate their effects, suggesting that it might be appropriate to combine them into the competition-frustration-aggression mechanism in some situations. For example, the competition mechanism commonly promotes discriminatory acts that seek to advantage one community, and discrimination is a powerful grievance that intensifies the frustration-aggression mechanism. Moreover, the competition mechanism often has difficulty promoting ethnic violence on its own because the costs of collective violence are usually very uncertain and can be enormous. Moreover, violence is a special type of action that seeks to harm or destroy another human being. It therefore has a vengeful and emotional element that is often absent from pure cost-benefit calculation. The frustration-aggression mechanism, however, can supplement the rational-choice-based competition mechanism with emotional grievances that cause actors to overlook unknown risks and act vengefully.

Besides the frustration-aggression and competition mechanisms, other educational mechanisms also complement and reinforce one another. For example, the socialization mechanism strengthens the frustration-aggression mechanism when it heightens ethnic difference and presents other communities in a negative light. In so doing, socialization pushes individuals to focus their frustration and aggression on ethnic communities. In Assam, Cyprus, interwar Germany, the Palestinian territories, and Sri Lanka, for example, educational socialization promoted ethnic-oriented frustration and aggression by portraying rival ethnic communities as nonnatives who either exploited the "true" community or stole their land and jobs. As a consequence, it caused individuals to blame ethnic communities for their frustration. Similarly, the socialization mechanism strengthens the competition mechanism by causing individuals to perceive other ethnic communities as rivals. Thus, anti-Semitism and race-based nationalism in German schools and anti-Tamil curricula in Sri Lanka heightened communal boundaries and thereby helped socialize people to see minorities as competitors. The socialization mechanism also helped remove Tamils and Jews from the moral community, thereby making the elimination of ethnic competitors an acceptable option.

The mobilization mechanism differs from the other three educational mechanisms because it helps mobilize violence instead of motivating it. As a consequence, it does not strengthen the motivational impulse of the socialization, frustration-aggression, and competition mechanisms but provides a means of broad-based violence when such motivation is already present. The mobilization mechanism is therefore most likely to contribute to ethnic violence in the presence of one or more motivational mechanism. This is evident in most of the case studies, as schools provided much of the organization and membership needed to make ethnic movements broad-based whereas the other three educational mechanisms provided much of the motivational thrust for the movements. Alternatively, university students in Burkina Faso and Benin have successfully mobilized protests in several instances, but these protests did not focus on ethnicity because the motivational mechanisms were weak. Similarly, universities provided considerable resources that could have mobilized ethnic violence in Quebec, but the FLQ's efforts to do just this largely failed because the three motivational educational mechanisms were not sufficiently strong to motivate violence among the student body. This lack of motivation helps explain why the enormous mobilizational resources available in wealthy countries with effective political institutions are only rarely used to organize violent movements.

The ultimate impact of the three motivational mechanisms, in turn, greatly depends on the mobilization mechanism. Most importantly, the mobilization mechanism amplifies the impact of the three motivational mechanisms by providing motivated individuals with the mobilizational resources to popularize grievances and organize ethnic movements. Even more, mobilizational resources help put ethnic motivations into action in another way: large demonstrations and movements create safety in numbers and thereby remove common impediments to violence. In these ways, education would likely have a much smaller impact on ethnic violence in the absence of the mobilization mechanism.

Besides finding that the educational mechanisms interact with and reinforce one another, I also provide consistent evidence that the mechanisms are context dependent and most likely to promote ethnic violence in particular environments. Three contextual factors commonly shape the impact of education on ethnic violence: ethnic divisions and antipathy, educational bubbles, and political institutions.

One notable but hardly surprising commonality evident in the case studies of countries that experienced severe ethnic violence is their ethnically divided and antagonistic social environments. Each case's history of ethnic violence, in turn, suggests that this common trait is not coincidental: education interacts with and intensifies the impact of ethnic divisions.

Explicit attempts to socialize students in schools frequently fail but are most successful when the educational message reflects the larger social environment, and the case studies in this book clearly show that the socialization mechanism depends on preexisting intercommunal divisions and antagonisms. In all cases, the elites controlling the educational systems shared ideas of community and intercommunal disfavor and created educational systems that socialized students in ways that intensified both. Their efforts, in turn, succeeded because teachers and students already perceived divisions and held ethnic stereotypes.

The frustration-aggression mechanism also logically depends on ethnic divisions. For example, the frustration and aggression of aggrieved and educated individuals can be directed against any number of actors, but ethnic rivals are common targets in social environments with preexisting divisions and hostilities. Most importantly, collective grievances are powerful sources of frustration and aggression, but they depend on preexisting ethnic identities and are more likely to be present in environments of heightened ethnic disfavor. In particular, ethnic-oriented communal grievances were present among the educated elite in Assam, Cyprus, Weimar/Nazi Germany, the Palestinian territories, and Sri Lanka and were promoted by a belief that the majority community was indigenous and that the minorities were intruders who threatened the well-being of the "true" community.

Notably, the competition mechanism depends on preexisting divisions in a similar fashion: ideas of ethnic difference and disfavor cause people to perceive other communities as rivals and to consider whether the rival community holds a disproportionate share of elite jobs. In interwar Germany, for example, the scapegoating of Jewish competitors would not have occurred without preexisting divisions and antipathy toward Jews.

Finally, the mobilizational resources of education are most likely to coordinate violent ethnic movements when strong and antagonistic ethnic divisions are already present. Most notably, preexisting divisions promoted ethnic-based student associations in nearly all the cases I analyzed in this book, and these associations were among the first and most influential actors mobilizing violent ethnic movements. The LTTE in Sri Lanka offers one notable example, as the organization was formed because of ethnic divisions and in an effort to increase them. Similarly, the AASU would not have become the main vehicle of Assamese chauvinism without preexisting ethnic divisions.

Ethnic divisions and intercommunal antagonisms hardly guarantee that education promotes ethnic violence; they are simply necessary for education to increase the risk of ethnic violence.[1] Quebec and contemporary Germany both show that education does not always exacerbate intercommunal divisions and antagonisms and might even help placate them in some instances. As such, other contextual factors also appear to shape whether the educational mechanisms promote ethnic violence. One of these is educational bubbles.

According to Tambiah (1996), the expansion of education in environments with limited economic opportunities is one of the most important causes of ethno-nationalist violence in South Asia. He writes:

The result [of ambitious literacy and educational programs] has been an explosion of literacy in the context of a population explosion, and the creation of large numbers of educated or semi-educated youths seeking employment in economies

---

[1] Preexisting ethnic divisions are not necessary conditions for education-induced ethnic violence because education has the potential to create ethnic divisions, although this is undoubtedly a very rare situation and one that depends on some sort of preexisting division.

slow in growth and unable to accommodate them. It is this category of unemployed youth in urban sites that has everywhere been the most visible and activist participant in ethnonationalist movements and ethnic riots. (17)

This book strongly supports Tambiah's findings. The statistical analysis in Chapter 3 finds that education is positively related to ethnic violence among nonwealthy countries but unrelated to ethnic violence among wealthy countries. The subsequent case studies, in turn, show that a large pool of educated individuals in an economic environment that offers them few opportunities for mobility increases the risk of ethnic violence by strengthening the frustration-aggression and competition mechanisms.

Considering the frustration-aggression mechanism, several of this book's case studies show that economic hardship increases the risk that the educated have powerful grievances. In particular, the educated commonly feel that they deserve prestigious white-collar jobs because of their educational merit and become very frustrated when they are unable to attain their employment aspirations. This frustration, in turn, increases the likelihood that the educated will participate in ethno-nationalist movements that scapegoat rival ethnic communities. The competition mechanism is equally dependent on the availability of resources, especially white-collar jobs. The cases with high levels of ethnic violence show how limited economic opportunities increase competition and thereby create incentives to eliminate rivals. This competition frequently focuses on ethnic competitors instead of individual competitors and thereby contributes to ethnic violence.

The case studies of Quebec and contemporary Germany also support these conclusions about the impact of educational bubbles on the frustration-aggression and competition mechanisms. Contrary to the cases that experienced high levels of ethnic violence, the unemployment rates of the educated in Quebec and contemporary Germany have been quite low and considerably lower than the rates for the less educated. In fact, unemployment throughout Europe and North America is strongly and negatively related to education level. As such, the abilities of the educated to find appropriate employment are great in wealthy environments, and this limits both frustration and competition for jobs and thereby helps reduce the risk that the educated will participate in ethnic violence. The Quebecois separatist movement, for example, has been overwhelmingly peaceful, and I find that good opportunities for mobility helped weaken both the frustration-aggression and competition mechanisms. Notably, it did not impede the mechanisms, as both were present and pushed many educated Quebecois to support the movement. Yet, because of the real opportunities for economic and social advancement and the negative impact violence would have on such opportunities, the mechanisms only rarely pushed individuals to support violence. Similarly, the educated had good opportunities for advancement in post-reunification Germany and faced little economic competition from ethnic minorities – factors that restrained their support of neo-Nazi violence.

The case studies suggest that the availability of jobs and other economic resources is not the only factor that limits ethnic violence in wealthy environments, however. In addition, wealthy countries commonly possess political institutions that impede ethnic violence, and this is a third contextual factor shaping the impact of education on ethnic violence. This finding coincides with many influential works showing that politics helps explain the intensity of violence. Most notably, Tilly (2003) claims that powerful states and robust democracies are strong deterrents of collective violence, and others point to formal political discrimination as an extremely influential cause of ethnic violence. These works, however, overlook the potential impact of education on ethnic violence and therefore do not consider how education and political institutions interact to affect ethnic violence. The case studies in this book suggest the competition mechanism and – especially – the frustration-aggression mechanism depend on political institutions.

Political institutions are common causes of grievances, although some are much better at limiting the grievances of their citizens. As a consequence, the strength of the frustration-aggression mechanism depends on political institutions. Effective states, for example, are able to limit ethnic violence by stopping it before it gets out of control. Alternatively, states sometimes use coercion against their own populations and thereby instigate violence. States that allow ethnic violence to occur and that use violence against particular ethnic communities, in turn, strengthen the frustration-aggression mechanism by creating new and powerful grievances. For example, the Sinhalese state's lack of effort to curtail anti-Tamil violence in 1983 and its own violence against Tamil separatists aggrieved educated Tamils and promoted their support for the separatist movement. In this way, the state not only failed to limit the motives of the educated to participate in violence, but actually provided them with motives for violent action. Alternatively, the Canadian and Quebec governments did not stomach ethnic violence, and they did not injure or kill members of the separatist movement. Both outcomes, in turn, helped restrain the frustration and aggression of separatists. Similarly, the states in Kerala and contemporary Germany have used their coercive powers to limit ethnic violence and have rarely created grievances that contribute to ethnic violence.

Beside the state's use and regulation of violence, formal political discrimination also affects the strength of the frustration-aggression mechanism and is the second way political institutions interact with education to affect ethnic violence. In Sri Lanka, formal discrimination against a relatively privileged minority sparked enormous frustration, as Tamils expected to use education as a means of upward mobility but found this route abruptly blocked – frustration that, in turn, contributed to a violent separatist movement. Such frustration can also be seen among Bengali Hindus in Assam, who felt their privileged positions severely threatened by pro-Assamese movements and legislation. As a consequence, they organized their own ethnic movements to counter pro-Assamese movements, and the subsequent clash between the rival movements contributed to severe ethnic violence. In Candada, on the other hand, neither the federal government nor the provincial government formally discriminated against educated Francophone Quebecois. In fact, they actually made considerable efforts to accommodate them, and the political institutions therefore did not create grievances that strengthened the frustration-aggression mechanism.

The ability to address grievances through formal channels is the third way through which political institutions shape the frustration-aggression mechanism. In Sri Lanka, Tamil efforts to limit the discrimination that they faced and increase communal autonomy could not be addressed through formal politics, causing many moderates to accept separatist violence as the only way to pursue change. Similarly, Greek Cypriots turned to violence after their efforts to pursue enosis through formal political channels failed. Most notably, EOKA emerged only after the British colonial government refused to recognize the results of a referendum overwhelmingly in favor of enosis. In Weimar Germany, one also sees a population who believed they were incapable of addressing their grievances through politics. This caused many Germans to disengage from the government and pursue radical political change. It also caused people to search for scapegoats, with Jews being a notable example.

The Quebec case study, on the other hand, clearly shows how the ability to address grievances through political channels helps limit the frustration-aggression mechanism. Francophone Quebecers have been able to effectively address their grievances through formal politics for more than a century. As a consequence, violence was not the only means available to them for change, and nonviolent means had considerably lower costs and risks. Kerala parallels Quebec in this instance, as effective government allowed individuals to pursue grievances through the government instead of violence.

Thus, the state's use and regulation of violence, political discrimination, and the ability of the public to address grievances through formal politics are three ways in which political institutions affect ethnic violence. In turn, effective political institutions are more likely to limit ethnic violence because they are better able to contain ethnic violence, provide formal channels for the public to address grievances, and implement policy that is not ethnically discriminatory. In doing so, effective political institutions limit the strength of the frustration-aggression mechanism and thereby weaken the impact of education on ethnic violence.

This book offers evidence that the competition mechanism also depends on political institutions. Political instability, for example, appears to have intensified competition in several cases. Most notably, colonial independence was a very unstable period, and several of the cases – including Cyprus, Assam/India, Nigeria, and Palestine/Israel – experienced ethnic-based mobilization and violence during the independence process, and this violence was promoted, in part, by educated individuals who mobilized their ethnic communities to fight for control of the postcolonial state. In particular, educated politicians mobilized their ethnic constituents in their pursuit of power, and educated ethnic constituents had the most to gain by having their ethnic leaders gain control of the state. Different case studies also provide evidence that ethnic clientelism strengthens the competition mechanism. In both Nigeria and Sri Lanka, for example, ethnicized states that maintained a power base through clientelist networks sparked competition for political power and became the focus of ethno-nationalist violence. This was also the situation in Benin and caused several ethnic-based coups, but political clientelism in Benin did not have the same impact on ethnic violence. One reason for this appears to be the limited competition among the educated for public-sector jobs, as low levels of education allowed nearly all educated individuals to find white-collar employment regardless of their ethnicity. The educated therefore did not have strong incentives to eliminate ethnic rivals.

Although consistent and supported by considerable evidence, these findings must be qualified in different ways given the nature of the analysis. First, and most fundamentally, I neither find nor argue that education is a universal cause of ethnic violence. Instead, the evidence from this book is probabilistic and suggests that education increases the risk of ethnic violence. Also, I neither find nor argue that education is incapable of limiting ethnic violence; it can and does in some instances. Indeed, a major finding of this book is that the impact of education depends on the context and content of education, and both vary greatly throughout the world, thereby causing education to have different effects in different places.

Another point of clarification concerns who acts violently. My case studies provide evidence that educated individuals play influential roles in violent ethnic movements. Yet in no way do I deny that less educated individuals partake in ethnic violence, as they most assuredly do. Even more, I do not find that all or even the majority of the educated participate in ethnic violence. In fact, the episodes of violence that I analyze involved only a minuscule segment of the educated. My analysis provides evidence, however, that education commonly increases one's motivation and capacity to participate in ethnic violence. Indeed, the educated usually play extremely important roles framing and popularizing ethnic grievances, organizing ethnic movements, and mobilizing large numbers of people – both educated and less educated – to participate in ethnic violence. Without the educated playing these roles, it seems likely that ethnic violence would have either been less intense or might not have even occurred in some instances.

Whereas the educated contribute to ethnic violence in diverse ways, my analysis suggests that their greatest impact on ethnic violence comes through the organizations that they control. Indeed, ethno-nationalist organizations played important roles instigating and mobilizing ethnic violence in the case studies, and the educated formed the core of each organization's membership. Ethno-nationalist organizations contributed to ethnic violence in different ways. Most obviously and most directly, organizations provide the mobilization means of broad-based collective violence: they have the mobilizational resources to politicize ethnicity, popularize ethnic grievances, designate ethnic scapegoats, and coordinate activities. In addition, ethnic organizations appear to have helped overcome aversions to violence in different ways: they can promote confidence through strength in numbers, use rituals to heighten emotions, provide resources for and training in violence, and pressure members to pursue communal interests at any cost.

Next, I need to clarify the actual effect education has on ethnic violence. In showing that education depends on different contextual factors, this analysis provides evidence that the impact of education on ethnic violence is primarily indirect. One might therefore conclude that education really does not contribute to ethnic violence; it is simply an intervening variable through which ethnic divisions, resource scarcity, and ineffective political institutions promote violence. Although this line of argument seems plausible, I provide evidence that one cannot discount the impact of education. The case studies show how the socialization, frustration-aggression, and competition mechanisms all intensify the effects of the contextual factors. Most notably, the socialization mechanism disseminates, strengthens, and legitimizes antagonisms; education can be a source of competition and exacerbate frustration; and the mobilization mechanism provides the resources for collective violence between ethnic communities. Through these mechanisms, education intensifies, legitimizes, and mobilizes ethnic divisions and disfavor and thereby increases the risk of severe violence.

My final point of clarification concerns the strength of my findings. This analysis is exploratory and, despite providing consistent evidence, is hardly definitive. Indeed, like nearly all analyses of ethnic violence, this book bases its conclusions on incomplete and imperfect data, and an analysis can only be as good as the data it uses. More research is badly needed to better understand how education affects ethnic violence.

BEYOND ETHNIC VIOLENCE? EDUCATION AND POLITICAL VIOLENCE

There are many types of violence, and scholars find that different types of violence have different dynamics and determinants. As a consequence, one cannot assume that education contributes to other types of violence. In this penultimate section, I briefly apply my findings to violence between a state and a domestic adversary to explore whether the findings can be applied to nonethnic types of violence as well.

Several of the cases analyzed in this book experienced both ethnic violence and political violence, a combination that is relatively common in regions experiencing ethno-nationalist movements. Education, in turn, appears to have contributed to each type of violence. The Sri Lankan case shows how ethnic violence can escalate into an ethnic-based civil war between an ethnic organization fighting for political autonomy and an ethnically dominated state fighting to maintain the boundaries of the national state. The educational mechanisms, in turn, contributed to both ethnic violence and the civil war. The Cypriot case shows how the educational mechanisms contributed to an anticolonial rebellion first and ethnic violence second. Similarly, Palestinian militants commonly target both the Israeli state and Jewish civilians, and the educational mechanisms help explain why Palestinian militants are relatively educated.

Beyond this book, several analyses of rebellions, revolutions, and civil wars find that educated individuals play vital roles organizing and participating in political violence. Goldstone (1991) and Riga (2008), for example, show how education contributed to revolutions through the frustration-aggression, competition, and mobilization mechanisms. Similarly, Wickham-Crowley analyzes all rebellions in Latin America since the 1950s and finds that education was a common determinant. More detailed analyses of Latin American rebellions arrive at similar conclusions. Wimmer's (2002) analysis of the Chiapas movement, for example, clearly highlights how education promoted violence through the frustration-aggression mechanism. He finds that the Mexican government's policy of expanding education among indigenous peoples contributed to the ethno-nationalist movement in Chiapas by increasing their expectations for mobility. These expectations could not be met because of rampant discrimination and limited opportunities and caused great frustration among educated segments of the indigenous population. Such frustration, in turn, helped motivate the educated indigenous elites to mobilize the Zapatista rebellion. Degregori's (1998) analysis of the Shining Path in Peru also notes the impact of education. He finds that the Shining Path was first organized by Peruvian university students and professors and that their mobilizational resources helped them organize a violent revolutionary movement. In addition, the movement's base of support was eventually strongest in Ayacucho, an indigenous region with exceptionally high rates of education but very limited opportunities for mobility. As a consequence, school graduates in Ayacucho joined the movement out of frustration and because the Shining Path offered them a sense of power.

Education also appears to have contributed to more recent political movements in North Africa and the Middle East. Tunisia, the country that kicked off the spree of movements, offers a notable example. On December 17, 2010, Mohamed Bouazizi set himself afire to protest the loss of livelihood and the humiliation he experienced when government officials confiscated his fruit and vegetable stand, and his self-immolation served as a catalyst for the subsequent Tunisian Revolution. The media almost universally reported that Bouazizi was a university graduate who was forced to sell fruits and vegetables illegally to support himself in an environment that offered no opportunities for the educated, but

Bouazizi's sister claims he never completed high school. This misinformation appears to have become so widespread because it struck a chord with many educated youth in Tunisia, a country where nearly half of the unemployed have completed their secondary education and where nearly 40 percent of recent university grads remained unemployed several years after graduation (Solletty 2011; World Bank 2008b: 214). And because of the severe frustration experienced by the educated unemployed and their active involvement in the antigovernment protests, many conclude that educated unemployment was the driving force behind the movement (Carney 2011; Solletty 2011). Notably, the movement proliferated throughout much of the region, and it tended to spread to other countries afflicted by educated unemployment: the percentage of the total unemployed who have completed their secondary education is 80 percent in Egypt and 59 percent in Bahrain (World Bank 2008b: 214).[2] Educational bubbles caused by rapid educational advances and limited opportunities therefore help explain turmoil and antistate violence throughout the region.

The mobilizational resources of the educated also appear to have contributed to political movements in North Africa and the Middle East. Different from the cases analyzed in this book, however, the most important resources used to mobilize the mass movements were Twitter, Facebook, and other recent communication and information technologies. Although not a direct outcome of education, Facebook and Twitter are resources used primarily by educated youth in North Africa and the Middle East because they have the skills – literacy, typing, computer, and the like – and resources needed to use them to organize mass movements.

Although this evidence suggests that education commonly contributes to rebellions, civil wars, and revolutions in many of the same ways that it appears to promote ethnic violence, statistical analyses consistently find that education does not increase the risk of civil war but actually reduces its risk (Dixon 2009; Thyne 2006). Such findings therefore offer evidence that education does not have the same impact on political violence as ethnic violence. Two factors likely explain this empirical discrepancy between the qualitative and quantitative analyses of civil war.

The first concerns the type of statistical analysis. Previous statistical analyses that explore the relationship between education and civil war do not analyze how change in education affects civil violence. Instead, they

---

[2] Data on educated unemployment are unavailable for Libya and Syria, but their levels appear similar to their neighbors.

simply use cross-sectional analysis to see if a country's level of education is related to a country's history of civil war. This book and the findings of other qualitative works on political violence, however, offer evidence that the rapid expansion of education is more influential than the level of education. A focus on the former instead of the latter might therefore offer different results.

The second potential reason for the empirical discrepancy between my findings and the statistical work on civil war is that ethnic violence and civil war are inherently different. Most notably, civil war necessarily involves states, and this difference might be important for two reasons: states are the main providers of education, and education is a powerful proxy for the state.

First, states are the most common providers of education, but some offer considerably more educational opportunities than others. States that offer educational services to their populations are less likely to provoke antistate violence, suggesting that places with high levels of education should have low levels of anti-state violence. Most notably, education is a service valued by people all over the world, so states that offer educational opportunities are less likely to face violent opposition because the population appreciates their educational outlays. Similarly, states commonly provoke antistate violence through predatory practices, but states that offer educational opportunities to their citizens are generally concerned for the well-being of their citizens and are less likely to prey on them and violently attack political demonstrators. Finally, states are able to control the educational system when they offer educations to their citizens and can therefore prevent antistate material from being taught and impede antistate activities from being organized on school premises. Alternatively, when a state does not control the educational system, schools can promote antistate violence through both the socialization and mobilization mechanisms.[3]

Besides limiting opposition to the state, education is an excellent proxy for a state's infrastructural power, fiscal resources, and organizational capacity; and all three allow states to contain antistate violence once it begins. Indeed, because states are the primary providers of education, countries with high levels of educational attainment almost always have states with the fiscal and organizational powers and geographical presence

---

[3] For example, the Taliban – whose name means "students" in Arabic – were largely recruited from Islamic schools (most in Pakistan), and the curricula taught in these schools was not controlled by the Afghan state and encouraged violence against it (Rashid 2000).

needed to provide educations to their citizens. Antistate movements, in turn, require space and resources for oppositional forces to organize and mount an attack against the government and to resist government capture. States with high levels of infrastructural power, resources, and organizational capacity are therefore quite capable of containing antistate movements before they get sufficiently organized to mount a sustained attack on the government (Fearon and Laitin 2003; Goldstone et al. 2000; Goodwin 2001; Herbst 2000). Notably, this book finds that powerful states can also help limit ethnic violence. Yet, whereas state leaders always have the will to stop antistate violence, they commonly lack the will to stop ethnic violence. Indeed, governments are commonly ethnicized and either provoke or simply stand on the sidelines watching ethnic violence. Moreover, ethnic violence commonly occurs on a small scale, rapidly, and with little warning, meaning that officials of even the most effective state might be unable to prevent it and only capable of containing it after considerable violence has already occurred.

Thus, the educational mechanisms appear to contribute to rebellions, civil wars, and revolutions; and this book therefore appears to offer important insight into the determinants of violent political movements. At the same time, violence between a state and a domestic adversary has a different dynamic than ethnic violence because the former necessarily involves the state. States that offer educational opportunities to their citizens are both less likely to instigate antistate violence and more capable of containing it. The impact of education on rebellions, civil wars, and revolutions therefore appears more complex than for ethnic violence.

POLICY IMPLICATIONS

When discussing my findings with others, I commonly receive the same reaction: with different mixtures of concern, surprise, jest, and disdain in their voices, I am asked, "So, you're saying that we should cut education to limit ethnic violence?" For several reasons, my answer to this question is no. In this final section, I review my reasoning and, in so doing, briefly address the policy implications of this study.

A simple reason one cannot conclude that limiting education will reduce ethnic violence is that the insight provided by the analysis is incomplete and uncertain. Additional analysis is therefore needed before concrete policy implications can be made. But even if future studies provide strong evidence supporting my findings, one cannot justify scaling back education over a heightened risk of ethnic violence for the simple fact that a good education has important benefits for both individual and society. Any attempt to restrict education to limit ethnic violence would therefore throw the baby out with the bathwater.

Even if one ignores the multitude of benefits provided by quality education, there are reasons to believe that efforts to limit ethnic violence through educational restrictions would be counterproductive. In most instances, restricting education would simply increase competition for it (unless the supply of education was already greater than demand for it), and heightened competition in an ethnically divided social environment fuels ethnic violence. Such restrictions would also almost certainly disproportionately affect – or be perceived as disproportionately affecting – particular ethnic communities, thereby promoting grievances and increasing intercommunal resentment and antipathy. As the case study of Sri Lanka clearly shows, heightened competition, grievances, and resentment can have deadly consequences; and educational restrictions contributed to all three.

So, if restricting education is not the answer, what policy implications – if any – can be drawn from the book? Overall, this analysis offers evidence that both the content and context of education shape the impact of education on ethnic violence and therefore suggests that policy should focus on adjusting both. Considering educational content, the analysis offers evidence that educational socialization affects ethnic violence and that curricular reforms can therefore help limit ethnic violence. Despite providing evidence that education is more likely to promote intolerance in certain social environments, the analysis does not suggest that educational socialization is incapable of promoting tolerance. On the contrary, the case studies show that curricular reforms are badly needed because many curricula actually increase intercommunal divisions and hostilities instead of minimizing them. I therefore strongly support Sen's (2006) claim that there is a dire need for "school education that expands, rather than reduces, the reach of reasoning" (119). To this, I add that we need schools that create unity and empathy rather than division and hatred.

Next, this analysis highlights how education interacts with its social environment to promote ethnic violence, and policy can also attempt to limit the impact of education by adjusting the social context. For one thing, education promotes ethnic violence in environments experiencing educational bubbles, thereby creating another reason for governments to implement policies that enhance the abilities of individuals to pursue their economic needs. These findings also suggest that the pursuit of development policy that overlooks economic development and simply promotes human development – while having very beneficial effects – might also increase the risk of violence in ethnically divided societies.

This policy prescription is obviously difficult to implement, as increasing economic growth is extremely difficult because one needs to both implement the proper policy and have the institutional capacity to implement it. Moreover, it can create a catch-22 in terms of educational policy. A focus on economic growth, for example, suggests a need to align one's educational system with the economy and to use the educational system to produce only those workers needed for the economy. Such a policy helps limit unemployment among the educated and contributes to economic growth, thereby limiting ethnic violence. At the same time, Nussbaum (2010) notes that making economic growth an imperative of the educational system limits the ability of education to promote critical thinking, heightens competition, and makes mobility the sole reason for education. Because of the latter, students have greater expectations for mobility and are more frustrated when their expectations are not met. By limiting critical thinking skills and increasing competition, in turn, students are more likely to find scapegoats to blame for their hardships and have incentives to eliminate them. In this way, one must be very weary of giving the educational system too much of an economic focus, although planners must consider the fit between the economy and the educational system.

Political institutions are a second contextual factor that helps determine whether education promotes ethnic violence, and I find that the construction of more effective institutions will help limit the impact of education on violence. By effective, I mean political institutions that are capable of implementing difficult policy noncoercively and that are responsive to the population and allow the population to address grievances through formal political channels. Such institutions allow governments to stop violence before it gets out of control, limit state violence against citizens, reduce grievances, and allow people to address their grievances through formal and nonviolent means. Even more, the aforementioned policy recommendations – curricular reform and pro-growth economic reforms – require effective political institutions for their implementation. Policy aimed at strengthening political institutions can therefore help limit ethnic violence, a policy prescription shared by different scholars of collective violence (Fearon and Laitin 2003; Tilly 2003; Wimmer, Cederman, and Min 2009).

Whereas changing the social context might help reduce the risk that education promotes ethnic violence, one must also recognize that policy prescriptions depend on the social context and cannot be implemented in a cookie-cutter fashion. Still, this analysis' focus on mechanisms and scope conditions allows one to apply the findings on a case-by-case basis. As Rueschemeyer (2009) emphasizes, mechanisms are largely overlooked in the policy world but are the best way to apply insight to complex, real-world conditions. And a critical understanding of the four educational mechanisms, the contextual conditions that affect them, and their complementarity allows governments and donors to analyze particular social environments on a case-by-case basis. In so doing, it allows them to minimize the risk that education promotes ethnic violence while maximizing education's considerable potential.

Bibliography

Abernethy, David. 1969. *The Political Dilemma of Popular Education: An African Case*. Stanford: Stanford University Press.

Abernethy, David. 2000. *The Dynamics of Global Dominance: European Overseas Empires, 1415–1980*. New Haven: Yale University Press.

Abramowitz, Isidore et al. 1948. "Letters to the Times: New Palestine Party; Visit of Menachen Begin and Aims of Political Movement Discussed." The New York Times (December 2).

Abu-Amr, Ziad. 1993. "Hamas: A Historical and Political Background." *Journal of Palestine Studies*, 22, 4: 5–19.

Abu-Saad, Ishmael and Duane Champagne. 2006. "Introduction: A Historical Context of Palestinian Arab Education." *American Behavioral Scientist*, 49, 8: 1035–1051.

Ahmad, Rafiq. 1984. *The Assam Massacre 1983: A Documentary Record*. Lahore: Centre for South Asian Studies.

Alexander, Thomas and Beryl Parker. 1929. *The New Education in the German Republic*. New York: John Day Company.

Allardt, Erik. 1981. "Ethnic Mobilization and Minority Resources." *Zeitschrift für Soziologie*, 10: 427–437.

Allen, Chris. 1988. "Benin." *Benin, the Congo, Burkina Faso: Politics, Economics and Society*. New York: Printer Publishers.

Alles, A.C. 1990. *The J.V.P.: 1969–1989*. Colombo: Lake House Investments LTD.

Altbach, Philip. 1968. "Student Politics and Higher Education in India." *Turmoil and Transition: Higher Education and Student Politics in India*. P. Altbach ed. New York: Basic Books, 17–73.

Altbach, Philip. 1989. *Student Political Activism: An International Reference Handbook*. New York: Greenwood Press.

Anabtawi, Samir. 1986. *Palestinian Higher Education in the West Bank and Gaza: A Critical Assessment*. New York: KPI.

Anandhi, S., J. Jeyaranjan, and Rajan Krishnan. 2002. "Work, Caste and Competing Masculinities: Notes from a Tamil Village." *Economic and Political Weekly*, 37, 43: 4397–4406.

Anderson, Benedict. 1983. *Imagined Communities: Reflections on the Origin and Spread of Nationalism*. London: Verso.

Anderson, James. 1995. "The Neo-Nazi Menace in Germany." *Studies in Conflict and Terrorism*, 18, 1: 39–46.

Anderson, Perry. 2008. "The Divisions of Cyprus." *London Review of Books*, 24, 8. Accessed June 22, 2009. www.lrb.co.uk/v30/n08/print/ande01_.html.

Angrist, Joshua. 1995. "The Economic Returns to Schooling in the West Bank and Gaza Strip." *American Economic Review*, 85, 5: 1065–1087.

Ansell, Ben. 2010. *From the Ballot to the Blackboard: The Redistributive Political Economy of Education*. New York: Cambridge University Press.

Anstey, Roger. 1970. "Belgian Rule in the Congo and the Aspirations of the 'Evolué' Class." *Colonialism in Africa, 1870–1960: Volume 2: The History and Politics of Colonialism, 1914–1960*. L. H. Gann and Peter Duignan eds. New York: Cambridge University Press, 194–225.

Arminger, Gerhard. 1984. "Involvement of German Students in NS Organizations Based on the Archive of the Reichsstudentenwerk." *Historical Social Research*, 80: 3–34.

Attanayake, Anula. 2001. *Sri Lanka: Constitutionalism, Youth Protest and Political Violence*. Matera: Ajith Printers.

Balasingham, Anton. 2004. *War and Peace: Armed Struggle and Peace Efforts of Liberation Tigers*. Mitcham: Fairmax Publishing Ltd.

Bandarage, Asoka. 1998. "College Degrees Bear Bitter Fruit in Sri Lanka." *The Chronicle of Higher Education*, 45, 17: B8.

Bannon, Alicia, Edward Miguel, and Daniel Posner. 2004. "Sources of Ethnic Identification in Africa." *Afrobarometer Working Papers* No. 44. Accessed August 10, 2010. http://pdf.usaid.gov/pdf_docs/PNADF393.pdf.

Barham, Richard W. 1982. "Enosis: From Ethnic Communalism to Greek Nationalism in Cyprus, 1878–1955." PhD Dissertation, Columbia University, New York.

Barro, Robert and Jong-Wha Lee. 2000. "International Data on Educational Attainment: Updates and Implications." Center for International Development at Harvard University, Working Paper No. 42. Accessed April 5, 2007. http://www.cid.harvard.edu/ciddata/ciddata.html.

Barry, Tammy, Alice Thompson, Christopher Barry, John Lochman, Kristy Adler, and Kwoneathia Hill. 2007. "The Importance of Narcissism in Predicting Proactive and Reactive Aggression in Moderately to Highly Aggressive Children." *Aggressive Behavior*, 33: 185–197.

Barua, Sandhya. 1978. "Language Problem in Assam." *Social Scientist*, 6, 12: 66–74.

Baruah, Sanjib. 1986. "Immigration, Ethnic Conflict, and Political Turmoil: Assam, 1979–1985." *Asian Survey*, 26, 11: 1184–1206.

Baruah, Sanjib. 1994. "'Ethnic' Conflict as State-Society Struggle: The Poetics and Politics of Assamese Micro-Nationalism." *Modern Asian Studies*, 28, 3: 649–671.

Baruah, Sanjib. 1999. *India Against Itself: Assam and the Politics of Nationality*. Philadelphia: University of Pennsylvania Press.

Basedau, Matthias, and Alexander Stroh. 2009. "Ethnicity and Party Systems in Francophone Sub-Saharan Africa." GIGA Working Paper No. 100. Accessed August 10, 2010. http://repec.giga-hamburg.de/pdf/giga_09_wp100_basedau-stroh.pdf.

Bates, Robert. 1974. "Ethnic Competition and Modernization in Contemporary Africa." *Comparative Political Studies*, 6: 457–484.

Baumeister, Roy. 1996. "Relation of Threatened Egotism to Violence and Aggression: The Dark Side of High Self-Esteem." *Psychological Review*, 103: 5–33.

Baumeister, Roy, Laura Smart, and Joseph Boden. 1996. "Relation of Threatened Egotism to Violence and Aggression: The Dark Side of High Self-Esteem." *Psychological Review*, 103, 1: 5–33.

Baumslag, Naomi. 2005. *Murderous Medicine: Nazi Doctors, Human Experimentation, and Typhus*. Westport: Praeger Publishers.

BBC. 2006. "Most Hamas Ministers Linked to Palestinian Islamic Universities." *BBC Worldwide Monitoring*.

Beck, Nathan and Jonathan Katz. 1995. "What to Do (and Not to Do) with Time-Series Cross-Section Data." *American Political Science Review*, 89: 634–647.

Bédard, Éric. 1998. *Chronique d'une Insurrection Appréhendée: La Crise d'Octobre et le Milieu Universitaire*. Saint-Laurent: Septentrion.

Behiels, Michael. 1985. *Prelude to Quebec's Quiet Revolution: Liberalism versus Neo-Nationalism, 1945–1960*. Montreal: McGill-Queen's University Press.

Belenger, Sarah and Maurice Pinard. 1991. "Ethnic Movements and the Competition Model: Some Missing Links." *American Sociological Review*, 56, 4: 446–457.

Benmelech, Efraim, Claude Berrebi, and Esteban Klor. 2010. "Economic Conditions and the Quality of Suicide Terrorism." NBER Working Paper No. 16320. Accessed January 19, 2010. http://www.nber.org/papers/16320.

Bennett, Scott D. and Christian Davenport. 2003. *Minorities at Risk Project (MARGene v1.0)*. Accessed May 1, 2006. http://www.cidcm.umd.edu/inscr/mar/.

Bergmann, Werner. 1997. "Antisemitism and Xenophobia in Germany since Unification." *Antisemitism and Xenophobia in Germany After Unification*. Hermann Kurthen, Werner Bergmann, and Reiner Erb eds. New York: Oxford University Press, 21–38.

Berman, Bruce J. 1998. "Ethnicity, Patronage, and the African State: the Politics of Uncivil Nationalism." *African Affairs*, 97: 305–341.

Berman, Sherri. 1997. "Civil Society and the Collapse of the Weimar Republic." *World Politics*, 49, 3: 401–429.

Berrebi, Claude. 2007. "Evidence about the Link between Education, Poverty and Terrorism among Palestinians." *Peace Economics, Peace Science and Public Policy*, 13, 1: 1–36.

Bhasin, Avtar Singh. 2004. *India in Sri Lanka: Between Lion and Tiger*. Colombo: Vijitha Yapa Publications.

Bhattacharjee, Arunima De. 2002. "Student Activism in the Barak Valley 1947–73." Baruah Apurba ed. *Student Power in North East India*. New Delhi: Regency Publications, 116–131.
Bhattacharya, A. K. 1982. *The Problem of Educated Unemployment in India*. New Delhi: Meenakshi Prakashan.
Blackburn, Gilmer W. 1985. *Education in the Third Reich: A Study of Race and History in Nazi Textbooks*. Albany: State University of New York Press.
Blalock, Hubert M. 1967. *Toward a Theory of Minority-Group Relations*. New York: Wiley.
Blanton, Robert, David Mason, and Brian Athow. 2001. "Colonial Style and Post-Colonial Ethnic Conflict in Africa." *Journal of Peace Research*, 38: 473–491.
Blau, Peter and Joseph Schwartz. 1984. *Crosscutting Social Circles*. Orlando: Academic Press.
Bobo, Lawrence and Frederick Licari. 1989. "Education and Political Tolerance: Testing the Effects of Cognitive Sophistication and Target Group Affect," *Public Opinion Quarterly* 53: 258–308.
Bonacich, Edna. 1973. "A Theory of Middleman Minorities." *American Sociological Review*, 38: 583–594.
Boren, Mark Edelman. 2001. *Student Resistance: A History of the Unruly Subject*. New York: Routledge.
Boruah, Kaustavmoni. 1980. "'Foreigners' in Assam and Assamese Middle Class." *Social Scientist*, 8, 11: 44–57.
Bossuroy, Thomas. 2006. "Déterminants de l'Identification Ethnique en Afrique de l'Ouest." *Afrique Contemporaine*, 4, 220: 119–136.
Bourdieu, Pierre. 1984. *Distinction: A Social Critique of the Judgement of Taste*. Cambridge, MA: Harvard University Press.
Boyden, Jo and Paul Ryder. 1996. *Implementing the Right to Education in Areas of Armed Conflict*. Oxford: Refugee Studies Centre.
Bozic-Roberson, Agneza. 2004. "Words before the War: Milosevic's Use of Mass Media Band Rhetoric to Provoke Ethnopolitical Conflict in Former Yugoslavia." *East European Quarterly*, 38, 4: 395–409.
Bracher, Karl D. 1970. *The German Dictatorship: The Origins, Structure, and Effects of National Socialism*. New York: Praeger Publishers.
Brady, Henry and David Collier (eds.). 2004. *Rethinking Social Inquiry: Diverse Tools, Shared Standards*. New York: Rowan and Littlefield Publishers.
Brass, Paul. 1997. *Theft of an Idol*. Princeton: Princeton University Press.
Breton, Albert. 1964. "The Economics of Nationalism." *Journal of Political Economy*, 72, 4: 376–386.
Breusch, T. S. and A. R. Pagan. 1979. "A Simple Test for Heteroskedasticity and Random Coefficient Variation." *Econometrica*, 47: 1287–1294.
Brilleau, Alain, François Roubaud, and Constance Torelli. 2004. "L'Emploi, le Chômage et les Conditions d'Activité dans le Principales Agglomérations de Sept Etats Members de l'UEMOA." *DIAL Document de Travail*. Accessed September 10, 2010. www.dial.prd.fr/dial_publications/PDF/Doc_travail/ 2004-06.pdf.

Brown, Nathan. 2001. "Democracy History and the Contest over the Palestinian Curriculum." *Adam Institute*. Accessed August 20, 2009. http://gush-shalom.org/archives/nathan_textbook.pdf.
Brubaker, Rogers and David Laitin. 1998. "Ethnic and Nationalist Violence." *Annual Review of Sociology*, 24: 423–452.
Bruhn, Crista. 2006. "Higher Education as Empowerment: The Case of Palestinian Universities." *American Behavioral Scientist*, 49, 8: 1125–1142.
Brush, Stephen. 1996. "Dynamics of Theory Change in the Social Sciences: Relative Deprivation and Collective Violence." *Journal of Conflict Resolution*, 40, 4: 523–545.
Brustein, William. 1996. *The Logic of Evil: The Social Origins of the Nazi Party, 1925–1933*. New Haven: Yale University Press.
Brustein, William. 2003. *Roots of Hate: Anti-Semitism in Europe before the Holocaust*. Cambridge: Cambridge University Press.
Brusten, Manfred. 1997. "Knowledge, Feelings, and Attitudes of German University Students toward the Holocaust." *Antisemitism and Xenophobia in Germany After Unification*. Hermann Kurthen, Werner Bergmann, and Reiner Erb eds. New York: Oxford University Press, 88–109.
Bryan, Audrey and Frances Vavrus. 2005. "The Promise and Peril of Education: The Teaching of In/Tolerance in an Era of Globalisation." *Globalisation, Societies and Education* 3:183–202.
Bryant, Rebecca. 1998a. "An Education in Honor: Patriotism and Rebellion in Greek Cypriot Schools." *Cyprus and Its People: Nation, Identity, and Experience in an Unimaginable Community, 1955–1997*. Vangelis Calotychos ed. Boulder: Westview Press, 53–68.
Bryant, Rebecca. 1998b. "Educating Ethnicity: On Cultures of Nationalism in Cyprus." PhD Dissertation Department of Anthropology University of Chicago Chicago.
Bryant, Rebecca. 2004. *Imagining the Modern: The Cultures of Nationalism in Cyprus*. New York: I.B. Tauris.
Bryjak, George. 1986. "Collective Violence in India." *Asian Affairs: An American Review*, 13, 2: 35–55.
Burdman, Daphne. 2003. "Education, Indoctrination and Incitement: Palestinian Children on Their Way to Martyrdom." *Terrorism and Political Violence*, 15, 1: 96–123.
Burton, James, Terence Mitchell, and Thomas Lee. 2005. "The Role of Self-Esteem and Social Influences in Aggressive Reactions to Interactional Injustice." *Journal of Business and Psychology*, 20: 131–170.
Bush, Kenneth D. 2003. *The Intra-Group Dimensions of Ethnic Conflict in Sri Lanka: Learning to Read between the Lines*. New York: Palgrave Macmillan.
Bush, Kenneth and Diana Saltarelli. 2000. *The Two Faces of Education in Ethnic Conflict*. Florence: UNICEF Innocenti Research Centre.
Bushman, Brad and Roy Baumeister. 1998. "Threatened Egotism, Narcissism, Self-Esteem, and Direct and Displaced Aggression: Does Self-Love or Self-Hate Lead to Violence." *Journal of Personality and Social Psychology*, 75: 219–229.
Calhoun, Craig. 1993. "Nationalism and Ethnicity." *Annual Review of Sociology*, 19: 211–239.

Callaway, Archibald. 1963. "Unemployment among African School Leavers." *Journal of Modern African Studies*, 1, 3: 351–371.
Campbell, Donald. 1975. "'Degrees of Freedom' and the Case Study." *Comparative Political Studies*, 8: 178–193.
Cardin, Jean-François. 1990. *Comprendre Octobre 1970: Le FLQ, la Crise et le Syndicalisme*. Montreal: Meridien.
Carney, John. 2011. "Here's the Real Story of What's Happening in Tunisia: A Higher Education Bubble." Accessed February 21, 2011. http://www.cnbc.com/id/41237865/Here_s_The_Real_Story_of_What_s_Happening_in_Tunisia_A_Higher_Education_Bubble.
Chakrapani, C. 1995. *Unemployment Stress: A Study of Educated Unemployed*. New Delhi: Vikas Publishing House.
Chandraprema, C. A. 1991. *Sri Lanka: The Years of Terror. The JVP Insurrection 1987–1989*. Colombo: Lake House Bookshop.
Chattopadhyay, Dilipkumar. 1990. *History of the Assamese Movement since 1947*. Calcutta: Minerva Associates.
Chhabra, K. M. L. 1992. *Assam Challenge*. Delhi: Konark Publishers.
Chickering, Roger. 1984. *We Men Who Feel Most German: A Cultural Study of the Pan-German League, 1886–1914*. Boston: Allen & Unwin.
Childers, Thomas. 1983. *The Nazi Voter: The Social Foundations of Fascism in Germany, 1919–1933*. Chapel Hill: University of North Carolina Press.
Clift, Dominique. 1982. *Quebec Nationalism in Crisis*. Montreal: McGill-Queen's University Press.
Cogneau, Denis. 2003. "Colonisation School and Development in Africa: An Empirical Analysis." DIAL Document de Travail. Accessed June 3, 2009. http://www.dial.prd.fr/dial_publications/PDF/Doc_travail/ 2003-01.PDF.
Coleman, William. 1984. *The Independence Movement in Quebec, 1945–1980*. Toronto: University of Toronto Press.
Collier, David, James Mahoney, and Jason Seawright. 2004. "Claiming Too Much: Warnings about Selection Bias." *Rethinking Social Inquiry: Diverse Tools, Shared Standards*. Henry Brady and David Collier eds. New York: Rowman and Littlefield, 85–102.
Colonial Office. 1952. "Makarious, 20.3.52, 'To All Greek Teachers of Cyprus.'" Public Records Office (Kew) CO 926/10.
Colonial Office. 1955. "18.10.55, Cyprus Intelligence Committee: The Nature of EOKA, Its Political Background and Sources of Direction." Public Records Office (Kew) CO926/455.
Colonial Office 1956a. "Note from Director of Education." Public Records Office (Kew) CO 926/157.
Colonial Office. 1956b. "PEKA (Political Committee of the Cyprus Struggle) [associated with EOKA]Proclamation distributed in Yialousa 29.9.56." Public Records Office (Kew) CO 926/166.
Colonial Office. 1956c. "13.12.1956, 'From Cyprus.'" Public Records Office (Kew) CO 926/454.
Colonial Office. 1959. "19.1.59, EOKA Intimidation of Pupils in Inter-communal Schools." Public Records Office (Kew) CO 926/589.

Conradt, David. 1980. "Changing German Political Culture." *The Civic Culture Revisited*. Gabriel Almond and Sidney Verba eds. Toronto: Little, Brown and Company.

Cook, Ramsay. 1967. "French Canadian Interpretations of Canadian History." *Journal of Canadian Studies*, 2: 3–17.

Copeaux, Etienne. 2002. "Otherness in the Turkish Historical Discourse: General Considerations." *Clio in the Balkans: The Politics of History Education*. Christina Koulouri ed. Thessaloniki: Center for Democracy and Reconciliation in Southeast Europe, 397–405.

Copeaux, Etienne and Claire Mauss-Copeaux. 2005. *Taksim! Chypre dévisée, 1964–2005*. Lyon: Aedelsa Éditions.

Corea, J. C. A. 1968. "One Hundred Years of Education in Ceylon." *Modern Asian Studies*, 3, 2: 151–175.

Coulby, David and Crispin Jones. 2001. *Education and Warfare in Europe*. London: Ashgate.

Crawshaw, Nancy. 1978. *The Cyprus Revolt: An Account of the Struggle for Union with Greece*. Boston: George Allen & Unwin.

Cronin, Peter. 2004. "Developing National Unity by Educating Students about Their Enemies: The Case of Israel and Palestine." *Education in Emergencies and Post-Conflict Situations: Problems, Responses and Possibilities*. Dana Burde ed. New York: Society for International Education.

Crouzet, François. 1973. *Le Conflit de Chypre, 1946–1959*. Bruxelles: Etablissements Emile Bruylant.

Cuneo, Carl and James Curtis. 1974. "Quebec Separatism: An Analysis of Determinants within Social-Class Levels." *Canadian Review of Sociology*, 11, 1: 1–29.

Curle, Adam. 1973. *Educational Problems of Developing Societies: With Case Studies of Ghana, Pakistan, and Nigeria*. New York: Praeger Publishers.

Das, Amiya Kumar. 1982. *Assam's Agony: A Socio-Economic and Political Analysis*. New Delhi: Lancers Publishers.

Das, Bhakta. 1992. *Unemployment in Assam: An Account of Human Error*. New Delhi: Cosmo Publications.

Das, Maitreyi Bordia. 2002. "Employment and Social Inequality in India: How Much Do Caste and Religion Matter?" PhD dissertation, University of Maryland, College Park.

Das, Maitreyi Bordia. 2008. *Minority Status and Labour Market Outcomes: Does India Have Minority Enclaves?* World Bank Policy Research Working Paper Series.

Das, Samir Kumar. 2002. "On the Question of Students' Hegemony: A Study of the Assam Movement (1979–1985)." *Student Power in North East India*. Baruah Apurba ed. New Delhi: Regency Publications, 132–148.

Dasgupta, Jyotirindra. 1997. "Community, Authenticity, and Autonomy: Insurgence and Institutional Development in India's Northeast." *Journal of Asian Studies*, 56, 2: 345–370.

Davies, Lynn. 2004. *Education and Conflict: Complexity and Chaos*. New York: Routledge Falmer.

Debroy, Bibek, Laveesh Bhandari, and Nilanjan Banik. 2003. "How Are the States Doing?" New Delhi: Rajiv Gandhi Institute for Contemporary Studies.

Degregori, Carlos Ivan. 1998. "Harvesting Storms: Peasant *Rondas* and the Defeat of Sendero Luminoso in Ayacucho." *Shining and Other Paths: War and Society in Peru, 1980–1995*. Steve Stern ed. Durham: Duke University Press, 128–157.

Deka, Meeta. 1996. *Student Movements in Assam*. New Delhi: Vikas Publishing House.

Demetriou, Chares. 2007. "Political Violence and Legitimation: The Episode of Colonial Cyprus." *Qualitative Sociology*, 30: 171–193.

de Silva, Chandra Richard. 1984a. "Sinhala-Tamil Ethnic Rivalry: The Background." *From Independence to Statehood: Managing Ethnic Conflict in Five African and Asian States*. R. Goldmann and A. Jeyaratnam Wilson eds. London: Frances Pinter Publishers, 111–124.

de Silva, Chandra Richard. 1984b. "Sinhala-Tamil Relations and Education in Sri Lanka: The University Admissions Issue – The First Phase, 1971–7." *From Independence to Statehood: Managing Ethnic Conflict in Five African and Asian States*. R. Goldmann and A. Jeyaratnam Wilson eds. London: Frances Pinter Publishers, 125–146.

de Silva, Chandra Richard. 1997. *Sri Lanka – A History*. New Delhi: Vikas Publishing House PVT Ltd.

de Silva, K. M. 1984. "University Admissions and Ethnic Tension in Sri Lanka, 1977–82." *From Independence to Statehood: Managing Ethnic Conflict in Five African and Asian States*. R. Goldmann, and A. Jeyaratnam Wilson eds. London: Frances Pinter Publishers, 97–110.

de Silva, K. M. 1986. *Managing Ethnic Tensions in Multi-Ethnic Societies: Sir Lanka 1880–1985*. New York: University Press of America.

de Silva, K. M. 1995. "The University of Peradeniya 1987–94: From Deep Crisis to Modest Recovery." *The University System of Sri Lanka: Vision and Reality*. K. M. de Silva and G. H. Peiris eds. Kandy: International Centre for Ethnic Studies, 54–73.

de Silva, K. M. 2007. *Sri Lanka's Troubled Inheritance*. Kandy: International Centre for Ethnic Studies.

Des Forges, Alison. 1969. "Kings without Crowns: The White Fathers in Ruanda." *Eastern African History, Volume III*. Daniel McCall, Norman Bennett, and Jeffrey Butler eds. New York: Praeger Publishers.

Dharmadasa, K. N. O. 1972. "Language and Sinhalese Nationalism: The Career of Munidasa Cumaratunga." *Modern Ceylon Studies – A Journal of the Social Sciences*, 3, 2: 125–143.

Dharmadasa, K. N. O. 1992. *Language, Religion, and Ethnic Assertiveness – The Growth of Sinhalese Nationalism in Sri Lanka*. Ann Arbor: University of Michigan Press.

Diamond, Larry. 1983. "Class, Ethnicity, and the Democratic State: Nigeria, 1950–1966." *Comparative Studies in Society and History*, 25: 457–489.

Dickovick, James. 2008. "Legacies of Leftism: Ideology, Ethnicity, and Democracy in Benin, Ghana, and Mali. *Third World Quarterly*, 29, 6: 1119–1137.

Dixon, Jeffrey. 2009. "What Causes Civil Wars? Integrating Quantitative Research Findings." *International Studies Review*, 11, 4: 707–735.

Dollard, John. 1939. *Frustration and Aggression*. New Haven: Yale University Press.

Dufour, Desmond, and Michel Amyot. 1972. "Evolution de la Scolarisation de la Population d'Âge Scolaire du Québec, 1961–1981." *L'Actualité Économique*, 48: 487–502.

Durkheim, Émile. 1934. *L'Éducation Morale*. Paris: Librarie Felix Alcan.

Durkheim, Émile. 1973. *Éducation et Sociologie*. Paris: Presses Universitaires de France.

Education Advisory Committee. 1966. *Cyprus School History Textbooks: A Study in Education for International Misunderstanding*. Sussex: Oliver Burridge.

Edwards, Bob and John McCarthy. 2004. "Resources and Social Movement Mobilization." *The Blackwell Companion to Social Movements*, D. Snow, S. Soule, and H. Kriesi eds. Malden: Blackwell Publishing, 116–152.

Eley, Geoff. 1980. *Reshaping the German Right: Radical Nationalism and Political Change after Bismarck*. New Haven: Yale University Press.

Emmerij, Louis. 1972. "Some Reflections on the Link between Education and Unemployment." *Higher Education*, 1, 4: 483–495.

Englebert, Pierre. 1998. *Burkina Faso: Unsteady Statehood in West Africa*. Boulder: Westview Press.

Fair, Christine. 2008. *The Madrassah Challenge: Militancy and Religious Education in Pakistan*. Washington, DC: United States Institute of Peace Press.

Falleti, Tulia and Julia Lynch. 2009. "Context and Causal Mechanisms in Political Analysis." *Comparative Political Studies*, 42: 1143–1166.

Falter, Jurgen. 1986. "Unemployment and Left-Wing Radicalism in Weimar Germany, 1930–33." *Unemployment and the Great Depression in Weimar Germany*. P. D. Stachura ed. Basingstoke: Macmillan, 209–225.

Falter, Jurgen. 1988. "The Economic Crisis of the 1930s and the Nazi Vote." *Journal of Interdisciplinary History*, 19, 1: 55–85.

Falter, Jurgen. 1990. "The Two Hindenburg Elections of 1925 and 1932: A Total Reversal of Voter Coalitions." *Central European History*, 23, 2/3: 225–241.

Falter, Jurgen. 1991. *Hitlers Wähler*. Munich: C. H. Beck.

Farmer, B. H. 1963. *Ceylon: A Divided Nation*. London: Oxford University Press.

Fearon, James. 2003. "Ethnic and Cultural Diversity by Country." *Journal of Economic Growth*, 8: 195–222.

Fearon, James and David Laitin. 2000. "Violence and the Social Construction of Ethnic Identity." *International Organization*, 54, 4: 845–877.

Fearon, James and David Laitin. 2003. "Ethnicity, Insurgency and Civil War." *American Political Science Review*, 97, 1: 75–90.

Feldman, Gerald. 1993. *The Great Disorder: Politics Economic, and Society in the German Inflation, 1914–1924*. New York: Oxford University Press.

Fernando, Tissa. 1979. "Aspects of Social Stratification." *Modern Sri Lanka: A Society in Transition*. T. Fernando and R. Kearney eds. Syracuse: Syracuse University Press, 29–42.

Foley, Charles ed. 1965. *The Memoirs of General Grivas*. New York: Frederick A. Praeger.
Foley, Charles and W. I. Scobie. 1975. *The Struggle for Cyprus*. Stanford: Hoover Institution Press.
Foreign Office. 1955. "Cyprus Intelligence Committee: Security Implications of the System of Education in Cyprus." Public Records Office (Kew) FO 371/117665.
Foreign Office. 1956a. "Background Statement on Secondary Education Policy." Public Records Office (Kew) FO 371/123949.
Foreign Office. 1956b. "Translations from Greek Elementary School Readers Used in Greek Orthodox Elementary Schools in Cyprus, 22. 11.1956." Public Records Office (Kew) FO 371/123949.
Foreign Office. 1957. "Education in Cyprus." Public Records Office (Kew) FO 371/130161.
Fortin, Pierre. 1984. "Le Chômage de Jeunes au Québec: Aggravation et Concentration, 1966–1982." *Industrial Relations*, 39, 3: 419–448.
Friedman, Willa, Michael Kremer, Edward Miguel, and Rebecca Thornton. 2011. "Education as Liberation?" NBER Working Paper No. 16939. Accessed July 7, 2011. http://www.nber.org/papers/w16939.
Fritzsche, Peter. 1990. *Rehearsals for Fascism: Populism and Political Mobilization in Weimar Germany*. Oxford: Oxford University Press.
Fritzsche, Peter. 1998. *Germans into Nazis*. Cambridge, MA: Harvard University Press.
Gaasholt, Oystein and Lise Togeby. 1995. "Interethnic Tolerance, Education, and Political Orientation: Evidence from Denmark," *Political Behavior* 17: 265–285.
Gaborieau, Marc. 1985. "From Al-Beruni to Jinnah: Idiom, Ritual and Ideology of the Hindu-Muslim Confrontation in South Asia." *Anthropology Today*, 1, 3: 7–14.
Gagnon, Alain and Mary Beth Montcalm. 1990. *Quebec Beyond the Quiet Revolution*. Toronto: Nelson Canada.
Gallagher, Hugh Gregory. 1990. *By Trust Betrayed: Patients, Physicians, and the License to Kill in the Third Reich*. New York: Henry Holt and Company.
Gallagher, Tony. 2004. *Education in Divided Societies*. New York: Palgrave Macmillan.
Gamson, William. 1987. "Introduction." *Social Movements in an Organizational Society*. M. Zald and J. McCarthy eds. New Brunswick: Transaction, 1–7.
Gasanabo, Jean-Damascene. 2006. "School History and mechanisms for the Construction of Exclusive Identities: The Case of Rwanda from 1962 to 1994." *Textbooks and Quality Learning for All: Some Lessons Learned from International Experiences*. C. Braslavsky ed. New York: UNESCO, 365–404.
Geary, Dick. 1983. "The Industrial Elite and the Nazis in the Weimar Republic." *The Nazi Machtergreifung*. Peter Stachura ed. Boston: George Allen and Unwin, 85–100.
Geary, Dick. 1987. "Unemployment and Working Class Solidarity: The German Experience, 1929–33." *The German Unemployed: Experiences and Consequences of Mass Unemployment from the Weimar Republic to the Third Reich*. R. J. Evans and D. Geary, eEds. London: Croom Helm, 261–280.

Geddes, Barbara. 1990. "How the Cases You Choose Affect the Answers You Get: Selection Bias in Comparative Politics." *Political Analysis*, 2: 131–150.
Geertz, Clifford. 1973. *The Interpretation of Cultures*. New York: Basic Books.
Gellner, Ernest. 1983. *Nations and Nationalism*. Ithaca: Cornell University Press.
George, Alexander and Andrew Bennett. 2005. *Case Studies and Theory Development in the Social Sciences*. Cambridge, MA: MIT Press.
Gifford, Prosser, and Timothy Weiskel. 1971. "African Education in Colonial Context: French and British Styles." *France and Britain in Africa: Imperial Rivalry and Colonial Rule*. Prosser Gifford and W. M. Roger Louis eds. New Haven: Yale University Press, 663–711.
Giles, Geoffrey. 1978. "The Rise of the National Socialist Students' Association and the Failure of Political Education in the Third Reich." *The Shaping of the Nazi State*. P. Stachura ed. New York: Barnes & Noble Books.
Giles, Geoffrey. 1983. "National Socialism and the Educated Elite in the Weimar Republic." *The Nazi Machtergreifung*. Peter Stachura ed. Boston: George Allen and Unwin, 49–67.
Gohain, Hiren. 1973. "Origins of the Assamese Middle Class." *Social Scientist*, 2, 1: 11–26.
Goldberg, Brett, Mark Serper, Michelle Sheets, Daniel Beech, Charles Dill, and Kristine Duffy. 2007. "Predictors of Aggression on the Psychiatric Inpatient Service: Self-Esteem, Narcissism, and Theory of Mind." *The Journal of Nervous and Mental Disease*, 195, 5: 436–442.
Goldhagen, Daniel. 1996. *Hitler's Willing Executioners: Ordinary Germans and the Holocaust*. New York: Vintage Books.
Goldstone, Jack. 1991. *Revolution and Rebellion in the Early Modern World*. Berkeley: University of California Press.
Goldstone, Jack. 1997. "Population Growth and Revolutionary Crises." *Theorizing Revolutions*. John Foran ed. New York: Routledge, 102–120.
Goldstone, Jack, Ted Gurr, Barbara Harff, Marc Levy, Monty Marshall, Robert Bates, David Epstein, Colin Kahl, Pamela Surko, John Ulfelder, and Alan Unger. 2000. "State Failure Task Force Report: Phase III Findings." Accessed October 14, 2005. http://globalpolicy.gmu.edu/pitf/SFTF%20Phase%20III%20Report%20Final.pdf.
Goodwin, Jeff. 2001. *No Other Way Out: States and Revolutionary Movements, 1945–1991*. New York: Cambridge University Press.
Goswami, Sandhya. 1997. *Language Politics in Assam*. Delhi: Ajanta Publications.
Gour, P. N. 1984. *Student Unrest: In the Universities of Bihar*. Patna: Library Publications.
Government of Assam. 2003. *Assam Human Development Report 2003*. Guwahati: Planning and Development Department.
Government of India. 2006. *Social, Economic and Educational Status of the Muslim Community of India*. New Delhi: Government of India.
Government of Quebec. 2010. "The Labour Market: Integration of Graduates Into the Labour Market." Accessed March 24, 2010. http://www.mels.gouv.qc.ca/STAT/indic01/indic01A/ia01603.PDF.
Graham-Brown, Sarah. 1994. "The Role of the Curriculum." *Education Rights and Minorities*. Minority Rights Group ed. Manchester: Manchester Free Press.

The Guardian. 1990. " Paralyzed by Student Jobs Riots." New Delhi.
Guha, Amalendu. 1980. "Little Nationalism Turned Chauvinist: Assam's Anti-Foreigner Upsurge, 1979–80." *Economic and Political Weekly*, 15, 41/43: 1699–1720.
Guindon, Hubert. 1964. "Social Unrest, Social Class, and Quebec's Bureaucratic Revolution." *Queen's Quarterly*, 71: 150–162.
Gunaratna, Rohan. 1998. *Sri Lanka's Ethnic Crisis and National Security.* Colombo: South Asian Network on Conflict Research.
Guntzel, Ralph. 2000. "'Rapprocher les Lieux du Pouvoire': The Quebec Labour Movement and Quebec Sovereigntism, 1960–2000." *Labour/Le Travail*, 46: 369–395.
Gurr, Ted. 1970. *Why Men Rebel.* Princeton: Princeton University Press.
Gurr, Ted. 1993. *Minorities at Risk: A Global View of Ethnopolitical Conflict.* Washington, DC: United States Institute of Peace Press.
Gurr, Ted. 2000. *People versus States: Minorities at Risk in the New Century.* Washington, DC: United States Institute for Peace Press.
Guruge, Ananda. 1965. *Return to Righteousness: A Collection of Speeches, Essays and Letters of the Anagarike Dharmapala.* Colombo: Ministry of Education and Cultural Affairs.
Hagendoorn, Louk and Shevrin Nekuee eds. 1999. *Education and Racism: A Cross National Inventory of Positive Effects of Education on Ethnic Tolerance.* Aldershot: Ashgate.
Hahn, H. J. 1998. *Education and Society in Germany.* New York: Berg.
Halliburton, Murphy. 1995. "Suicide: A Paradox of Development in Kerala." *Economic and Political Weekly*, 33, 36/37: 2341–2345.
Hamilton, Richard. 1982. *Who Voted for Hitler?* Princeton: Princeton University Press.
Hamilton, Richard and Maurice Pinard. 1976. "The Bases of Parti Quebecois Support in Recent Quebec Elections." *Canadian Journal of Political Science*, 9, 1: 3–26.
Hannan, Michael. 1979. "The Dynamics of Ethnic Boundaries in Modern States." *National Development and the World System: Educational, Economic and Political Change, 1959–1970.* John W. Meyer and Michael Hannan eds. Chicago: University of Chicago Press.
Hansen, Thomas B. 1996. "Recuperating Masculinity: Hindu Nationalism, Violence and the Exorcism of the Muslim 'Other.'" *Critique of Anthropology*, 16, 2: 137–172.
Harber, Clive. 1996. "Educational Violence and Education for Peace in Africa." *Peabody Journal of Education*, 71, 3: 151–169.
Harding, John. 1956a. "1956.2.9, From Cyprus, Field Marshal J. Harding." Public Records Office (Kew) FO 371/123949.
Harding, John. 1956b. "Cyprus Ref: S.206/54/II." Public Records Office (Kew) CO 926/166.
Harries, Patrick. 1991. "Exclusion, Classification and Internal Colonialism: The Emergence of Ethnicity among the Tsonga-Speakers of South Afria." *The Creation of Tribalism in Southern Africa.* LeRoy Vail ed. Berkeley: University of California Press, 82–117.

Hausman, J. A. 1978. "Specification Tests in Econometrics." *Econometrica*, 46: 1251–1271.
Hazary, Subas Chandra. 1987. *Student Politics in India*. New Delhi: Ashish Publishing House.
Hechter, Michael. 1975. *Internal Colonialism: The Celtic Fringe in British National Development, 1536–1966*. Berkeley: University of California Press.
Hechter, Michael. 2000. *Containing Nationalism*. New York: Oxford University Press.
Hedstrom, Peter and Richard Swedberg eds. 1998. *Social Mechanisms: An Analytical Approach to Social Theory*. New York: Cambridge University Press.
Heintzman, Ralph. 1983. "The Political Culture of Quebec, 1840–1960." *Canadian Journal of Political Science*, 16, 1: 3–59.
Heller, Patrick. 1999. *The Labor of Development: Workers and the Transformation of Capitalism in Kerala, India*. Ithaca: Cornell University Press.
Hellmann-Rajanayagam, Dagmar. 1986. "Educational Standards and Social Distance: Two Tamil Minorities in Sri Lanka." *Education and the Integration of Ethnic Minorities*. Dietmar Rothermund and John Simon eds. London: Frances Pinter, 129–150.
Hellmann-Rajanayagam, Dagmar. 1994. "Tamils and the Meaning of History." *The Sri Lankan Tamils – Ethnicity and Identity*. C. Manogaran and Bryan Pfaffenberger eds. Boulder: Westview Press.
Herbst, Jeffrey. 2000. *States and Power in Africa: Comparative Lessons in Authority and Control*. Princeton: Princeton University Press.
Heston, Alan, Robert Summers, and Bettina Aten. 2002. "Penn World Table Version 6.1." Center for International Comparisons at the University of Pennsylvania (CICUP). Accessed May 1, 2005. http://pwt.econ.upenn.edu/.
Heston, Alan, Robert Summers, and Bettina Aten. 2009. "Penn World Table Version 6.3." Center for International Comparisons of Production Income and Prices. University of Pennsylvania. Accessed June 8, 2010. http://pwt.econ.upenn.edu/.
Hettige, S. T. 1991. "Human Resources Development in Sri Lanka: A Sociological Perspective." *Sri Lanka Journal of Social Sciences*, 14: 49–64.
Hewitt, Christopher. 1977. "Majorities and Minorities: A Comparative Survey of Ethnic Violence." *Annals of the American Academy of Political and Social Sciences*, 433: 150–160.
Hill, George. 1952. *A History of Cyprus* (Vol. IV). Cambridge: Cambridge University Press.
Hitler Adolf. 1925/1971. *Mein Kampf*. New York: Houghton Mifflin.
Hodgetts, A. B. 1968. *What Culture, What Heritage? A Study of Civic Education in Canada*. Toronto: Ontario Institute for Studies in Education.
Holland, Robert. 1998. *Britain and the Revolt in Cyprus 1954–1959*. Oxford: Clarendon Press.
Hornung, Carlton, B. Claire McCullough, and Taichi Sugimoto. 1981. "Status Relationships in Marriage: Risk Factors in Spouse Abuse." *Journal of Marriage and the Family*, 43: 675–692.

Horowitz, Donald. 1985. *Ethnic Groups in Conflict*. Berkeley: University of California Press.
Horowitz, Donald. 2001. *The Deadly Ethnic Riot*. New York: Oxford University Press.
Houngnikpo, Mathurin. 2001. *Determinants of Democratization in Africa: A Comparative Study of Benin and Togo*. New York: University Press of America.
Hsiao, Cheng. 2003. *Analysis of Panel Data*. New York: Cambridge University Press.
Huber, Evelyne and John Stephens. 2001. *Development and Crisis of the Welfare State: Parties and Policies in Global Markets*. Chicago: University of Chicago Press.
Huntington, Samuel. 1968. *Political Order in Changing Societies*. New Haven: Yale University Press.
Hussain, Monirul. 1993. *The Assam Movement: Class, Ideology, and Identity*. Delhi: Manak Publications.
Hussain, Zahid. 2007. *Frontline Pakistan: The Struggle with Militant Islam*. New York: Columbia University Press.
Ichilov, Orit. 2004. *Political Learning and Citizenship Education under Conflict: The Political Socialization of Israeli and Palestinian Youngsters*. New York: Routledge.
IndiaStat. 2010. Accessed 23 June, 2010. http://www.indiastat.com.
Intelligence and Terrorism Information Center. 2004. "The Suicide Bombers and Martyr Culture at Al-Najah University in Nablus." Accessed August 20, 2009. http://www.terrorism-info.org.il/site/html/search.asp.
International Labour Organisation. 2010. *LABORSTA Internet*. Accessed August 10, 2010. http://laborsta.ilo.org/STP/guest.
Jaffrelot, Christophe. 1996. *The Hindu Nationalist Movement in India*. New York: Columbia University Press.
Jarausch, Konrad 1978. "Liberal Education as Illiberal Socialization: The Case of Students in Imperial Germany." *Journal of Modern History*, 50, 4: 610–630.
Jarausch, Konrad. 1982. *Students, Society, and Politics in Imperial Germany: The Rise of Academic Illiberalism*. Princeton, Princeton University Press.
Jarausch, Konrad. 1984. "German Students in the First World War." *Central European History*, 17, 4: 310–329.
Jarausch, Konrad. 1985. "The Crisis of German Professions 1918–33." *Journal of Contemporary History*, 20, 3: 379–398.
Jarausch, Konrad. 1986. "The Perils of Professionalism: Lawyers, Teachers, and Engineers in Nazi Germany." *German Studies Review*, 9, 1: 107–137.
Jayasuriya, Laksiri. 2004. "Social Policy and the Sri Lankan Welfare State: The British Colonial Legacy." *Social Policy and the Commonwealth: Prospects for Social Inclusion*. C. Jones Finer and P. Smyth eds. New York: Palgrave Macmillan, 109–124.
Jayawardena, Kumari. 2004. *Ethnic and Class Conflict in Sri Lanka: The Emergence of Sinhala-Buddhist Consciousness 1883–1983*. Colombo: Sanjiva Books.
Jayawardene, C. H. S. and H. Jayawardene. 1987. *Terror in Paradise: The Battle for Eelam*. Ottawa: Crimcare Publications.

Jayaweera, Swarna. 1971. "Language and Colonial Educational Policy in Ceylon in the Nineteenth Century." *Modern Ceylon Studies: A Journal of the Social Sciences*, 2, 2: 151–169.

Jayaweera, Swarna. 1979. "Education." *Modern Sri Lanka: A Society in Transition*. T. Fernando and R. Kearney eds. Syracuse: Syracuse University, 131–153.

Jayaweera, Swarna. 1990. "Education and Socio-Economic Development." *Sri Lanka Journal of Social Sciences*, 13: 47–72.

Jeffrey, Craig. 2009. "Fixing Futures: Educated Unemployment through a North Indian Lens." *Comparative Studies in Society & History*, 51, 1: 182–211.

Jeffrey, Craig, Patricia Jeffery, and Roger Jeffery. 2005. "When Schooling Fails: Young Men, Education and Low-Caste Politics in Rural North India." *Contributions to Indian Sociology*, 39, 1: 2–38.

Jeffrey, Craig, Roger Jeffery, and Patricia Jeffery. 2008. "School and Madrasah Education: Gender and the Strategies of Muslim Young Men in Rural North India." *Compare: A Journal of Comparative Education*, 38, 5: 581–593.

Jensen, Michael. 2006. "'Re-Islamising' Palestinian Society 'From Below': Hamas and Higher Education in Gaza." *Holy Land Studies: A Multidisciplinary Journal*, 5, 1: 57–74.

Jewsiewicki, Bogumil. 1991. "The Formation of the Political Culture of Ethnicity in the Belgian Congo, 1920–1959." *The Creation of Tribalism in Southern Africa*. LeRoy Vail ed. Berkeley: University of California Press, 324–349.

Johnson, David and Frances Stewart. 2007. "Editorial." *International Journal of Educational Development*, 27: 247–251.

Kalberg, Stephen. 1994. *Max Weber's Comparative-Historical Sociology*. Chicago: University of Chicago Press.

Kandel, Isaac L. 1970. *The Making of Nazis*. Westport: Greenwood Press.

Kar, M. 1975. "Assam's Language Question in Retrospect." *Social Scientist*, 4, 2: 21–35.

Karagiorges, Andreas Georghiou. 1986. *Education Development in Cyprus, 1960–1977*. Nicosia: MAM.

Kater, Michael. 1983. *The Nazi Party: A Social Profile of Members and Leaders, 1919–1945*. Oxford: Basil Blackwell.

Kater, Michael. 1984. "Everyday Antisemitism in Prewar Nazi Germany: The Popular Bases." *Yad Vashem Studies*, 16: 129–159.

Kater, Michael. 1985. "Professionalization and Socialization of Physicians in Wilhelmine and Weimar Germany." *Journal of Contemporary History*, 20, 4: 677–701.

Kater, Michael. 1986. "The Nazi Physicians' League of 1929: Causes and Consequences." *The Formation of the Nazi Constituency, 1919–1933*. Thomas Childers ed. Totowa: Barnes and Noble Books.

Kater, Michael. 1987. "Hitler's Early Doctors: Nazi Physicians in Pre-Depression Germany." *Journal of Modern History*, 59, 1: 25–52.

Kater, Michael. 1989. *Doctors under Hitler*. Chapel Hill: University of North Carolina Press.

Kater, Michael. 2002. "Criminal Physicians in the Third Reich." *Medicine and Medical Ethnics in Nazi German: Origins, Practices, Legacies*. Francis Nicosia and Jonathan Huener eds. New York: Berghahn Books.

Kearney, Robert. 1975. "Educational Expansion and Political Volatility in Sri Lanka: The 1971 Insurrection." *Asian Survey*, 15, 9: 727–744.
Kearney, Robert. 1978. "Language and the Rise of Tamil Separatism in Sri Lanka." *Asian Survey*, 18, 5: 521–534.
Kearney, Robert. 1979. "Politics and Modernization." *Modern Sri Lanka: A Society in Transition*. T. Fernando and R. Kearney eds. Syracuse: Syracuse University, 57–81.
Kearney, Robert and Barbara Miller. 1985. "The Spiral of Suicide and Social Change in Sri Lanka." *Journal of Asian Studies*, 45, 1: 81–101.
Kelling, George Horton. 1990. *Countdown to Rebellion: British Policy in Cyprus, 1939–1955*. New York: Greenwood Press.
Kernis, Michael, Bruce Grannemann, and Lynda Barclay. 1989. "Stability and Level of Self-Esteem as Predictors of Anger Arousal and Hostility." *Journal of Personality and Social Psychology*, 56: 1013–1022.
Kimura, Makiko. 2003. "Memories of the Massacre: Violence and Collective Identity in the Narratives on the Nellie Incident." *Asian Ethnicity*, 4, 2: 225–239.
King, Gary, Robert Keohane, and Sidney Verba. 1994. *Designing Social Inquiry: Scientific Inference in Qualitative Research*. Princeton: Princeton University Press.
Koshar, Rudy. 1990. "Cult of Associations? The Lower Middle Classes in Weimar Germany." *Splintered Classes: Politics and Lower Middle Classes in Interwar Europe*. Rudy Koshar ed. New York: Holmes and Meier, 31–54.
Koullapis, Loris. 2002. "The Subject of History in the Greek Cypriot Education System: A Subset of the Greek Nation." *Clio in the Balkans: The Politics of History Education*. Christina Koulouri ed. Thessaloniki: Center for Democracy and Reconciliation in Southeast Europe, pp. 406–413.
Krueger, Alan and Jitka Maleckova. 2003. "Education, Poverty and Terrorism: Is There a Causal Connection?" *Journal of Economic Perspectives*, 17: 119–144.
Kumar, D. P. 1990. *Challenge to India's Unity: Assam Student's Agitation and Government*. New Delhi: B.R. Publishing Corporation.
Kurthen, Hermann. 1997. "Antisemitism and Xenophobia in United Germany: How the Burden of the Past Affects the Present." *Antisemitism and Xenophobia in Germany after Unification*. Hermann Kurthen, Werner Bergmann, and Reiner Erb eds. New York: Oxford University Press, 39–87.
Kurthen, Hermann, Werner Bergmann, and Reiner Erb. 1997. "Introduction: Postunificatiion Challenges to Germany Democracy." *Antisemitism and Xenophobia in Germany after Unification*. Hermann Kurthen, Werner Bergmann, and Reiner Erb eds. New York: Oxford University Press, 3–17.
Laczko, Leslie. 1987. "Perceived Communal Inequalities in Quebec: A Multidimensional Analysis." *Canadian Journal of Sociology*, 12, 1/2: 83–110.
Lange, Matthew. 2009. *Lineages of Despotism and Development: British Colonialism and State Power*. Chicago: University of Chicago Press.
Lange, Matthew and Hrag Balian. 2008. "Containing Conflict or Instigating Unrest? A Test of the Effects of State Infrastructural Power on Civil Violence." *Studies in Comparative International Development*, 43: 314–333.

Lange, Matthew and Andrew Dawson. 2009. "Dividing and Ruling the World? A Statistical Test of the Effects of Colonialism on Postcolonial Civil Violence." *Social Forces*, 88: 785–818.

Lange, Matthew and Andrew Dawson. 2010. "Education and Ethnic Violence: A Cross-National Time-Series Analysis." *Nationalism and Ethnic Politics*, 16: 216–239.

Lange, Ralf. 2003. *Promoting Livelihood and Employment in Post-Conflict Situations: Approaches and Lessons Learned*. Stuttgart: FAKT.

Langton, Kenneth, and M. Kent Jennings. 1968. "Political Socialization and the High School Civic Curriculum in the United States." *American Political Science Review*, 62: 852–867.

Latouche, Daniel. 1974. "La Vrai Nature de . . . la Revolution Tranquille." *Canadian Journal of Political Science*, 7, 3: 525–536.

Lavoie, Constance. 2008. "Éducation Bilangue et Développment Humain Durable au Burkina Faso." PhD Thesis Department of Second Language Education. McGill University Montreal.

Lebovics, Herman. 1969. *Social Conservatism and the Middle Classes in Germany, 1914–1933*. Princeton: Princeton University Press.

Lebrun, Johanne, Yves Lenoir, Mario Laforest, Francois Larose, Gerard-Raymond Roy, Carlo Spallanzani, and Mary Pearson. 2002. "Past and Current Trends in the Analysis of Textbooks in a Quebec Context." *Curriculum Inquiry*, 32, 1: 51–83.

Leirvik, Oddbjørn. 2004. "Religious Education, Communal Identity and National Politics in the Muslim World." *British Journal of Religious Education*, 26, 3: 223–236.

Lennox-Boyd, A. 1956. "19 March 1956, Letter from A. Lennox-Boyd." Public Records Office (Kew) CO 926/166.

Levitt, Matthew. 2006. *Hamas: Politics, Charity, and Terrorism in the Service of Jihad*. New Haven: Yale University Press.

Lian, Jason and David Matthews. 1998. "Does the Vertical Mosaic Still Exist? Ethnicity and Income in Canada, 1991." *Canadian Review of Sociology and Anthropology*, 35, 4: 461–481.

Lichtenberger, Henri. 1937. *The Third Reich*. New York: Greystone Press.

Linden, Ian. 1977. *Church and Revolution in Rwanda*. Manchester: Machester University Press.

Linteau, Paul-André, René Durocher, Jean-Claude Robert, and François Ricard. 1991. *Quebec Since 1930*. Trans. Robert Chodos and Ellen Garmaise. Toronto: James Lorimer & Co.

Lipset, Seymour Martin. 1963. *Political Man: The Social Bases of Politics*. Garden City: Doubleday.

Locke, Kenneth. 2009. "Aggression, Narcissism, Self-Esteem, and the Attribution of Desirable and Humanizing Traits to Self Versus Others." *Journal of Research in Personality*, 43: 99–102.

Loizos, Peter. 1974. "The Progress of Greek Nationalism in Cyprus, 1878–1970." *Choice and Change: Essays in Honour of Lucy Mair*. J. Davis ed. New York: Humanities Press, 114–133.

Loizos, Peter. 1975. *The Greek Gift: Politics in a Cypriot Village*. Oxford: Basil Blackwell.

Madhab, Jayanta. 2005. *Survey on the Unemployeds in Assam*. Guwahati: Navanita Printers.

Magnusson, Bruce. 2005. "Democratic Legitimacy in Benin: Institutions and Identity in a Regional Context." *The Fate of Africa's Democratic Experiments: Elites and Institutions*. Leonardo Villalon and Peter Von Doepp eds. Bloomington: Indiana University Press, 75–95.

Mahoney, James. 2000. "Strategies of Causal Inference in Small-N Analysis." *Sociological Methods and Research*, 28, 4: 387–424.

Majumdar, Swapna. 2005. "In India, Domestic Violence Rises with Education." *Gender and History*, 16, 3: 24–26.

Mamdani, Mahmood. 2001. *When Victims Become Killers: Colonialism, Nativism, and Genocide in Rwanda*. Princeton University Press.

Mann, Michael. 2000. "Were the Perpetrators of Genocide 'Ordinary Men' or 'Real Nazis'? Results from Fifteen Hundred Biographies." *Holocaust and Genocide Studies*, 14, 3: 331–366.

Manogaran, Chelvadurai. 1987. *Ethnic Conflict and Reconciliation in Sri Lanka*. Honolulu: University of Hawaii Press.

Markides, Diana Weston. 2001. *Cyprus 1957–1963: From Colonial Conflict to Constitutional Crisis*. Minneapolis: Minnesota Mediterranean and East European Monographs.

Markides, Kyriacos C. 1977. *The Rise and Fall of the Cyprus Republic*. New Haven: Yale University Press.

Marshall, Monty G. and Keith Jaggers. 2003. "Polity IV Dataset." College Park MD: Center for International Development and Conflict Management University of Maryland. Accessed May 1, 2005. http://www.cidcm.umd.edu/inscr/polity/index.htm.

Mazawi, Andre. 1998. "Contested Regimes, Civic Dissent and the Political Socialization of Children and Adolescents: The Case of the Palestinian Uprising." *Citizenship and Citizenship Education in a Changing World*. Orit Ichilov ed. London: Woburn Press, 83–97.

Mbonimana, Gamaliel. 1978. "Christianisation Indirecte et Cristallisation des Clivages Ethniques au Rwanda, 1925–1931." *Enquêtes et Documents d'Histoire Africaine*, 3: 125–163.

Mbonimana, Gamaliel. 1995. "Ethnies et Eglise Catholique: Le Remodelage de la Société par l'Ecole Missionnaire, 1900–1931." *Cahiers Centre Sainte-Dominique*, 1: 34–44.

McAdam, Doug. 1982. *Political Process and the Development of Black Insurgency, 1930–1970*. Chicago: Chicago University Press.

McCarthy, John and Mayer Zald. 1987. "Resource Mobilization and Social Movements: A Partial Theory." *Social Movements in an Organizational Society*. M. Zald and J. McCarthy eds. New Brunswick: Transaction Book, 15–42.

McCully, Bruce. 1940. *English Education and the Origins of Indian Nationalism*. New York: Columbia University Press.

McHenry, James A. Jr. 1981. "The Uneasy Partnership on Cyprus, 1919–1939: The Political and Diplomatic Interaction between Great Britain Turkey, and

the Turkish Cypriot Community." PhD Dissertation University of Kansas, Lawrence.
McRoberts, Kenneth. 1975. "Mass Acquisition of a Nationalist Ideology: Quebec Prior to the 'Quiet Revolution.'" PhD Dissertation University of Chicago Chicago.
McRoberts, Kenneth and Dale Posgate. 1980. *Quebec: Social Change and Political Crisis*. Toronto: McClelland and Stewart Limited.
Melson, Robert and Howard Wolpe. 1970. "Modernization and the Politics of Communalism: A Theoretical Perspective." *American Political Science Review*, 64: 1112–1130.
Menon, Dilip. 1994. *Caste, Nationalism, and Communism in South India: Malabar, 1900–1948*. New York: Cambridge University Press.
Merelman, Ricard. 1971. *Political Socialization and Educational Climates: A Study of Two School Districts*. New York: Holt, Rinehart and Winston.
Midlarsky, Manus. 1988. "Rulers and the Ruled: Patterned Inequality and the Onset of Mass Political Violence." *American Political Science Review*, 82, 2: 491–509.
Miguel, Edward. 2004. "Tribe or Nation? Nation Building and Public Goods in Kenya versus Tanzania." *World Politics*, 56, 3: 327–362.
Milner, Henry. 1978. *Politics in the New Quebec*. Toronto: McClelland and Steward.
Mishal, Shaul and Avraham Sela. 2000. *The Palestinian Hamas: Vision, Violence, and Coexistence*. New York: Columbia University Press.
Mommsen, Hans. 1996. *The Rise and Fall of Weimar Democracy*. Chapel Hill: University of North Carolina Press.
Moore, Laura and Seth Ovadia. 2006. "Accounting for Spatial Variation in Tolerance: The Effects of Education and Religion." *Social Forces*, 84: 2205–2222.
Moore, M. P. 1981. "Unemployment of Educated Youth: A Problem for Whom?" *Marga Quarterly Journal*, 6, 2: 97–105.
Morris, Aldon. 1981. "Black Southern Student Sit-in Movement: An Analysis of Internal Organization." *American Sociological Review*, 46, 6: 744–767.
Morris, Aldon and Suzanne Staggenborg. 2004. "Leadership in Social Movements." *The Blackwell Companion to Social Movements*. D. Snow, S. Soule, and H. Kriesi eds. Malden: Blackwell, 171–196.
Mosse, George. 1964. *The Crisis of German Ideology: Intellectual Origins of the Third Reich*. New York: Universal Library.
Muhlberger, Detlef. 1991. *Hitler's Followers: Studies in the Sociology of the Nazi Movement*. New York: Routledge.
Muhlberger, Detlef. 2003. *The Social Basis of Nazism 1919–1933*. Cambridge: Cambridge University Press.
Muller, Edward N. and Mitchell A. Seligson. 1987. "Inequality and Insurgency." *American Political Science Review*, 81: 425–451.
Nair, P. R. Gopinathan. 1981. *Primary Education, Population Growth, and Socio-Economic Change*. New Delhi: Allied Publishers Private Limited.
Narayanan, M. G. S. 1972. *Cultural Symbiosis in Kerala*. Trivandrum: Kerala Historical Society.

Nicholls, Anthony J. 2000. *Weimar and the Rise of Hitler*. New York: St. Martin's Press.
Nissan, Elizabeth. 1996. *Sri Lanka: A Bitter Harvest*. London: Minority Rights Group International.
Nordbruch, Goetz. 2001. "Narrating Palestinian Nationalism: An Inquiry into the New Palestinian Textbooks." Accessed July 21, 2009. http://www.jewishvirtuallibrary.org/jsource/Peace/paltext.html.
Nuñez, Imanol and Ilias Livanos. 2010. "Higher Education and Unemployment in Europe: An Analysis of the Academic Subject and National Effects." *Higher Education*, 59: 475–487.
Nussbaum, Martha. 2010. *Not For Profit: Why Democracy Needs the Humanities*. Princeton: Princeton University Press.
Oberschall, Anthony. 2000. "The Manipulation of Ethnicity: From Cooperation to Violence and War in Yugoslavia." *Ethnic and Racial Studies*, 23, 6: 982–1001.
Olzak, Susan. 1992. *The Dynamics of Ethnic Competition and Conflict*. Stanford: Stanford University Press.
Olzak, Susan and Joane Nagel eds. 1986. *Competitive Ethnic Relations*. Orlando: Academic Press.
Orr, C. W. J. 1972. *Cyprus under British Rule*. London: Zeno Publishers.
Oswald, Hans. 1999. "Political Socialization in the New State of Germany." *Roots of Civic Identity: International Perspectives on Community Service and Activism in Youth*. Miranda Yates and James Youniss eds. New York: Cambridge University Press, 97–113.
Paden, John. 1971. "Communal Competition, Conflict and Violence in Kano." *Nigeria: Modernization and the Politics of Communalism*. Robert Melson and Howard Wolpe eds. East Lansing: Michigan State University Press, 113–144.
Papadakis, Yiannis. 2008. *History Education in Divided Cyprus: A Comparison of Greek Cypriot and Turkish Cypriot Schoolbooks on the "History of Cyprus"*. Oslo: International Peace Research Institute.
Pape, Robert. 2005. *Dying to Win: The Strategic Logic of Suicide Terrorism*. New York: Random House.
Parvathamma, C. 1984. *Employment Problems of University Graduates*. New Delhi: Ashish Publishing House.
Paulsen, Friedrich. 1906. *The German Universities and University Study*. London: Longmans.
Paz, Reuven. 2000. "Higher Education and the Development of Palestinian Islamic Groups." *Middle East Review of International Affairs*, 4, 2. Accessed August 20, 2009. http://meria.idc.ac.il/journal/2000/issue2/jv4n2a6.html.
Paz, Reuven. 2003. "The Development of Palestinian Islamic Groups." *Revolutionaries and Reformers: Contemporary Islamist Movements in the Middle East*. Barrt Rubin ed. New York: SUNY Press, 23–40.
Peiris, Gerald. 1995. "The Campus Community at Paradeniya: Travails of a Residential University." *The University System of Sri Lanka: Vision and Reality*. K. M. de Silva and G.H. Peiris eds. Kandy: International Centre for Ethnic Studies, 185–236.

Peiris, Gerald. 1999. "Insurrection and Youth Unrest in Sri Lanka." *History and Politics: Millennial Perspectives. Essays in Honour of Kingsley de Silva*. Gerald Peiris and SWR de A Samarasinghe eds. Colombo: Law and Society Trust, 165–199.
Perera, Sasanka. 1991. "Teaching and Learning Hatred: The Role of Education and Socialization in Sri Lankan Ethnic Conflict." PhD Dissertation University of California, Santa Barbara.
Persell, Caroline Hodges, Adam Green, and Liena Gurevich. 2001. "Civil Society, Economic Distress, and Social Tolerance." *Sociological Forum*, 16, 2: 203–230.
Persianis, Panayiotis. 1978. *Church and State in Cyprus Education : The Contribution of the Greek Orthodox Church of Cyprus to Cyprus Education During the British Administration (1878–1960)*. Nicosia: Violaris Press.
Petersen, Roger. 2002. *Understanding Ethnic Violence: Fear, Hatred, and Resentment in Twentieth-Century Eastern Europe*. New York: Cambridge University Press.
Pfaffenberger, Bryan. 1990. "Ethnic Conflict and Youth Insurgency in Sri Lanka: The Social Origins of Tamil Separatism." *Conflict and Peacemaking in Multiethnic Societies*. Joseph Montville ed. Toronto: Lexington Books.
Pfaffenberger, Bryan. 1994. "Introduction: The Sri Lankan Tamils." *The Sri Lankan Tamils: Ethnicity and Identity*. C. Manogaran and B. Pfaffenberger eds. Boulder: Westview Press, 1–27.
Phadnis, Urmila. 1984. *Ethnic Conflict in Sri Lanka – An Overview*. New Delhi: Ghandi Peace Foundation.
Phukan, Monuj. 2005. *Students' Politics in Assam: A Study of All Tai Ahom Students' Union*. Dehli Anshah Publishing House.
Pinard, Maurice and Lisa Kowalchuk. Forthcoming. "New Middle Class and Other Segments or Intellectuals, as Class Bases of the Quebec Movement: An Empirical Assessment." *The Quebec Independence Movement*. Montreal: McGill-Queen's University Press.
Pollis, Adamantia. 1998. "The Role of Foreign Powers in Structuring Ethnicity and Ethnic Conflict in Cyprus." *Cyprus and Its People: Nation, Identity, and Experience in an Unimaginable Community, 1955–1997*. Vangelis Calotychos ed. Boulder: Westview Press, 85–102.
Post, Jerrold, Ehud Sprinzak, and Laurita Denny. 2003. "The Terrorists in Their Own Words: Interviews with 35 Incarcerated Middle Eastern Terrorists." *Terrorism and Political Violence*, 15, 1: 171–184.
Proctor, Robert. 1988. *Racial Hygiene: Medicine under the Nazis*. Cambridge, MA: Harvard University Press.
Proctor, Robert. 1994. "Racial Hygiene: The Collaboration of Medicine and Nazism." *Medicine, Ethics, and the Third Reich: Historical and Contemporary Issues*. J. J. Michalczyk ed. Kansas City: Sheed & Ward.
Qazzaz, Hadeel. 2009. "Palestine: West Bank and Gaza Strip." *From Charity to Social Change*. Barbara Ibrahim and Dina. H. Sherif eds. Cairo: American University in Cairo Press, 87–110.
Quillian, Lincoln. 1996. "Group Threat and Regional Change in Attitudes Toward African-Americans." *American Journal of Sociology*, 102: 816–860.

Quinley, Harold and Charles Glock. 1979. *Anti-Semitism in America*. New York: Free Press.
Ranger, Terence. 1991. "Missionaries, Migrants and the Manyika: The Invention of Ethnicity in Zimbabwe." *The Creation of Tribalism in Southern Africa*. LeRoy Vail ed. Berkeley: University of California Press, 118–150.
Rashid, Ahmed. 2000. *Taliban: Militant Islam, Oil and Fundamentalism in Central Asia*. New Haven: Yale University Press.
Riga, Liliana. 2008. "The Ethnic Roots of Class Universalism: Rethinking the Russian Revolutionary Elite." *American Journal of Sociology*, 114, 3: 649–705.
Ringer, Fritz. 1967. "Higher Education in Germany in the Nineteenth Century." *Education and Social Structure: In the Twentieth Century*. Walter Laqueur and George Mosse eds. New York: Harper and Row, 123–138.
Roberts, Allen. 1991. "History, Ethnicity and Change in the 'Christian Kingdom' of Southeastern Zaire." *The Creation of Tribalism in Southern Africa*. LeRoy Vail ed. Berkeley: University of California Press, 193–214.
Roberts, Clayton. 1996. *The Logic of Historical Explanation*. University Park: Pennsylvania State University Press.
Roberts, Michael. 1977. "Elites, Nationalisms, and the Nationalist Movement in British Ceylon." *Documents of the Ceylon National Congress and Nationalist Politics in Ceylon 1929–1950*. Michael Roberts ed. Colombo: Department of National Archives, xxvii–ccxxii.
Rodgers, Harrell. 1973. "Civics Curricula and Southern School Children: The Impact of Segregated and Integrated School Environments. *Journal of Politics*, 35: 1002–1007.
Rogers, Martyn. 2008. "Modernity, Authenticity, and Ambivalence: Subaltern Masculinities on a South Indian College Campus." *Journal of the Royal Anthropological Institute*, 14, 1: 79–95.
Roosens, Eugeene. 1989. *Creating Ethnicity: The Process of Ethno-Genesis*. Newbury Park: Sage.
Roy, Sara. 1999. "De-development Revisited: Palestinian Economy and Society since Oslo." *Journal of Palestine Studies*, 28, 3: 64–82.
Roy, Sara. 2004. "The Palestinian-Israeli Conflict and Palestinian Socioeconomic Decline: A Place Denied." *International Journal of Politics, Culture, and Society*, 17, 3: 365–403.
Rudra, Nita. 2008. *Globalization and the Race to the Bottom in Developing Countries*. New York: Cambridge University Press.
Rueschemeyer, Dietrich. 2009. *Usable Theory: Analytical Tools for Social and Political Research*. Princeton: Princeton University Press.
Russell, Charles and Bowman Miller. 1978. "Profile of a Terrorist." *Contemporary Terrorism: Selected Readings*. John Elliot and Leslie Gibson eds. Gaithersburg: Bureau of Operations and Research, 81–95.
Ryan, Bruce. 1961. "Status, Achievement, and Education in Ceylon." *Journal of Asian Studies*, 20, 4: 463–476.
Sabaratnam, Lakshmanan. 2001. *Ethnic Attachments in Sri Lanka: Social Change and Cultural Continuity*. New York: Palgrave.

Sahedevan, P. and Neil DeVotta. 2006. *Politics of Conflict and Peace in Sri Lanka*. New Delhi: Manak Publications.

Salih, Halil Ibrahim. 1968. *Cyprus: An Analysis of Cypriot Political Discord*. Brooklyn: Theo Gaus Sons, Inc.

Samarasinghe, S. W. R. de A. 1984. "Ethnic Representation in Central Government Employment and Sinhala-Tamil Relations in Sri Lanka: 1948–1981." *From Independence to Statehood: Managing Ethnic Conflict in Five African and Asian States*. R. Goldmann and A. Jeyaratnam Wilson eds. London: Frances Pinter Publishers, 173-184.

Sambanis, Nicholas. 2001. "Do Ethnic and Non-Ethnic Civil Wars Have the Same Causes? A Theoretical and Empirical Inquiry (Part 1)." *Journal of Conflict Resolution*, 45, 3: 259–82.

Samuel, R. H. and R. Hinton Thomas. 1949. *Education and Society in Modern Germany*. London: Routledge and Kegan Paul Limited.

Sandbrook, Richard, Marc Edelman, Patrick Heller, and Judith Teichman. 2007. *Social Democracy in the Global Periphery: Origins, Challenges, Prospects*. New York: Cambridge University Press.

Sandstrom, Marlene, and Rachel Jordan. 2007. "Defensive Self-Esteem and Aggression in Childhood. *Journal of Research in Personality*, 42: 506–514.

Sanuey, J. 1955. "MED 22/52/01." Public Records Office (KEW) CO 926/409.

Sarmah, Alaka. 1999. *Immigration and Assam Politics*. Delhi: Ajanta Books International.

Sayles, Marnie. 2007. "Relative Deprivation and Collective Protest: An Impoverished Theory?" *Sociological Inquiry*, 54, 4: 449–465.

Sayre, E. A. 2009. "Labor Market Conditions, Political Events, and Palestinian Suicide Bombings." *Peace Economics, Peace Science and Public Policy*, 15, 1: 1–26.

Schmidt, Ulf. 2007. *Karl Brandt: The Nazi Doctor: Medicine and Power in the Third Reich*. New York: Hambledon Continuum.

Schubarth, Wilfred. 1997. "Xenophobia among East German Youth." *Antisemitism and Xenophobia in Germany after Unification*. Hermann Kurthen, Werner Bergmann, and Reiner Erb eds. New York: Oxford University Press, 143–158.

Seitz, Klaus. 2004. *Education and Conflict: The Role of Education in the Creation, Prevention and Resolution of Societal Crises – Consequences for Development Cooperation*. Eschborn: GTZ.

Semyonov, Moshe and Ephraim Yuchtman-Yaar. 1992. "Ethnicity, Education, and Occupational Inequality: Jews and Arabs in Israel." *International Perspectives on Education and Society*, 2: 215–224.

Sen, Amartya. 2006. *Identity and Violence: The Illusion of Destiny*. New York: W.W. Norton.

Senaratne, Jagath P. 1997. *Political Violence in Sri Lanka, 1977–1990: Riots, Insurrections, Counterinsurgencies, Foreign Intervention*. Amsterdam: VU University Press.

Shah, Ghanshyam. 1987. "Middle Class Politics: Case of Anti-Reservation Agitations in Gujarat." *Economic and Political Weekly*, 22, 19/21: AN155–AN172.

Shapiro, D. M. and M. Stelcner. 1987. "Earnings Disparities among Linguistic Groups in Quebec, 1970–1980." *Canadian Public Policy*, 13, 1: 97–104.
Shastri, Amita. 1994. "The Material Basis for Separatism: The Tamil Eelam Movement in Sri Lanka." *The Sri Lankan Tamils: Ethnicity and Identity*. C. Manogaran and B. Pfaffenberger eds. Boulder: Westview Press.
Sikand, Yoginder. 2003. "Islamist Assertion in Contemporary India: The Case of the Students Islamic Movement of India." *Journal of Muslim Minority Affairs*, 23, 2: 335–345.
Singh, Bhawan. 1984. *Politics of Alienation in Assam*. Delhi: Ajanta Publications.
Singh, Lal Bahadur. 1996. "Alienation: A Symptomatic Reaction of Educated Unemployed Youth in India." *International Journal of Psychology*, 31, 2: 101–110.
Singh, Lal Bahadur, Renu Kumari, and Indra Kumar Singh. 1992. "Extent of Hostility in Educated Indian Unemployed Youth: A Micro Analysis." *International Journal of Psychology*, 27, 1: 89–97.
Singh, Prerna. 2010. "We-ness and Welfare: A Longitudinal Analysis of Social Development in Kerala, India." *World Development*, 39,
Siriwardena Reggie, K. Indrapala, Sunil Bastian, and Sepali Kottegoda. 1985. *School Text Books and Communal Relations in Sri Lanka*. Colombo: Council for Communal Harmony through the Media.
Skrypietz, Ingrid. 1994. "Militant Right-Wing Extremism in Germany." *German Politics*, 3, 1: 133–140.
Smith, Anthony D. 1983. *Theories of Nationalism*. New York: Holmes and Meier.
Solletty, Marion. 2011. "Le Chômage des Diplômés Moteur de la Révolte Tunisienne." *Le Monde*. Accessed February 21, 2011. http://www.lemonde.fr/afrique/article/2011/01/07/le-chomage-des-diplomes-moteur-de-la-revolte-tunisienne_1462244_3212.html.
South China Morning Post. 2003. "India's University Students Graduating to Terrorism." New Delhi.
Speier, Hans. 1986. *German White-Collar Workers and the Rise of Hitler*. New Haven: Yale University Press.
Stachura, Peter. 1983. "The Nazis, the Bourgeoisie and the Workers during Kampfzeit." *The Nazi Machtergreifung*. Peter Stachura ed. Boston: George Allen and Unwin, 15–32.
Stackelberg, Roderick. 2009. *Hitler's Germany: Origins, Interpretations, Legacies*. New York: Routledge.
Steinberg, Michael. 1977. *Sabers and Brown Shirts: The German Students' Path to National Socialism, 1918–1935*. Chicago: Chicago University Press.
Steinmetz, George. 1997. "Social Class and the Reemergence of the Radical Right in Contemporary Germany." *Reworking Class*. John R. Hall ed. Ithaca: Cornell University Press, 335–368.
Stepan, Alfred, Juan Linz, and Yogendra Yadav. 2011. *Crafting State-Nations: India and Other Multinational Democracies*. Baltimore: Johns Hopkins University Press.
Stephens, John and Dietrich Rueschemeyer. 1997. "Comparing Social Historical Sequences – A Powerful Tool for Causal Analysis." *Comparative Social Research*, 17: 55–72.

Stevenson, Garth. 2006. *Parallel Paths: The Development of Nationalism in Ireland and Quebec.* Montreal: McGill Queen's University Press.
Svindseth, Marit, Jim Aage Nottestad, Juliska Wallin, John Olav Roaldset, and Alv Dahl. 2008. "Narcissism in Patients Admitted to Psychiatry Acute Wards: Its Relation to Violence, Suicidality and Other Psychopathology." *BMS Psychiatry*, 8, 13: 1-11.
Tambiah, Stanley. 1986. *Sri Lanka – Ethnic Fratricide and the Dismantling of Democracy.* Chicago: University of Chicago Press.
Tambiah, Stanley. 1996. *Leveling Crowds: Ethnonationalist Conflicts and Collective Violence in South Asia.* Berkeley: University of California Press.
Tampoe, Mahen. 2006. *From Spices to Suicide Bombers and Beyond: A Study of Power, Politics and Terrorism in Sri Lanka.* Twickenham: Athena Press.
Thangarajah, C. Y. 2002. "Youth, Conflict and Social Transformation in Sri Lanka." *Sri Lankan Youth: Challenges and Responses.* Colombo: Friedrich Ebert Stiftung, 172–207.
Thomaes, Sander, Brad Bushman, Hedy Stegge, and Tjeert Olthof. 2008. "Trumping Shame by Blasts of Noise: Narcissism, Self-Esteem, Shame, and Aggression in Young Adolescents." *Child Development*, 79, 6: 1792–1801.
Thyne, Clayton. 2006. "ABC's, 123's, and the Golden Rule: The Pacifying Effects of Education on Civil War, 1980–1999." *International Studies Quarterly*, 50, 4: 733–754.
Tilly, Charles. 2001. "Mechanisms in Political Processes." *Annual Review of Political Science*, 4: 21–41.
Tilly, Charles. 2003. *The Politics of Collective Violence.* New York: Cambridge University Press.
Tiruchelvam, Neelan. 1984. "Ethnicity and Resource Allocation." *From Independence to Statehood: Managing Ethnic Conflict in Five African and Asian States.* R. Goldmann and A. Jeyaratnam Wilson eds. London: Frances Pinter Publishers, 85–195.
Torney, Judith, A. N. Oppenheim, and Russell Farnen. 1975. *Civic Education in Ten Countries: An Empirical Study.* New York: Wiley.
Torney-Purta, Judith. 2000. "Review: Comparative Perspectives on Political Socialization and Civic Education." *Comparative Education Review*, 44, 1: 88–95.
Torney-Purta, Judith and John Schwille. 1986. "Civic Values Learned in School: Policy and Practice in Industrialized Countries." *Comparative Education Review*, 30, 1: 30–49.
Tremayne, Penelope. 1958. *Below the Tide.* London: Hutchinson.
Trottier, Claude. 1982. "Les Enseignants Comme Agents de Socialisation Politique au Quebec." *Canadian Journal of Education*, 7, 1: 15–43.
Trudel, Marcel and Genevieve Jain. 1970. *Canadian History Textbooks: A Comparative Study.* Ottawa: Queen's Printer.
Tuch, Steven. 1987. "Urbanism, Region, and Tolerance Revisited: The Case of Racial Prejudice." *American Sociological Review* 52: 504–510.
Udagama, P. 1990. "Education and National Integration in Sri Lanka." *Sri Lanka Journal of Social Sciences*, 13: 9–17.

UNESCO. 1995. *Declaration of Principles on Tolerance.* Accessed July 17, 2008. http://www.unesco.org/cpp/uk/declarations/tolerance.pdf.
United Nations. 2009. *Human Development Report.* New York: Oxford University Press.
United Nations. 2007. *UN Population Division Quinquennial Estimates and Projections.* Accessed July 26, 2007. http://unstats.un.org.
Upadhyay, R. 2003. "Students Islamic Movement of India (SIMI)." South Asia Analysis Group, paper no. 825. Accessed August 16, 2009. http://www.southasiaanalysis.org/%5Cpapers9%5Cpaper825.html.
Vail, LeRoy. 1991. "Introduction: Ethnicity in Southern African History." *The Creation of Tribalism in Southern Africa.* LeRoy Vail ed. Berkeley: University of California Press, 1–20.
Vail, LeRoy and Landeg White. 1991. "Tribalism in the Political History of Malawi." *The Creation of Tribalism in Southern Africa.* LeRoy Vail ed. Berkeley: University of California Press, 151–192.
Vaillancourt, Francois, Dominique Lemay, and Luc Vaillancourt. 2007. "Laggards No More: The Changed Socioeconomic Status of Francophones in Quebec. No. 103." C.D. Howe Institute.
van den Berghe, Pierre. 1981. *The Ethnic Phenomenon.* New York: Elsevier.
Vanniasingham, Somasundaram. 1988. *Sri Lanka – The Conflict Within.* New Delhi: The Lancer Group.
Varnavas, Andreas. 2001. *A Brief History of the Liberation Struggle of EOKA (1955–1959).* Nicosia: Theopress Ltd.
Varshney, Ashutosh. 2002. *Ethnic Conflict and Civic Life.* New Haven: Yale University Press.
Verwimp, Philip. 2005. "An Economic Profile of Peasant Perpetrators of Genocide: Micro-Level Evidence from Rwanda." *Journal of Development Economics,* 77: 297–323.
Volkan, Vamik. 1979. *Cyprus: War and Adaptation: A Psychoanalytic History of Two Ethnic Groups in Conflict.* Charlottesville: University Press of Virginia.
Walker-Keleher, Jessica. 2006. "Reconceptualizing the Relationship between Conflict and Education: The Case of Rwanda." *Praxis: The Fletcher Journal of Human Security,* 31: 35–53.
Walter, Enders and Todd Sandler. 2006. *The Political Economy of Terrorism.* New York: Cambridge University Press.
War Office. 1959. "Report on the Cyprus Emergency." Public Records Office (Kew) WO 106/6020.
War Office. 1960. "A History of EOKA 1954–1959." Public Records Office (Kew) WO 33/2736.
Ward, J. G. 1956. "1956.5.28, J.G. Ward." Public Records Office (Kew) FO 371/123949.
Warnapala, W. A. Wiswa. 1994. *Ethnic Strife and Politics in Sri Lanka: An Investigation into Demands and Responses.* New Delhi: Navrang.
Weber, Eugen. 1976. *Peasants into Frenchmen: The Modernization of Rural France, 1870–1914.* Stanford: Stanford University Press.
Weber, Max. 1921. *Gesammelte Politische Schriften.* Munich: München Drei Masken Verlag.

Weber, R. G. S. 1986. *German Student Corps in the Third Reich.* London: Macmillan.
Wegner, Gregory. 2002. *Anti-Semitism and Schooling under the Third Reich.* New York: RoutledgeFalmer.
Weil, Frederick. 1997. "Ethnic Intolerance, Extremism, and Democratic Attitudes in Germany since Unification." *Antisemitism and Xenophobia in Germany after Unification.* Hermann Kurthen, Werner Bergmann, and Reiner Erb eds. New York: Oxford University Press, 110–140.
Weiner, Myron. 1978. *Sons of the Soil: Migration and Ethnic Conflict in India.* Princeton: Princeton University Press.
Weiner, Myron. 1991. *The Child and the State in India: Child Labor and Education Policy in Comparative Perspective.* Princeton: Princeton University Press.
Weiner, Myron and Mary Katzenstein. 1981. *India's Preferential Policies: Migrants, the Middle Classes, and Ethnic Equality.* Chicago: University of Chicago Press.
Weir, W. W. 1952. *Education in Cyprus: Some Theories and Practices in Education in the Island of Cyprus since 1878.* Nicosia: Cosmos Press.
Weiss, John. 1996. *Ideology of Death: Why the Holocaust Happened in Germany.* Chicago: Ivan R. Dee.
Weiss, John. 2003. *The Politics of Hate: Anti-Semitism, History, and the Holocaust in Modern Europe.* Chicago: Ivan R. Dee.
Weyers, Wolfgang. 1998. *Death of Medicine in Nazi Germany: Dermatology and Dermatopathology under the Swastika.* A. Bernard Ackerman ed. Philadelphia: Ardor/Scribendi.
Weymar, Erich. 1961. *Das Selbstverständnis der Deutschen.* Stuttgart: Jahrhundert.
Wickham-Crowley, Timothy. 1992. *Guerrillas and Revolution in Latin America: A Comparative Study of Insurgents and Regimes since 1956.* Princeton: Princeton University Press.
Wijesinghe, C. P. 1969. "Youth in Ceylon." *Youth: A Transcultural Psychiatric Approach.* J. Masserman ed. New York: Grune and Stratton, 31–44.
Wijesinghe, C. P. 1973. "Youth Unrest and the Psychiatrist in Sri Lanka." *Australian and New Zealand Journal of Psychiatry,* 7: 313–317.
Wijesinghe, Rajiva. 2004. "Education Policy in Sri Lanka: The Failure of Good Intentions and Little Learning." *Protection of Minority Rights and Diversity.* Nanda Wanasundera ed. Colombo: International Centre for Ethnic Studies, 251–309.
Wilgoren, Jodi. 2001. "After the Attacks: The Hijackers; A Terrorist Profile Emerges that Confounds the Experts." *The New York Times* (September 15), A2.
Wilkinson, Steven. 2004. *Votes and Violence: Electoral Competition and Ethnic Riots in India.* New York: Cambridge University Press.
Williams, R. L. 2000. "A Note on Robust Variance Estimation for Cluster-Correlated Data." *Biometrics,* 56: 645–646.

Wilson, A. Jeyaratnam. 2000. *Sri Lankan Tamil Nationalism: Its Origins and Development in the Nineteenth and Twentieth Centuries*. Vancouver: UBC Press.

Wimmer, Andreas. 2002. *Nationalist Exclusion and Ethnic Conflict: Shadows of Modernity*. New York: Cambridge University Press.

Wimmer, Andreas, Lars-Erik Cederman, and Brian Min. 2009. "Ethnic Politics and Armed Conflict: A Configurational Analysis." *American Sociological Review*, 74, 2: 316–337.

Windolf, Paul. 1997. *Expansion and Change: Higher Education in Germany, the United States, and Japan, 1870–1990*. Boulder: Westview Press.

Winslow, Deborah and Michael Woost. 2004. "Articulations of Economy and Ethnic Conflict in Sri Lanka." *Economy, Culture, and Civil War in Sri Lanka*. D. Winslow and M. Woost eds. Bloomington: Indiana University Press, 1–27.

Woodberry, Robert. 2004. "The Shadow of Empire: Christian Missions, Colonial Policy, and Democracy in Postcolonial Societies." PhD Thesis. Department of Sociology. University of North Carolina, Chapel Hill.

World Bank. 2002. *World Development Indicators*. ESDS International, (MIMAS) University of Manchester.

World Bank. 2008a. *Data & Statistics: Country Classification*. Accessed August 13, 2008. http://go.worldbank.org/K2CKM78CC0.

World Bank. 2008b. *The Road Not Traveled: Education Reform in the Middle East and North Africa*. Accessed February 21, 2011. http://sitesources.worldbank.org/INTMENA/Resources/EDU_Flagship_Full_ENG.pdf.

World Bank. 2009. *World Development Indicators On-Line*. Accessed August 20, 2009. http://data.worldbank.org/data-catalog/world-development-indicators.

Yashin, Neshe. 2002. "School is a Textbook: Symbolism and Rituals in Turkish Cypriot Schools." *Clio in the Balkans: The Politics of History Education*. Christina Koulouri ed. Thessaloniki: Center for Democracy and Reconciliation in Southeast Europe, 414–422.

Young, Crawford. 1976. *The Politics of Cultural Pluralism*. Madison: University of Wisconsin Press.

Ziegler, Herbert. 1989. *Nazi Germany's New Aristocracy: The SS Leadership, 1925–1939*. Princeton: Princeton University Press.

Index

AASU, see All Assam Students Union
Abidjan (Cote d'Ivoire), 150
Afghanistan, 202n
Agrarian Bund (Germany), 177
Alberta (Canada), 167
Alexander, Thomas, 176
All Assam Students Union (AASU) (India), 127–34, 193
Alles, A.C., 69n
American Ceylon Mission, 62
Anandhi, S., 122
Angrist, Joshua, 119
Anti-Semitism, 170, 175–88 passim, 191
Archbishop of Cyprus, 86; Archbishop Kyprianos, 94; Archbishop Makarios III, 94, 104–5
Arendt, Hannah, 1
Assam (India), 125–34, 138, 196, 197; case selection, 114; competition mechanism, 130–3; ethnic violence, 127–30; frustration-aggression mechanism, 130–3; mobilization mechanism, 133–4, 193; socialization mechanism, 191
Assam Literary Society (India), 127, 128
Assam Movement (India), 128–33
Assam Popular Struggle Association (AAGSP) (India), 134
Assertiveness, see frustration-aggression mechanism
Association of Greek Cypriot Intellectuals (Cyprus), 93
Athow, Brian, 141
Ataturk, Kemal, 106

Atta, Mohammed, 2
Ayacucho (Peru), 200

Bahrain, 201
Bandarage, Asoka, 74
Bangladeshis, 128, 132–4
Bannon, Alicia, 144–5
Barro, Robert, 39
Baruah, Sanjib, 129, 130
Basedau, Matthias, 146
Bates, Robert, 23
Bédard, Éric, 165
Belgian colonialism, 140–4, 150–2; see also Rwanda
Bengalis, 125, 127–33, 196
Benin, 148–9, 191, 197
Berlin, 171
Berman, Sherri, 180
Berrebi, Claude, 115
Bildung (Germany), 178
Bill 101 (Quebec), 158, 168
Bharatiya Janata Party (BJP) (India), 136
Bhattacharya, A.K., 122
BJP, see Bharatiya Janata Party
Blanton, Robert, 141
Bloc Québécois, 168
Bossuroy, Thomas, 145
Botswana, 144
Bouazizi, Mohamed, 200–1
Bourassa, Robert, 160
Bourdieu, Pierre, 20–1, 187
Boy Scouts, 103
Brass, Paul, 16

Breton, Albert, 161
Brilleau, Alain, 149
British colonialism, 43n; in Cyprus, 86–107 passim; in Sri Lanka, 62–6; in sub-Saharan Africa, 140–5, 147, 150
Bruhn, Crista, 117, 121
Brustein, William, 179–80, 187
Bryant, Rebecca, 95–6, 101, 111
Buddhism, 61, 63, 65, 70; Buddhists, 59, 60, 64, 65
Burghers, 60–62 passim, 78, 79
Burkina Faso, 144, 145–6, 148–9, 191
Burma, 148n
Burundi, 150
Byzantine Empire, 85, 87

Canada, *see* Quebec
Catholic Church, 156–7, 158n
Center for Monitoring the Impact for Peace, 116
Central African Republic, 144
Centrale des Syndicats du Québec, 160
Ceylon, *see* Sri Lanka
Chad, 144
Chakrapani, C., 122
Chamberlain, H.S., 177
Chandraprema, C.A., 67
Chiapas (Mexico), 200
Chickering, Roger, 174
Christianity, 63, 65, 147; Christians in Cyprus, 85, 100; Christians in Kerala, 134, 137; Christians in Sri Lanka, 60, 62, 66, 76, 78–9
Church Mission Society, 62
Civil rights movement, 25–27 passim
Civil war, *see* political violence
Cogneau, Denis, 142
Colombo (Sri Lanka), 62, 78, 80n, 82
Colonial Society (Germany), 174
Communist Party of India (CPI), 137
Comparative-historical methods, 6–9; case selection, 9–11
Competition mechanism, 3, 22–4, 190; in Assam, 130–3; in Cyprus, 96–9; in Nazi Germany, 178–80, 182–3; in Quebec, 164–5; in Sri Lanka, 70–1, 77–83; in sub-Saharan Africa, 142–50 passim; *see also* Mechanistic complementarity; Scope conditions affecting mechanisms
Competition theory, 23; *see also* competition mechanism

Confédération des Syndicats Nationaux (Quebec), 160
Congo, Democratic Republic of, 150
Congress Party (India), 137
Constructivism, 16–7, 19; *see also* socialization mechanism
Contonou (Benin), 149
Copeaux, Etienne, 90
Cote d'Ivoire, 150
Crawshaw, Nancy, 87
Cross, James Richard, 159, 166
Cuba, 25
Cumaratunga, Mundisa, 65–6
Curriculum, 15, 18–9, 32, 190; in Assam, 132; in Cyprus, 98–105 passim, 112; in Germany, 175–7; in the Palestinian territories, 117–8, 121; in Rwanda, 151–2; in Sri Lanka, 82; *see also* socialization mechanism
Cyprus, 84–112; case selection, 9; competition mechanism, 96–100, 197; educated elites, 93–5; education, 92–3; enosis movement, 87–112 passim; frustration-aggression mechanism, 96–7, 193, 196; history of foreign domination, 85–7; mobilization mechanism, 109–12; socialization mechanism, 100–9, 111–2, 191; violence, 90–1, 199–200

Dalits, 122
Das, Amiya Kumar, 133–4
Das, Maitreyi Bordia, 124
Das, Samir, 131
Dawson, Andrew, 40
de Lagarde, Paul, 177
de Silva, K.M., 79–82 passim
Degregori, Carlos Ivan, 200
Dharmadasa, K.N.O., 78
Dharmapala, Anagarika, 65
Discrimination, 19–20, 28–9, 33, 190, 195; in Cyprus, 97; in Germany, 170, 177; in India, 122, 124; in Israel, 118–20 passim; in Kerala, 136, 153; in Mexico, 200; in Nigeria, 147; operationalization, 39; in Quebec, 167; in Rwanda, 151; in Sri Lanka, 75–6, 80, 83, 196
Doctors, 2, 66, 93–5 passim, 172–3, 180–5
Dollard, John, 20
Durkheim, Émile, 17

Eastern Marches Society (Germany), 174

Economic development: in Assam, 125; in Cyprus, 96–7; in Kerala, 135; operationalization, 40; in the Palestinian territories, 118; in Quebec, 164; as scope condition, 4, 31–2, 41–2, 46–8, 193–5, 204–5; in Sri Lanka, 72
Education: conceptualization, 14–5; operationalization, 38–9
Educational bubbles, 32, 192–4 passim, 204; in Africa, 145; in India, 134, 152; in the Middle East, 201; in Sri Lanka, 83
Egypt, 201
Einsatzgruppen, (Germany), 173
Einstein, Albert, 1
Eley, Geoff, 174
Empowerment and education, 26–7
Englebert, Pierre, 146
EOKA, *see* National Organization of Cypriot Struggle
EROS (Cyprus), 68
Ethnic violence: in Assam 127–30; in Cyprus, 89–91; definition, 12–4; in Germany, 185–6; in Nigeria, 148; operationalization, 37–8; in the Palestinian territories, 114; in Quebec, 158–9; in Rwanda, 151–2; in Sri Lanka, 60–2; theories of, 12
Ethnicity: in Assam, 125; in Cyprus, 84; definition, 13; in Kerala, 134; in Quebec, 155–6; in Rwanda, 151; in Sri Lanka, 59–60; as scope condition, 5, 30–1, 41, 45–51, 192–3; *see also* ethnic violence
Eugenics, *see* Racial hygiene

Facebook, 201
Falter, Jurgen, 171, 178
Farmer, B.H., 64
Fearon, James, 39, 40
Fédération des Travailleurs et Travailleuses du Québec, 160
Food Movement (India), 127, 132
France, 25, 93n, 141; *see also* French colonialism
French colonialism, 140–150 passim
Friedman, Willa, 145
Fritsch, Theodor, 177
Front de la Libération du Québec (FLQ), 158–9, 162–8 passim, 191
Frustration-aggression mechanism, 3, 19–22, 26–7, 190; in Assam, 130–3, 193; in Cyprus, 96–7, 193; in Germany, 178–80, 183–4, 193; in the Palestinian territories, 118–20, 193; in Quebec, 164–5; in Sri Lanka, 70–7, 82–3, 193; in sub-Saharan Africa, 142–50 passim; *see also* Mechanistic complementarity; Scope conditions affecting mechanisms

Gabon, 144
Gallagher, Hugh Gregory, 181
Geertz, Clifford, 24
Genocide, 152, 170, 176
German Conservative Party, 175, 177
German Peace Society, 174
Germany, 154–5; 169–88; case selection 10–1; competition and frustration-aggression mechanisms, 178–80, 182–4, 187–8, 193, 194–5; East Germany, 187; education level, 93n; mechanistic complementarity, 191; mobilization mechanism, 180, 184–5; political institutions, 187–8, 196; socialization mechanism, 175–7, 181–2, 188, 193
Goldstone, Jack, 23, 200
Goswami, Sandhya, 130
Gour, P.N., 122
Great Britain, 62, 86, 91, 93n; *see also* British colonialism
Great Idea (Greece), 87–8, 101, 106
Greece, 86–93 passim, 94n, 98, 101–8 passim
Grievances, *see* frustration-aggression mechanism
Grivas, George, 88, 89, 106, 110
Gujarat (India), 124

Halliburton, Murphy, 138n
Ham, 151
Hamas, 115, 118, 120, 121
Hamburg, 171
Hamilton, Richard, 171, 181
Hansen, Thomas, 123
Harding, John, 100
Hausa-Fulani, 147–8
Hela movement (Sri Lanka), 65–6
Hellenism, 85, 101, 105, 107
Hinduism, 65; Hindus in India, 123–5, 134, 136; Hindus in Sri Lanka, 60, 64, 65
Hitler, Adolf, 170, 174–6 passim, 180, 181; *Mein Kampf*, 176

Horowitz, Donald, 23
Hussain, Monirul, 130–1
Hutu Revolution (Rwanda), 151

Ideal types, see Weber, Max
Igbo, 147–8
India, 16, 59, 121–39, 152–3; case selection, 10, 113–4; see also Assam; Kerala
Indo-Sri Lankan Accord, 67
Instrumentalist theory, 22
Internal colony, 157
Irgun, 1–2
Irish Republican Army, 169
Islamic Bloc (the Palestinian territories), 121
Islamic Center (the Palestinian territories), 121
Israel, see Palestinian territories

Jaffna (Sri Lanka), 63, 75
Jaffrelot, Christophe, 123
Jama'at (India), 124
Jarausch, Konrad, 179
Jayasuriya, Laksiri, 59
Jayawardena, Kumari, 66
Jayaweera, Swarna, 69
Jeffery, Patricia, 123
Jeffery, Roger, 123
Jeffrey, Craig, 122, 123
Jensen, Michael, 118
Jews: in Germany, 170, 177–86 passim, 191–3, 196; in Israel and the Palestinian territories, 114–21 passim, 200; see also Anti-Semitism
Jeyaranjan, J., 122
JVP, see People's Liberation Front

Kano (Nigeria), 148
Karagiorges, Andreas, 107
Karens (Burma), 148n
Kater, Michael, 179, 184, 185
Katzenstein, Mary, 131
Kearney, Robert, 67, 73, 74n
Kelling, George Horton, 99n
Kenya, 145
Kerala (India), 134–8, 153; case selection, 114; political institutions, 154, 195–6, 197
Kérékou, Mathieu, 149
King David Hotel (Palestine), 2

Koshar, Rudy, 180
Kowalchuk, Lisa, 159
Knights of Templar, see Cyprus, history of foreign domination
Kremer, Michael, 145
Krishnan, Rajan, 122
Kumari, Renu, 122
Kurthen, Hermann, 187

Laitin, David, 40
Langbehn, Julius, 177
Lange, Matthew, 40, 43n
Language Association (Germany), 174
Language Movement (India), 128, 132
Laporte, Pierre, 159, 165, 166
Latin America, 25, 200
Lebanon, 115, 120
Lee, Jong-Wha, 39
Lemay, Dominique, 165
Lesage, Jean, 157, 158, 160
Lévesque, René, 158
Liberation Tigers of Tamil Eelam (LTTE) (Sri Lanka), 61–2, 66–9, 74–6, 81–83 passim, 193
Loizos, Peter, 97
LTTE, see Liberation Tigers of Tamil Eelam

Mamdani, Mahmood, 16
Manitoba (Canada), 168
Mann, Michael, 173
Markides, Kyriacos, 93, 95
Marwaris, 125, 127
Mason, David, 141
Materialist theory, 19
Mauss-Copeaux, Claire, 90
Mazawi, Andre, 118
McAdam, Doug, 27
McHenry, James Jr., 99
Mechanistic complementarity, 3–4, 28–30, 190–2
Medicine, 74, 78, 79, 80, 181–4
Meech Lake Accord (Canada), 168
Megali Idea, see Great Idea
Methodology, 6–11; see also statistics; comparative-historical methods
Mexico, 200
Middle East, 200–1
Miguel, Edward, 144–5
Miller, Barbara, 74n

Millet system (Ottoman Empire), 85–6, 100
Milosevic, Slobodan, 22
Mishal, Shaul, 121
Missionaries: in Burma, 148n; in Sri Lanka, 62–5 passim; in sub-Saharan Africa, 16, 141, 147, 150–1
Mobilization mechanism, 3, 24–7, 190; in Assam, 133–4; in Cyprus, 109–12; in Germany, 180, 185; in India, 124–5; in the Palestinian territories, 120–2; in Quebec, 191; in Sri Lanka, 68–9; *see also* Mechanistic complementarity; Scope conditions affecting mechanisms
Mommsen, Hans, 175
Montreal (Canada), 155, 167
Morris, Aldon, 25
Mosse, George, 177, 181
Mughols, 137
Muhlberger, Detlef, 171
Museum of Barbarism (Cyprus), 108–9
Muslim Brotherhood, 117
Muslims: in Cyprus, 84, 85; in India, 123–4, 134, 137; in the Palestinian territories, 114–5, 118, 120; in Sri Lanka, 60, 65, 66, 76; *see also* Bengalis

Narayanan, M.G.S., 137
Narrative comparison, *see* comparative-historical methods
National History Project (Canada), 163
National Organization of Cypriot Struggle (EOKA), 88–91, 94–100 passim, 106, 109–11, 196; EOKA-B, 91, 95, 97, 98
National Socialist German Physicians' League (NSAB), 181, 185
National Socialist German Students' Association, 181, 185
National Socialist German Workers' Party (NSDAP), *see* Nazis
Nationalism, 13–4, 93; in Cyprus, 89, 93–6, 101–12 passim; in Germany, 170, 175–81; in Greece, 87, 98, 99, 101; in India, 123; in the Palestinian territories, 117, 120–1; in Quebec, 155–8, 168; in Sri Lanka, 64–6
Navalar, Arumuga, 65
Navy League (Germany), 174
Nazis (Germany), 11, 154, 170–88
Nellie massacre (India), 128–9, 130, 134
Neo-Nazis, 11, 154, 169–70, 185–8, 195

Nepalis, 125
Newfoundland and Labrador (Canada), 168
Nicosia (Cyprus), 89, 90, 106
Nigeria, 146–9, 197
Nissan, Elizabeth, 70
Noah, 151
Nordbruch, Goetz, 117
North Africa, 200–201
Northern Ireland, 169
Nussbaum, Martha, 205

Ontario (Canada), 155, 156
Orr, C.W.J., 97
Orthodox Church, 86–8, 94, 98, 100, 104–5
Oslo Accord, 114
Ottoman Empire, 85–8, 92, 93, 100

Paden, John, 148
Pakistan, 115n, 202n
Palestinian Islamic Jihad, 115, 120
Palestinian territories, 1–2, 114–21, 152; case selection, 9–10, 113; frustration-aggression mechanism, 118–20, 193; mobilization mechanism, 120–1; political instability and violence, 114–6, 197, 200; socialization mechanism, 116–8, 191; unemployment, 119, 164
Pancyprian National Youth Organization (PEON) (Cyprus), 94, 110
Pan-German League, 174, 177
Papadakis, Yiannis, 108
Pape, Robert, 115
Parker, Beryl, 176
Parti Québécois (PQ), 158–63 passim, 169
Pattern matching, *see* comparative-historical methods
Paz, Reuven, 117, 121
Pelletier, Gerard, 163
People's Liberation Front (JVP), 66–9, 74, 76–7, 80, 81n
Persianis, Panayiotis, 95, 100, 104, 105, 110n
Peru, 200
Pfaffenberger, Bryan, 75
Pinard, Maurice, 159
Political Committee of the Cyprus Struggle (PEKA), 88, 94

Political institutions: in Germany, 187–8; impact on civil war, 202–3; in Kerala, 136–8; in Quebec, 166–9, 191–2; as scope condition, 4–5, 32–3, 42–3, 49–55, 195–7, 205
Political Violence, 199–203
Portugal, 93n
Posner, Daniel, 144–145
Process tracing, *see* comparative-historical methods
Proctor, Robert, 182
Prussia, 179, 182

Quebec, 154–69; case selection, 10–1; competition and frustration-aggression mechanisms, 162, 164–9, 194–5; educated elites, 159–60, 161–3; education, 160–1; mobilization mechanism, 191; political institutions, 166–9, 195–7; separatist movement, 156–9; socialization mechanism, 163, 193
Quiet Revolution (Quebec), 165

Racial hygiene, 151, 175–6, 182
Ralliement National (RN) (Quebec), 157–8
Rassemblement pour l'Indépendance Nationale (RIN) (Quebec), 157–8
Rational-choice theory, 22; *see also* competition mechanism
Rebellion, *see* political violence
Resource mobilization theory, 24; *see also* mobilization mechanism
Resource scarcity, *see* economic development
Revolution, *see* political violence
Riga, Liliana, 200
Roberts, Michael, 66
Roman Empire, 85
Roubaud, François, 149
Rueschemeyer, Dietrich, 206
Rule of law, 136
Russia, 25, 86
Rwanda, 16, 144, 150–2

Sandbrook, Richard, 137
Scapegoating, 21–2, 29–31 passim, 194, 198, 205; in Assam, 131–3; in Germany, 179, 187–8, 193, 196; in Sri Lanka, 75–6, 82; in sub-Saharan Africa, 145, 146, 149

School Association (Germany), 174
Scope conditions affecting mechanisms, 4–5, 30–3, 192–7, 198–9; *see also* Statistics: statistical interactions; Economic development, as scope condition; Ethnicity, as scope condition; Political institutions, as scope condition
Sela, Avraham, 121
Self-esteem, *see* frustration-aggression mechanism
Sen, Amartya, 204
Senaratne, Jagath, 77
Senegal, 144
Seven Years' War, 155
Shah, Ghanshyam, 123
Shining Path (Peru), 200
Sikand, Yoginder, 124
Singh, Indra Kumar, 122
Singh, Lal Bahadur, 122
Singh, Prerna, 137
Sinhala Only Act (Sri Lanka), 75
Siriwardena, Reggie, 70
Social movements, 24–7
Socialist Students Union (Sri Lanka), 69
Socialization mechanism, 3, 16–9, 189–90; in Cyprus, 100–9, 112; in Germany, 175–7, 181–2, 188; in the Palestinian territories, 116–8; in Sri Lanka, 69–70; in sub-Saharan Africa, 150–2; *see also* Mechanistic complementarity; Scope conditions affecting mechanisms
Society of Friends (Cyprus), 86, 94
South Africa, 144
Spain, 93n
Sri Lanka, 59–83, 204; case selection, 9; civil war, 199; competition mechanism, 70–1, 77–83, 197; educated elites, 64–6; education, 62–4; ethnicity and ethnic violence, 59–62; frustration-aggression mechanism, 70–7, 82–3, 193, 195–6; mobilization mechanism, 68–9, 193; socialization mechanism, 69–70, 191
SS (Germany), 173, 181
Staggenborg, Suzanne, 25
Statistics, 6, 35–7; statistical interactions, 41–3, 46–55
Stevenson, Garth, 165
St. Léonard (Canada), 158
Storm-Troopers (SA), 181
Storrs, Ronald, 103

Yashin, Neshe, 108
Yoruba, 147
Young People's Christian Orthodox Union (OXEN) (Cyprus), 94, 110

Yugoslavia, 22–3

Zapatistas (Mexico), 200
Zimbabwe, 144

Stroh, Alexander, 146
Strong Youth of EOKA (ANE) (Cyprus), 88, 110
Students, 14–5; in Assam, 126–31, 133; in Cyprus, 88, 92–5, 98, 100–12; frustration-aggression mechanism, 205; in Germany, 172–3, 175–7, 180–5, 188; in India, 122, 124–5; in Latin America, 25, 200; mobilization mechanism, 25–6; in the Palestinian territories, 117–8, 120–1; in Quebec, 163–5; socialization mechanism, 3, 17–9, 31, 192; in Sri Lanka, 62–3, 66–70, 73, 79–82; in sub-Saharan Africa, 148, 151, 191; Taliban, 202n
Students' Action Committee (India), 125
Students Islamic Movement of India (SIMI), 124
Sub-Saharan Africa, 10, 114, 138–53
Suicide, 74n, 138n
Sweccha Sevak Bahini (SSB) (India), 130

Taliban, 202n
Tambiah, Stanley, 64–5, 76, 78, 193–4
Tamil Nadu (India), 70, 125
Tamil Students' Federation (Sri Lanka), 68, 69
Tamil Tigers, *see* Liberation Tigers of Tamil Eelam
Teachers, 5, 14–5, 19, 32, 192; in Cyprus, 93–5, 97, 99, 104–6, 110–2; in Germany, 172, 177, 188; in Quebec, 163; in Sri Lanka, 66, 70–1, in sub-Saharan Africa, 141, 152
Terrorism, 1–2, 67, 114–5, 124, 159
Thorton, Rebecca, 145
Tilly, Charles, 32, 195
Tiruchelvam, Neelan, 74
Torelli, Constance, 149
Toronto (Canada), 155, 167
TUF Youth Organisation (Sri Lanka), 68
Tunisia, 200–201
Turkey, 84, 87, 90–1, 102, 106–8; *see also* Ottoman Empire
Turkish Resistance Organization (TMT) (Cyprus), 91
Twitter, 201

Udagama, P., 69
ULFA (India), 130

Unemployed Graduates Union (Sri Lanka), 68, 75
Unemployment: in Assam, 114, 125–7, 131; in Cyprus, 96–7; frustration-aggression mechanism, 32; in Germany, 178–9, 183, 187, 194; in India, 114, 122–4, 152; in Kerala, 114, 132–6, 138, 153; in the Middle East, 201; in the Palestinian territories, 118–9; in Quebec, 164, 167, 194; in Sri Lanka, 66, 68, 72–5; in sub-Saharan Africa, 139, 142, 144–7, 149–50; *see also* Educational bubbles
United States of America, 2, 62, 91
Universities: in Assam, 128–32; in Cyprus, 98, 101, 105; in Germany, 163n, 175–6, 180–85; in India, 124; in the Palestinian territories, 115, 117–21; in Quebec, 161, 163, 191; in Sri Lanka, 64, 67, 69, 74, 77–83

Vaillancourt, Francois, 165
Vaillancourt, Luc, 165
Vallières, Pierre, 162
Varnavas, Andreas, 109
Varshney, Ashutosh, 137
Venetians, 85, 86
Vernacular schools: in Sri Lanka, 62–3, 70, 71, 78, 79; in sub-Saharan Africa, 141, 150
Verwimp, Philip, 152
Volkan, *see* Turkish Resistance Organization (TMT)
Volkan, Vamik, 90
von Treitschke, Heinrich, 177

War Measures Act (Canada), 164–5, 166, 168
Weber, Max, 8–9
Weiner, Myron, 131, 132
Weiss, John, 176, 177, 178
Wesleyan Mission, 62
Weyers, Wolfgang, 185
Weymar, Eric, 176
Wickham-Crowley, Timothy, 25, 200
Wiesel, Ellie, 1
Wijesinghe, C.P., 73–4
Wilkinson, Steven, 136
Wimmer, Andreas, 200
Windolf, Paul, 173n
Woodberry, Robert, 141